W9-BJP-238

POOR,
YET MAKING
MANY
RICH

POOR, YET MAKING MANY RICH

The poor as agents of creative justice

Richard D. N. Dickinson

Commission on the
Churches' Participation in Development
World Council of Churches, Geneva

The title of this book is taken from 2 Corinthians 6:10

Cover: Michael Dominguez
ISBN No 2–8254–0732–1
© 1983 World Council of Churches, 150 route de Ferney,
1211 Geneva 20, Switzerland

Printed in Switzerland

Contents

Foreword vii
Introduction ix

PART ONE: THE CONTEXT OF THE CHURCHES DEVELOPMENT–
LIBERATION WORK
1. Some major elements in the socio-economic context 3
2. The ongoing development debate in the "secular" realm 25
3. Christian ethics in the World Council of Churches arena 43

PART TWO: TOWARDS A CHURCH IN SOLIDARITY WITH
THE POOR: FIVE MODES
Introduction 71
4. Relief and modified project assistance 76
5. Development education 93
6. Structural analyses 108
7. Theological and ethical reflection 127
8. Working alongside the poor 148

PART THREE: SOME PERSONAL REFLECTIONS ON PAST EXPERIENCE
AND FUTURE PROSPECTS
9. Some personal reflections 167

Bibliography 185

APPENDICES
1. A comment from Ghana, by Annie Jiagge 195
2. A comment from Indonesia, by T. B. Simatupang 209

Foreword

At its Fifth Assembly in Nairobi, Kenya, the World Council of Churches reaffirmed its concern for development, and called upon the churches to continue their participation in the process. The Council also reaffirmed its understanding of development as a process which seeks to bring about social justice, self-reliance and economic growth through the participation of the people directly involved in it. The report from the section dealing with human development said:

> The broader vision of development that we now have must be used to look at old problems in a new perspective. The church's concern for development has arisen primarily from the concern for the poor. But how does the church express its solidarity with the poor and fight along with them for liberation and justice? In this quest we are led to new understandings of the problem and of our tasks.[1]

After the Nairobi Assembly, the several sub-units of the WCC dealing with issues of social justice organized their programmes in the light of the main insights of the Assembly. Among these insights there are two directly related to the development process: first, that the poor and oppressed people are the chief protagonists and must be the main beneficiaries of development. And, second, that the way to tackle development challenges should be through a comprehensive approach.

Dr Richard Dickinson's input to the discussion of development at the Uppsala and Nairobi Assemblies had been of crucial importance.[2] In the present volume he reviews and analyzes the programme lines followed by the WCC during the post-Nairobi period. Dr Dickinson has been associated with WCC's work for many years; he sees it as a whole and he writes about it with critical appreciation. The result is a book which provides a comprehensive overview of what is happening in the area of development-liberation at the ecumenical level and a perceptive analysis of the implications of it. In the process, it suggests as well guidelines for future work.

The Commission on the Churches' Participation in Development warmly commends this book to the churches. We are passing through a period of history when there are more questions asked about development than answers given; when the lot of the poor seems to worsen and the structures that oppress seem more securely entrenched than ever before. All these pose a challenge to the Christian church and the ecumenical movement, which needs to be met with courage and faith.

We are deeply grateful to Dr Dickinson. We are also grateful to Justice Annie Jiagge of Ghana and General T. B. Simatupang of Indonesia whose comments from local and regional perspectives, included in the book as appendices, express the richness and plurality of our current thoughts on development.

Julio de Santa Ana
Director, Commission on the Churches'
Participation in Development

NOTES

1. David M. Paton, ed, *Breaking Barriers: Nairobi 1975*, London, SPCK, 1976, p. 123.
2. See Richard N. Dickinson, *Line and Plummet*, Geneva, WCC, 1968, and *To Set at Liberty the Oppressed*, Geneva, WCC, 1975.

Introduction

"Words, words, words . . . don't talk at all; show me," says Liza Doolittle in that saucy musical "My Fair Lady". An act, like a picture, is worth a thousand words. Enough official and unofficial reports, along with recommendations, have been published to fill a library. But the poor of the world seem to slide ever more uncontrollably into misery and oppression. Only the relatively few rich seem to benefit from business as usual, and apathy.

So why more words? Their only justification (aside from an invitation to write) is to provide an overview, primarily but not exclusively, for those attending an assembly, and those deeply committed to making the World Council an effective instrument of the churches in their ministries of justice and wholeness. Thus this book focuses on the experiences and efforts of the World Council of Churches, not because the Council is the only agent promoting justice, nor because its vision or efforts are distinctive or normative, but because the Council provides a diverse but common focus and framework for the churches' ministries. The narrowness of the focus, therefore, should not suggest ignorance of, or indifference to, the efforts of other religious and secular organizations to promote global justice. Rather it is a consequence of the specific purposes of this volume.

Even within the World Council there is a richness and fullness not evident in this study. Some very significant efforts, like the Commission of the Churches on International Affairs, or the Programme to Combat Racism, or the Commission on Faith and Order, receive scarce mention. Why are they omitted? Actually they are not omitted; they are not included. An effort has been made to illustrate certain theses about the Council's work, and illustrative programmes have been lifted up; others could have been, but the point is not to mention everything.

The title of this volume may be confusing. Perhaps it is only the author's idiosyncrasy which leads him to biblical titles, even when

they are obscure, or even downright misleading. With this title my
intention was to symbolize the very significant movement since my
1967 *Line and Plummet* (Uppsala), which displayed the mentality of
the day in focusing on the moral responsibility of the rich to act
sacrificially to help the poor. My 1974 *To Set at Liberty the Oppressed*
(Nairobi) was built upon a deeper perception of the phenomenon of
centre-periphery relationships and the significance of people's participation. With this volume, *Poor, Yet Making Many Rich* (Vancouver), the crucial role of the poor as agents of change for justice
which liberates and enriches all has become more evident and central. It is *not* suggested that the poor are again to be used or exploited
for the enrichment of the rich, but that the poor are special agents
of God's redemptive work in history. These changing emphases
have been deeply influenced by the ongoing development-liberation
debate within the ecumenical movement.

Certain terminological problems persist. No satisfactory alternative to "third world" has yet been found, though terms like "poorer
nations", "less-materially-developed nations" etc. may sometimes
attenuate the difficulty. It would perhaps help, but not resolve, the
semantic difficulty if the history of the term could be kept in mind
– a term to my knowledge first used by a French author (*tiers monde*)
to refer to countries not in the "free market" or "socialist" orbits
of influence. That historical reference reduces its potential pejorative
connotation, though it does not eliminate it.

Similarly, it has been difficult to find a felicitous term to cover
the process sometimes referred to as "development", at other times
referred to as "liberation". Unwilling to relinquish certain advantageous connotations of each word, this book often takes recourse
in what must be a confusing ploy of referring to "development-
liberation", directed towards global justice and wholeness. Suffice
it to say that new, more adequate, concepts would be of great
benefit to all of us working in this area.

The purpose of this volume, following up the previous volumes
for the Uppsala and Nairobi Assemblies, is to review how the World
Council of Churches' thinking on development, liberation and
global justice issues has continued to evolve since the Nairobi Assembly, and to stimulate fresh reflection on appropriate and faithful
action by the churches generally, and the World Council of
Churches particularly, in fostering global justice in the years ahead.
An effort is made to put that action and discussion in the context of
social pressures, the secular debate on development-liberation, and
the longer-term ecumenical discussion on ethics.

Further, the study claims that the dominant theme of the World

Council of Churches during the post-Nairobi period has been "towards a church in solidarity with the poor", though there are differing ways to understand the implications of solidarity for action. Thus, five differing ways of being in solidarity, obviously overlapping, are specified and illustrated, and an effort made to demonstrate that each of these should be understood as partial, experimental, and complementary to other modes of being in solidarity. Overall, there is a concern to show that at the current stage of the World Council of Churches' effort it is desirable to highlight the provisional, tentative and sometimes groping character of all efforts to be in solidarity, and that there is an urgent need to sense a partnership in faithfulness rather than a sense of competitiveness and non-cooperation.

Included in the book are comments by two of the World Council of Churches presidents from third world continents, reflecting on the descriptions and arguments in the first part of the volume. In this way it is hoped that the predominantly "first world" views expressed in the preliminary part of the study will be challenged and enriched by those contributors with deep and radically different experiences.

Finally, a few words of appreciation: to the two current World Council presidents (Justice Annie Jiagge and General T. B. Simatupang) who have kindly consented to share their criticisms and perspectives; to Julio de Santa Ana and CCPD staff who issued the invitation to share my ideas and ministry in this way, and who made critical contributions to my work; to former colleagues and friends at the World Council who offered time, information and ideas as this study was being shaped and prepared; to the several different typists who helped with the various drafts (Margareta Andersson, Katherine Parker, Linda McCrae, Harry Brown, Ruth Ann Krieg); to President T. J. Liggett and colleagues at Christian Theological Seminary who understood why a seminary dean needs to invest significant energies in a project like this. Finally, a special word of gratitude and appreciation to Elizabeth, my oldest child and only daughter, who not only made a long summer in Geneva (away from Lake Michigan) much more pleasant, but who contributed many refreshing ideas, considerable information, and above all a commitment to the church as an instrument in the struggle for justice and wholeness. She is an intellectual and spiritual partner in every sense.

Indianapolis, Indiana
Palm Sunday, 1982

Part One:
The context of the churches' development-liberation work

1: Some major elements in the socio-economic context

We live in the midst of paradoxes. The more powerful the rich become, the less secure they feel. The more possibilities for freedom the poor sense, the more impatient they become for rapid or revolutionary change. The more it seems reasonable to hope that science and technology can help to resolve the fundamental problems of world hunger, disease and ignorance, the less it seems possible to mobilize those human and material resources for a just society. The more there is cause for hope and risk, the more we seem paralyzed by primal fears.

It is one of the most perplexing paradoxes that over the last decade a series of blue ribbon studies have emerged (e.g. Club of Rome, New Futures, Brandt Commission, Global 2000, the numerous Special Session reports of the United Nations family).[1] All these call for basic changes in the world economic order, all challenge the rich nations to new thinking and new institutions and all argue both moral and self-interest reasons for changes in the policies of rich nations. Yet response has been appallingly feeble: deteriorating aid commitments, recalcitrance of economically powerful nations to modify trading policies and patterns leading to a New International Economic Order, tardy progress in establishing the seas and space as a global human "commons", or escalation of "national security" measures symbolized in the haemorrhaging of human and material resources out of vital human productivity into unproductive military hardware for "preparedness". It seems as if the analysis of issues is perceived as sufficient response; as if we believe social transformation will take place mysteriously when rational human beings are presented with scientifically and cogently argued data highlighting the need for change.

After two development decades, and notwithstanding numerous high-level reports, we are still groping for the way ahead towards global social and economic justice, but too often looking for a painless, effortless formula. After two decades it has become clearer how complex the issues of socio-economic development are, how difficult it is to change the socio-economic forces which have characterized the world for the past three hundred years, how difficult it is to raise the level of the discussion from the morality of good or bad actors, to the level of the adequacy or inadequacy of those basic political, economic and cultural myths, and of institutions which have been fashioned to express those myths. The tenacity of those myths, the fear of change and loss of privilege, the complexity of development-liberation issues, and a paucity of imagination concerning alternative futures, prompted the Brandt Commission to conclude that, bad as things are at the beginning of the 1980s, there is little room for optimism for the year 2000.

> For these trends to continue [poverty, hunger, stagflation, international monetary disorder, growing world population, unemployment, environmental destruction, protectionism] is dangerous enough, but they can easily worsen. Such developments are not improbable; but we do not believe them to be inevitable.[2]

A cherished part of the mythos of the enlightened rational intelligentsia is that problems can be solved with more personal morality, and/or more facts and analysis. However, more facts, without policy and institutional change, will not eliminate the global misery and injustices which now prevail. If more facts and voluminous reports in themselves could solve the problems, we would be in good shape. A future simply extrapolated from the present, without significant changes in economic, political and cultural relationships between nations, will produce a world in 1990 or 2000 even worse off than today. This is likely to be the kind of world we will have, unless there is significant change, generated from both the richer and poorer countries. The record of the past two decades, does not generate much hope. It is a record marked by increasing polarization between rich and poor countries, and between the rich and poor within countries – a polarization which makes the victimized ever more ready to use violent means to overcome the oppressive systems which dominate them, and a parallel readiness on the part of incumbent political and economic authorities to reinforce themselves through centralization of power and intensification of "security" measures.

This kind of world is probable, but not necessary. The decade ahead will sorely test Christians who believe that God continues to make all things new, and that God's people are called to faithful, though riskful, participation in that continuing creation. *Metanoia* is not natural or easy, but it is possible. Some, even though rich and comfortable, can be turned around; others, though poor (perhaps *because* they are poor), can be quickened by the Spirit to new visions of their own capacities and to new hopes for their own communities and for society as a whole. God can and does use the voices of the faithful to restore sight to the blind; in inscrutable ways God does use acts of hope and love, wherever they are manifest among the poor or the rich, to bring about new creation.

It is chic to say that the past two development decades were unmitigated disasters. By some calculations they have been: when judged by the enormous and growing need of the poor; when assessed by the criteria of their own objectives; when compared with what would have been possible, given the will and inventiveness to move forward resolutely. On all three counts, the decades have been failures. Yet in retrospect important things have been achieved: population growth has been somewhat slowed (enough to make the difference of half a billion people by the year 2000): literally hundreds of millions now enjoy better health and longer lives; literacy, even adult literacy, has increased remarkably, though absolute and relative statistics are still appalling; new instruments for international cooperation have emerged; a new ethos of international cooperation and interdependency is slowly evolving (despite keen disappointments in the NIEO, the SALT, and Law of the Sea); limits to old patterns are more starkly visible; our understandings of the issues of development and liberation have matured, and continue to change, in significant ways. Most important of all, there is a growing sense of identity, dignity, self-reliance and assertiveness taking root among the poor and oppressed of the world.

We do not stand, in 1982, where we stood at the time of the WCC assemblies in New Delhi (1960), Uppsala (1968), or even Nairobi (1975). That fact may be more consoling to a middle class social ethicist living in a rich country than to a mother and father in Bangladesh or Namibia who cannot feed and educate their children, or find a health professional when they lie sick. It is probably no consolation to a Kampuchean refugee in Thailand, a Haitian refugee being deported from the United States, or a boat refugee seeking asylum in Malaysia.

Yet, whatever achievements have been made, the situation of the poor and oppressed remains bleak. As Robert McNamara so eloquently reminded us in 1973, "absolute poverty is a condition of life so degraded by disease, illiteracy, malnutrition and squalor as to deny its victims basic human necessities; a condition of life so limited as to prevent realization of the potential of the genes with which one is born; a condition of life so degrading as to insult human dignity; and yet a condition of life so common as to be the lot of 40% of the people of the developing countries. And are not we who tolerate such poverty, when it is within our power to reduce the number of people afflicted by it, failing to fulfill the fundamental obligations accepted by civilized men since the beginning of time?"[3] Several dominant factors characterize the current world environment, and will greatly influence prospects for increasing global justice in the years just ahead.

Continuing marginalization

The first is the continuing marginalization (an active process, not just a static condition) of hundreds of millions of people. The bleak statistics are so readily available that it seems superfluous, almost disarming, to enumerate them.

- sixteen million refugees;
- 1.3 billion people chronically malnourished, and 462 million actually so malnourished that they are starving, one half of these being children under 5 years;[4]
- adult literacy in 38 low income countries, with a total population of 1.3 billion, at 38%;[5]
- per capita food production in those same 38 countries *less* (97%) than in 1970;[6]
- life expectancy in those 38 countries of 50 years;[7]
- 77% of the primary school age population (64% for females) actually enrolled in school; with 24% in secondary, and 4% in higher education;[8]
- 28% of the population in these 38 poorest countries having access to safe drinking water and only $1/16$ to health professionals (nurses and doctors); still, in 1978, one of every five children dying between the ages of one and five years, in these poorest countries;[9]
- 500 million people, half of them adult women (evidence of cultural oppression of females) suffering anaemia, a common factor in fatigue and low performance in school, work, etc.;[10]
- unemployment and underemployment, often hidden and disguised, remaining high; ILO estimates that in 1975, 35% of the labour force in the third world was underemployed;[11] 36 million new jobs a year are needed between now and the year 2000; 120,000 new jobs per day.[12]

Such numbing human statistics only hint at the range and depth of suffering from lack of basic human needs among vast numbers of people. While we refer primarily to the poorest countries, where the proportions of poverty are most overwhelming, even in many middle and upper income countries (as measured by deceptive gross national product and per capita income statistics) there is widespread suffering from lack of basic human needs.

Five misconceptions about "basic human needs" need to be dispelled. One is that to meet basic human needs in food, health, education and housing would require impossibly large resources. The fact is that, while a major effort would be required, the goal of meeting basic human needs, even by 2000, is achievable. The World Bank estimates that a mere 2% redistribution of good resources could overcome malnutrition. To attain such a goal would require, however, considerably expanded short-term assistance from the more industrialized countries, stringent measures to increase self-reliance within the poorer nations themselves, and significant structural changes in global economic relationships to enhance economic growth in poorer countries.

A second misconception is that basic human needs can be met by simply expanding production, or "throwing more money at the problems". Yet food deficiencies are more a consequence of mal-distribution than of inadequate production. Already sufficient calories and proteins are produced worldwide to ensure an adequate diet for all people, if food were properly distributed. The World Bank argues that undernourishment (too few proteins) rather than mal-nourishment is the cause of serious and extensive nutritional deficiency.[13] Similarly in health care, a basic issue is not only the overall number of health professionals being trained, but how they are deployed throughout the country; how the limited resources spent on health care get disproportionately concentrated in services to the affluent – not to mention the large subsidy which poor countries provide to the rich through the brain drain in the health profession. Thus, basic human needs go unmet not only because of low productivity, but because of the way that structural forces in society allocate scarce resources. There is a causal relationship between islands of affluence and privilege and unmet needs.

A third fact about basic human needs is that they are closely linked to poverty, as poverty is to unemployment. Need is directly related to purchasing power – a rather trite observation were it not for a widespread notion that need is defined by absolute scarcity. Many poor people spend 80% of their income on food, and still are desperately hungry. Small wonder, then, that the World Bank concludes that "malnutrition is largely a reflection of poverty; people do not have enough income for food. The most effective long-term policies are those which raise the incomes of the poor."[14] Similar arguments can be adduced in relation to health care and education, though the problem often is not so acute in education because of

governmental policies of mass education, at least at the primary and
secondary levels.

A fourth misconception is that "it is only a matter of time";
gradually matters will improve if growth continues or accelerates
(now predicted at 5% in Asia and 3–4% in Africa for the first five
years of the 80s, though these fairly optimistic composite regional
figures obscure differences between countries of a region).[15] Indeed,
while increases in food production have been impressive, despite
lean years, the advances have not been uniform in all areas. In health
care the picture has not been one of steady and unrelieved progress.
The World Bank study shows a continuing high incidence of
gastro-intestinal ailments and respiratory infections (the former
causing between 5 and 10 million deaths annually, and the latter 4–
5 million).[16] Other diseases with a persisting high incidence are
tuberculosis, round worms, malaria, sleeping sickness and river
blindness. The study concludes that "attempts have been made to
control these diseases by eliminating disease carriers through chem-
ical and environmental mechanisms, but with only limited and in
some instances temporary success".[17] Overcoming deficiencies in
basic human needs, then, requires more than the "passing of time",
or simple quantitative increase in efforts along the same lines. Provision of basic human needs on the scale required for a decent life
for the hundreds of millions now deprived, requires both intensified
efforts and new strategies based on the primary principle of justice.

Finally, a strategy to meet basic human needs cannot be predicted
on a relief or charity approach. Basic human needs can be met, in
the long term, only through an increasing capacity on the part of
local communities to become more self-reliant. For this reason the
recent emphasis in international circles on a massive effort to meet
basic human needs is both morally right and dangerously deceptive.
It is morally right because the denial of fundamental human rights
and the wasting of human lives is an affront to humanity and to
God. But it is also dangerously deceptive if it does not also call for
new structures of justice and interdependence. No wonder, then,
that many third world persons oppose a basic human needs strategy
if it becomes a substitute for serious discussions about fundamental
changes in world trading systems and patterns, through a new
international economic order. Small wonder that many third world
persons oppose a basic needs approach if it does not aim first at
enhancing self-reliance in the poorer countries themselves, since
there is plentiful evidence that outside aid, without strategies of
self-reliance, has actually deepened dependency.

Thus a major force in the 1980s will be the continuing struggle of two-thirds to three-quarters of the world's people to enjoy the basic necessities of life. This struggle will probably become sharper, even more crucial, not only from the point of view of the moral scandal of deprivation, but as a factor intensifying stresses and strains along the whole range of national and international relations.

Increasing concentration of power

A second major factor in the decade or two just ahead is increasing concentration of power and decision-making, at both the national and international levels. Demands of modern urbanization and industrialization, supported by an ethos which stresses the "free" play of social power, enables power to become increasingly centralized. Power, whether economic, political, technological, scientific, cultural and military, or in the field of information and communication, coalesces to such a degree that even the presumed powerful decision-makers lose much of their power to control an interlocking system which seems impossible to attack effectively at any one point. Ironically, today these systems are so highly developed and interlocked that power holders have comparatively little power, at least as individuals or small groups, to initiate changes. At the same time, increasing concentration of power makes the system more vulnerable to those who want to disrupt it; society is so intricately interdependent that a breakdown in one critical point can threaten or paralyze the entire system. Hence, the greater the concentration of power, the greater is the tendency to escalate protective power to ensure the safety of the entire system.

Such concentration of power is already well-recognized in the political and economic spheres. The phenomenon of burgeoning transnationals and their ability to contravene government development policies has been well-documented, and the subject of considerable ethical debate. Far less publicized is the growth of transnational agribusiness in both rich and poorer countries.[18] This produces a dependency of even remote rural areas on national and international mechanisms which, though potentially beneficial in some respects, often control, distort and manipulate local production.

Recent United Nations' controversies swirling around the meaning of "freedom of the press" highlight the centralizing power in that area. The shibboleth "freedom of the press" is a two-edged sword which can be used to subvert and control as well as inform and emancipate. Many recent studies document the use of controlled information to enhance the power of those already in control.[19] Information is power. Malevolent or transnational corporate forces

are not behind every advocate of "freedom of information" or
"freedom of the press"; not all information gathering or dispersing
is used maliciously by the powerful to retain and enlarge their
power. Yet, the explosion of the technology of communication and
information gathering has not been the benign force fostering interdependence and the "global village", foreseen by Marshall Mc-
Luhan, where communication technology enables us to overcome
"the regime of time and space and pours upon us instantly and
continuously the concerns of all other men".[20]

> The *Declaration of Human Rights* and its advocacy of the "free flow" [of
> information] rests on the nineteenth century liberalism of thinkers like
> Adam Smith and John Stewart Mill. One wonders whether this is con-
> gruent with twentieth century requirements for participation in the "free
> flow," like electricity, know-how, capital and marketing mechanisms.
> Therefore, as Finnish President Kekkonen asked: "Could it be that the
> prophets who preach unhindered free communication are in fact not
> concerned with equality between nations, but are on the side of the
> stronger and wealthier?"[21]

Hamelink argues that "global interdependence is rather a dependence of developing nations upon rich, industrialized nations for their
information. The public access is really only granted to those with
the economic resources to afford the communication infrastructure.
The better understanding between peoples amounts in fact to the
imposition of the socio-cultural values of the powerful nations upon
the rest of the world."[22]

A further area of growing power is the patenting of biological
processes. In the USA a company now has the right to patent living
organisms which have been developed in the laboratory (comparable
to pharmaceutical patents) and thus to use these living organisms
for private commercial interests. These new genetic techniques,
often developed in the university, in part through public funds, are
made available to industry on commercial bases – often, ironically,
to keep the university financially solvent in a time when public and
other sources of funds are becoming more scarce. The capacity to
splice genes could open up significant economic advantages. Such
developments have wide possibilities for further concentration of
power, yet they are not, to date, attentive to the profound philosophical, religious and moral implications of such practices. There
is greater prospect that such questions will be pursued vigorously
in the university environment than in the scientific laboratories of
large corporations.

This is particularly crucial since recent research, as indicated in
the Vogelenzang report, suggests that DNA changes can be made

not only in somatic cells (affecting only those specific cells), but in "germ-line" cells which can cause changes to be passed on from generation to generation.[23] In the light of these possibilities in DNA modifications, the consultation suggested, among other conclusions:

Patent applications are likely to be granted soon for micro-organisms created by genetic manipulation, which contain biologically functional genes and which synthesize medically useful proteins and similar macro-molecules. This may not be significantly different from the granting of process patents for the production of pharmaceutical and therapeutic substances. Nonetheless, many would argue that patent protection in this form will allow existing and emergent corporations to make excessive profits out of human suffering, to sustain an unhealthy world-wide dependence on pharmaceutical products, and to ignore real health needs because they offer lesser economic returns.[24]

The US patent decision rested upon a scientific, highly reductive conception of life, which sought to remove any distinction between living and non-living matter that could serve as an obstacle to the patenting of living but unnatural organisms. It would be easy to underestimate the philosophical, moral and ideological importance of the abolition of such a distinction, precisely because it allows a shift in accepted ideas to what may be done to living things.[25]

The report noted with concern the patenting of plants, giving corporations the power to narrow down the base of crops in any given area, and ultimately making the world more dependent on, and vulnerable to, "plants dependent on fertilizers and pesticides [often] produced by the same corporation".[26] Thus, the extent and capacities of new bio-technologies "raises in an acute and massive way the issue of private ownership of the production of products needed for human welfare".[27] Such a statement implies, of course, fundamental questions about patents and legally-protected information in other areas as well.

In brief, some of the most profound and perplexing moral and human issues of our time are rooted in the concentration and interlocking character of many kinds of power which have been historically defended by tradition and law. That process of increased centralization promises to persist as a major feature of the decade, while at the same time it threatens to undermine, or render ineffectual, an emphasis on self-reliance.

Growing restiveness of the poor

Coupled with continuing privation on one hand, and concentration of power on another, is a growing restiveness of poor nations, and poor peoples within nations. The poor are becoming more and more aware of their rights, their power, their potentialities, and they are increasingly convinced that these will not be conceded voluntarily by those now holding power. Three areas illustrate this greater willingness to take matters into their own hands.

The first is a persisting determination for self-reliant economic development, though self-reliance as an ideal is being sorely tested in practice. The economic, political and cultural costs of becoming integrated into a global economic system are high; vulnerability to others' decisions increases dramatically; second-class status seems to be guaranteed. Yet it is premature to predict success for self-reliant development; even in China the advantages of interdependent, as distinguished from independent, development have been reasserted. The attractions of increased participation in a global economic nexus, despite its liabilities, appear great even for many nations which have adopted philosophies and national policies of self-reliance. The same kinds of dynamics appear within nations as between nations. The next decade will be a major test of whether experiments with self-reliance can slow the surge towards concentration of economic, political and cultural power.

A second dramatic manifestation of rising opposition to dependency is the resurgence of traditional religions and cultures, most visibly and compellingly of Islam. It remains to be seen whether Islamic political power will coalesce with and reinforce the dominant world economic system, or use its economic muscle and strategic geopolitical location to identify more fully with the aspirations of the third world. The test will be not only in the size of its petro-dollar aid programme (significant as that could be), but in endorsing goals and strategies of the poorer nations. Aside from how it uses its economic and political power, however, the revival of Islamic culture and religion represents a significant challenge to the invasion of third world societies by cultures and values emanating from either the first or second world. This resurgence of Islamic culture, and its confrontation with Western technological society, notably in Iran, parallels similar developments of a less volcanic nature in many parts of Asia, Africa, and Latin America.

This same phenomenon is evident among many third world Christian communities, who insist upon discovering anew what it means to be faithful in their own cultures, in the light of their own unique historical experience, and thereby to resist the domination of Christian theology and institutions as defined in a Western context and exported across the world. Indigenous Christian communities, notable in Zaire and Brazil, and active members of the ecumenical family, are vigorous expressions of opposition to cultural domination. Equally dramatic in recent years has been the brushfire development of "base communities" of Christians, almost always rooted among the poor and marginalized sectors of society. These *grupos de base* are forging a new kind of identity for Christian faith, most often through their solidarity in a struggle for justice and liberation. Despite oppression against them, they are a promising sign not only for the renewal of society but also for the renewal of the church.[28]

Finally, evidence is mounting on the level of direct political protest: through outbursts of passionate anger and frustration (1981 summer burning in English cities); indiscriminate terrorism often against innocent victims; guerilla activities typified by an overall plan and strategy for change; freedom movements; protest movements against public policy (demonstrations against nuclear energy plants in the USA, or against the placement of nuclear weapons in Western Europe). While statistics on anti-establishment actions are often skewed, there can be no doubt that there has been a dramatic increase during the past decade and a half.

Evidences of violence abound, though the media tend to focus attention on violence against established social systems: escalating crime, especially crimes of violence; apparently indiscriminate terrorism; guerilla attacks; *coups d'etat*; civil wars and wars between states. Stuart Kingma, Director of the Christian Medical Commission, refers to escalated violence in an article he wrote for *Contact*:

> Many observers of the human scene have noted that there is a significant escalation of violence in all its forms, both overt and subtle. In the last 25 years alone, more than 65 nations have been involved in civil and international war in over 120 identifiable conflicts. The toll is to be measured not only in casualties which itemize the dead and wounded. The greater toll is in human suffering and disability, the destruction of livelihood, the displacement of populations. . . . Violations of civil and human rights are reported from all corners of the world. Torture has become one of the plagues of the past 50 years, but the stories hardly stir our sensitivities.[29]

The past three decades have been enormously violent, and the frequency of violence appears to escalate.

Without minimizing the incredibly tragic aspects of such confrontations with the system, it is also important to reckon with the escalating violence of established regimes against people who, often justifiably, are desperate to change their condition: torture; imprisonment; violations of human rights; growing oppression of the masses of the people by their own leaders; suppression of poor nations by the rich, often under the guise of assisting or protecting them; the tyranny of a militaristic mentality on us all. Violence of repression and suppression works dialectically with the violence of people yearning for freedom. The objective realities of poverty, misery and oppression intensify so rapidly and massively that many sophisticated and veteran social philosophers almost despair of *The Human Prospect*.[30] Heilbroner sees runaway population, obliterative war, potential environmental collapse and science and technology as the four major external challenges to the human prospect.

But on the subjective side, much despair and violence stem from a collapse of cohering and compelling social and human values; humankind no longer is convinced it has the capacity to overcome its problems.[31]

Escalating militarism

A fourth dominant fact on the world scene is growing militarism and its twin, the "national security stage". We assume here the definition of militarism used by Ninan Koshy in *The Security Trap*: "the process whereby military values, ideology and patterns of behaviour achieve a dominating influence on the political, social, economic and external affairs of the state. As a consequence the structural, ideological and behavioural patterns of both the society and the government are militarized."[32] "Current world military spending is double the gross national product of the continent of Africa and equal to that of Latin America."[33] So prominent is this rise of militarism that Barnet, whose major work has been in the field of transnationals, writes that "the 1960s were the decade that established the Global Factory (TNCs); the 1970s was the decade of the global arsenal."[34]

The super-powers and their partners vastly increased military spending, in 1981 estimated at approximately $500 billion per year globally, and absorbing an estimated 50% of all scientific research and personnel. Equally stunning is increased arms expenditures by poorer countries, with arms purchases from the industrialized countries amounting to about 70% of the $14 billion spent in 1978 by third world countries (with $5.8 billion and $4 billion having been sold by the USA and USSR, respectively).[35] The USA is scheduled to export between $25–30 billion in arms in 1982–83, and France, too, is rapidly increasing its exports of armaments.[36] As Pierre shows, many of these exports are not to "stable" areas of the world, but to unstable areas, such as the Middle East.[37] A survey of Asian expenditures on health, on education and on the military, revealed that several countries spend a higher proportion of their GNP on the military budget than on health and education combined.[38]

The third world's share of total world arms sales has increased during the past decade, roughly from 15% to 25%.[39] Barnet puts the figure still higher, arguing that about a third of arms sales in 1979 were purchases by third world countries, with seventy-five third world countries importing sophisticated weaponry. The implication of these remarks is not that poor countries are less justified than the rich in spending huge amounts in the military sector. Rather, the argument is intended to convey the tragic fact that, worldwide, in a time of colossal human need, vast resources of the total human community are being squandered on almost completely unproductive military expenditures. No nation can afford such huge outlays.

Why have military expenditures expanded so rapidly, especially in the poorer countries? Various answers can be given: prestige, escalating costs of production, renewed or intensified external threats. This explains why military expenditures, especially for imported arms, tend to be concentrated in unstable regions of the world, especially the Middle East.

Is there a more basic reason? Some analysts point to the emerging "national security state". Given the volatile political situation in many countries, often due to social injustice, a strong military establishment is developed as a defence against one's own people. Incumbent local leaders, in collusion with international elites, maintain themselves in power through a powerful and expanding military establishment. "Security" thus becomes a euphemism for the security of incumbent political and economic leaders, not against external threats (though often the spectre of real or imagined external threats is used to justify repression) but against internal dissidents. This view is described by Barnet:

> These three developments – increasing integration of the world economy, increasing consciousness of resource scarcity and resource dependence, and increasingly sophisticated use of military systems for maintaining control over resources [and markets?] – produced a new military order for the world. The new order is in some ways a legacy of the old colonial military order, but it is new in striking and important ways. In the colonial system the imperial powers maintained control by stationing their own troops and naval forces in the area. In the new military order, the development of which was accelerated in response to the failure of counter-insurgency warfare in Indo-China, the emphasis is upon building up "indigenous" forces with the help of massive amounts of sophisticated military equipment supplied by outside powers.[40]

As the Churches' Commission on International Affairs concluded, "national security is a legitimate concern of nations and states, but in recent decades it has become a common pretext for many countries to clamp down on the fundamental rights of their citizens, to build up their war machinery and even to initiate aggression against other nations".[41]

The connection between growing militarization and continuing poverty is obvious: money is drained away from socially desirable productivity; scientists and highly trained personnel are diverted to non-productive work; inflation escalates nationally and globally hurting everyone, but especially the poor; scarce energy and minerals are wasted; a climate of fear, distrust and helplessness is created; an environment of secrecy, deception, and manipulation is generated; gross violations of human rights occur; productivity is skewed away from basic human needs to earn foreign exchange to purchase military hardware; research resources and investments are siphoned off; indebtedness and balance of payments problems are heightened; dependence on other nations and corporations is increased. The social costs of militarism are clearly huge, perhaps incalculable, even if no war is ever actually waged.

> No shot need ever be fired, no bomb dropped, and no missile launched, for people by the millions to feel first-hand the destruction and devastation that lie in the wake of the now worldwide race towards greater and greater military prowess.[42]

The threat of war is there, too. Hanging over all is the nuclear sword of Damocles which could incinerate or radio-activate all life on earth. Writing in preparation for the 1979 MIT conference, Prof. Oldak described the situation graphically:

> The future is like a sharp sword. Recognize opportunely the problems of the future and you will grasp the hilt of the sword in good time. Miss the opportune time and you are faced with the need to grasp the honed blade of the sword with your bare hands, that is to correct the unfavourable development of events hastily and at the cost of great losses, and not to use one's opportunities to the full.[43]

Resource depletion

Resource depletion constitutes a further overarching reality. Ecological limits significantly impact world development prospects in several ways, including both the fact of limits and the perception and fear of limits. Both of these accentuate existing tensions. The fear of further limits prompts industrialized nations to strengthen policies to protect privileged access to scarce minerals already in short supply in the richer countries. Driven by the fear of shortages, and by the prospects of hugh profits, the USA almost single-handedly thwarted (or at least postponed) a Law of the Sea, so painstakingly negotiated over seven years, and symbolically (as well as economically) important. Thus, the fact of resource depletion and limits encourages industrialized nations to adopt policies to protect their supply of strategic metals even when this means interference in the politics of the supplying nation. This is perhaps most evident currently in the scarcely veiled threat to use force to keep the oil fields open.

Added to worry about scarce resources, like oil and minerals, has been a heightened concern about fresh and clean water. Fresh water is a problem at two levels: there is far less of it than is generally realized; it is inequitably distributed. Scarcity and maldistribution of water is likely to become a volatile issue between nations, as well as within nations, especially in areas not blessed with natural watershed supplies (e.g. the density of rivers in Africa is consider- ably less than that in South America). Already water rights between nations is a subject of complex and controversial debate, and likely to become even more acute. The issues pertain not only to industrial and agricultural use, important as these are. They relate to issues of basic survival and health also. As many as 40% of the world's people do not have access to safe water. Because so much of the world's illness is caused by lack of safe water, this poses an enormous problem for supply and distribution. While the earth seems to have a plentiful supply of water (the earth is about two-thirds water), fresh water is less than 3% of the total.[44] In 1970 the World Health Organization estimated that only 15% of rural families had sufficient water, and they now argue that "the provision of a safe and con- venient water supply is the single most important activity that could be undertaken to improve the health of people living in rural areas".[45]

Ironically, one of the chief users of water is agriculture, with much of the world's increase in food production in recent decades attributable to newly irrigated land. Irrigation, however, is often highly inegalitarian, causing a further marginalization of the poor farm family, suggesting that every effort should be made to sustain water production for the very poorest elements of the population. Here the tensions between the supply problem, the quality problem, and the justice or distributional problem become readily apparent. It is evident, therefore, that in the years ahead the question of water will become increasingly prominent in development discussions. The urgency of fresh and safe water has been recognized in the UN decision to name the 1980s the "Water Decade".

Similarly, the need for firewood as fuel for cooking has progres- sively depleted forests and vegetation, with its attendant influence on soil erosion. Though many families even now spend up to seven hours each day gathering fuel, the situation is worsening. De-forestation goes on apace, causing flooding and erosion of precious soils. Dung and other materials, so desperately needed to replenish the soil, often are burned instead. "To meet their basic cooking and heating needs, some 1.5 billion people depend on wood fuels and nearly half a billion more, because they lack even wood, rely on dung and crop residues."[46] Though worldwide, this problem is particularly acute for people in the third world: "nine-tenths of the people in the poor countries where most of the world's population is concentrated use no fossil fuels at all. For the most part they burn wood. About 80% of the wood used in the third world is burned for cooking."[47]

Given the present rates of depletion (in the last 25 years the forest cover worldwide has been reduced by 20%), it has been estimated that by the year 2000 there will be only 10% of the wood necessary in the third world, unless drastic measures are taken to start countervailing programmes.[48] Though the problems of deforestation are caused in large measure by the survival needs of the local population, transnational corporations are among the chief exploiters of forests, with the benefits going to the richer countries. The denuding of huge areas, like the Amazon and Kalimantan, entail adverse side effects, such as the depletion of oxygen (the Amazon has been popularly described as "the lungs of the world"). It also tends to narrow plant and animal species important not only for medicines and food, but which have proven immunity to diseases. Thus deforestation has the unexpected side effect of increasing world reliance on a narrowing spectrum of plant and animal life.

New aspects of resource limitation are being revealed almost daily; these revelations heighten the anxiety of many who feel that their dreams are being thwarted by natural limits beyond their control, and by demands for social justice which many allege are exacerbated by uncontrolled and irresponsible population growth, especially among the poor. Others (often the poor) feel frustrated by the natural limits imposed upon them, but even more by the social limits imposed by those who have inordinate expectations and who make unfair demands on the ecosystem, and use their power and advantage to undermine the hopes of the poor to escape poverty. They resent, too, the audacity of those who insist on talking about population explosion rather than consumption explosion, and who have the temerity to talk about the need for a worldwide "steady-state" economy, thus implying a "freezing" of the current state of injustices.[49]

One of the most vivid descriptions of resource limits is offered by Hunter and Amory Lovins:

> If the earth were the size of an egg, then all of the water we will have, if collected together, would be one drop spread over most of the surface of that egg. All the air, condensed to the density of water, would be a droplet about a fortieth as big. All the arable land would be a not quite visible speck of dust. That drop, droplet and speck are all that make the earth enduringly different from the moon. Within this decade, if we remain unmindful, we will see still more unmistakable evidence that that drop, droplet and speck are unravelling, unable to repair the damage.[50]

Faced by absolute resource limits, and absorptive capacity limits, issues of justice become increasingly dominant. We can no longer afford the luxury of assuming that social justice questions can be resolved by the sleight of hand of economic growth alone.

Persisting North-South frictions on structural economic questions

Finally, frictions surrounding the international economic "order" will continue to be of paramount significance. It is widely believed that the Bretton Woods agreements, signed in 1944 by the rich nations, pegging currencies to fixed exchange rates and to the strength of the US dollar, have collapsed. "Stagflation" (high inflation and high unemployment, previously presumed to be incompatible) in most industrialized nations, coupled with widely fluctuating exchange rates and commodity prices, are both symptoms and causes of a fiscal turbulence which generates tensions both between the industrialized nations and the third world, as well as among nations in each of those groups. Similar, though not identical, problems affect the "ruble community" (working through the International Bank for Economic Cooperation), especially since an increasing amount of its trade is with members of the Bretton Woods community. Although Western Europe and Japan have become much more powerful actors in the world economy, their relative strength is not fully reflected in international fiscal policies: the US share of OECD productivity has declined from 60% to 40%, but "the dollar today accounts for over 80% of that part of international liquidity which consists of national currencies".[51]

At the same time transnational corporations and banking institutions play an increasingly influential role in economic stability or turbulence by shifting accounts into currencies most profitable at any given time (e.g. high interest rates, prospects for changes in currency exchange rates, favouring those based upon a floating rate).[52] Vast numbers of petro-dollars, in search of profitable absorption in the world economy, are another major element in the current fiscal morass. Bretton Woods, many assert, is a "system" broken down, where the anarchy of the strong hurts everyone, but especially the poorer and more vulnerable nations.

Among other things, the world economic system requires the development of international liquidity based upon something other than a national currency which depends on one set of national priorities and policies. As the Brandt Commission notes, some halting progress has been made to enhance liquidity through the International Monetary Fund's Special Drawing Rights. "The SDR represents a clear first step towards a stable and permanent international currency."[53] Along with the enlarged scope for an international SDR currency, several other components of a developing policy are advocated: a pluralistic basis for an international monetary system; greater and more equitable sharing in decision-making within international fiscal institutions; revision of the rules of conduct within the International Monetary Fund; adoption of basic changes such as those suggested in the New International Economic Order proposals.[54]

Disruptive as the current fiscal situation is for the more industrialized countries, it has been particularly devastating for many poorer countries. The spiralling cost of oil has been a major factor for many, but the oil factor must be seen in the context of more general pressures: erratic prices of primary product exports, continued quota and tariff pressures to keep poorer countries from processing products and from industrialization, escalating prices for imports from more industrialized countries, etc. Perhaps most visible of all third world countries' financial difficulties is their current indebtedness – estimated at $350 billion by the end of 1980, with $150 billion of this indebtedness being to commercial banks.[55] Although this indebtedness is largely concentrated in a few countries (Brazil, Argentina, Mexico and South Korea), and despite the International Monetary Fund report of August 1981, that most countries have been able to reschedule or otherwise meet their debt obligations, the issue of indebtedness continues to plague the world economy as well as the economies of poor countries.[56] It is in the obvious best interests of both rich and poor countries to develop a more rational, more just, more pluralistically defined, system. It is a matter of both justice and self-interest.

★ ★ ★

We face the decade of the 1980s with profound, recurring and complex problems, each of them fraught with technical and moral implications, each of them raising issues of justice and the exercise of power. Most of them also raise the question of not only physical sustainability, but of social sustainability as well. They are issues of survival. Militarism tramples onward implacably; stagflation persists; transnational corporations and commercial banking institutions broaden their influence and control; national elites suppress internal movements for participation and justice with ever firmer measures, under the guise of internal security; little progress is made on new international structures of trade leading to more justice for the poor; new indebtedness is being incurred through imports of energy and industrial goods; unemployment and underemployment are unlikely to ease, given the population profile particularly in poorer countries; the mood in many industrialized countries seems to be hardening towards the South, as shown by tighter conditions of aid and trade and more conservative social policies internationally as well as nationally; population growth is not slackening as quickly as some specialists had calculated (e.g. India); energy, armaments, pollution control absorb more and more resources; China's fuller emergence into the international market will mean greater competition for markets and fiscal resources; Islamic resurgence, supported by oil revenues, will challenge the economic and cultural hegemony of the West, and to some extent of Christianity. The challenges of the decade are enormous.

But there are also hopeful signs. In part, the magnitude of the challenges themselves is a hopeful element. The need for change, for justice, for new structures, will become increasingly imperious and unavoidable. A new awareness is growing across the world, despite frustrations and anxieties. People's movements for social justice spring up even where they are oppressed; base Christian communities, sometimes with tenuous connections with historic and institutional churches, manifest themselves on all continents; the ethos of self-reliance and the questioning of traditional views of development objectives are widespread; horizontal rather than vertical linkages are being developed among poor peoples and nations; commitment to meeting basic needs within the context of structures of justice is a far more conscious central commitment than just a few years ago; despite the dismal performance of most industrialized countries, a few have increased their aid efforts, and some ardently advocate systemic changes to foster justice and self-reliance; across the world there is new public consciousness of, and commitment to, justice and sustainability and participation, partly through new life-style commitments.

There *are* "signs of hope and justice". Many of these signs are

offered not by those in power, but by those who believe that an
alternative future is not only desirable, but possible – by those who
are determined to contribute to the shaping of that new alternative.

NOTES

1. For example, Willy Brandt, *North-South: a Program for Survival*, Cambridge,
   Massachusetts, MIT Press, 1980; Gerald Barney, *The Global 2000 Report to the
   President*, Washington, DC, US Government Printing Office, 1980; Pearson
   Commission, *Partners in Development*, New York, Praeger Publications, 1969;
   Gunnar Myrdal, *Challenge of World Poverty*, New York, Random House, 1970;
   Donella Meadows, *et al.*, *Limits to Growth*, New York, Universe Books, 1972;
   Mihajlo Mesarovic and Eduard Pestel, *Mankind at the Turning Point*, New York,
   New American Library, Inc., 1974; Presidential Commission on World Hunger,
   "Overcoming World Hunger: the Challenge Ahead", June 1980; Sixth Special
   Session of the General Assembly of the United Nations (1974), etc.
2. Brandt Commission Report, p. 47.
3. World Bank Annual Meeting, Nairobi, 24 September 1973.
4. Richard Barnet, *The Lean Years*, New York, Simon & Schuster, 1980, p. 152.
5. World Bank, *World Development Report, 1980*, London, Oxford University
   Press.
6. *Ibid.*, p. 110.
7. *Ibid.*, p. 110.
8. *Ibid.*, p. 154.
9. *Ibid.*, pp. 150 and 152.
10. *Ibid.*, p. 60.
11. John Sewell (ed.), *The United States and World Development: Agenda, 1980*,
    Washington, Overseas Development Council, 1980, p. 82.
12. Barnet, *op. cit.*, p. 257.
13. World Bank, *op. cit.* p. 59.
14. *Ibid.*, p. 59.
15. Similar composite statistics hide disparities within a nation. For example per
    capita growth rate in the poorest countries was only .9% in the period between
    1970 and 1977, and *minus* .1% in Africa during the same period. Sewell, *op. cit.*,
    p. 152; and *Newsweek* (European edition) 6 July 1981, pp. 38–41.
16. World Bank, *op. cit.*, p. 54.
17. *Ibid.*, p. 55.
18. This phenomenon is increasingly documented. On the US scene such books as
    the following introduce the issue. Wendell Berry, *The Unsettling of America*,
    New York, Avon Publishers, 1978; Charles Little, *Land and Food: the Preservation
    of US Farmland*, Washington, DC, American Land Forum Report Number 1,
    1979; Ross Talbot (ed.), *The World Food Problem and US Politics and Practices*,
    Ames, Iowa, Iowa State University, 1979.
19. Cees Hamelink, *The Corporate Village*, Rome, IDOC, 1977; see also Hamelink,
    Communication in the Eighties: a Reader on the McBride Report, Rome, IDOC
    International, 1980, p. 2.
20. *Ibid.*, p. 2.
21. *Ibid.*, pp. 2–3.
22. *Ibid.*, p. 5.
23. Church and Society, World Council of Churches, *Manipulating Life: Ethical*

Issues in Genetic Engineering, report of a working group, Vogelenzang, Netherlands, 15–18 June 1981, 1982, pp. 4ff. In August 1981, it was reported that "Stanford University (USA) plans to license its patented process for gene splicing to any company that wants to use it, for a minimum of $10,000 a year. The University predicted that it would earn several hundred thousand dollars per year at first, and as much as $1 million per year by the mid-'80s." *International Herald Tribune*, 6 August 1981, p. 9.

24. *Ibid.*, p. 21.

25. *Ibid.*, p. 22.

26. *Ibid.*, p. 23.

27. *Ibid.*, p. 25.

28. See, for example, Jether Ramalho, *Signs of Hope and Justice*, Geneva, CCPD/WCC, 1980; and Sergio Torres and John Eagleson (eds.), *The Challenge of Basic Christian Communities*, Maryknoll, New York, Orbis Books, 1981.

29. "Beyond Mere Survival to the Abundant Life", *Contact*, No. 62, June 1981, pp. 2–3.

30. Robert Heilbroner, *An Inquiry Into the Human Prospect*, New York, W. W. Norton & Company, Inc., 1974.

31. *Ibid.*, Chapters 2 and 5.

32. Jose-Antonio Viera-Gallo (ed.), *The Security Trap*, Rome, IDOC International, 1979, p. 6.

33. Ernie Regehr, *Militarism and the World Military Order*, Geneva, WCC/CCIA, 1980, p. 3.

34. Barnet, *op. cit.*, p. 223.

35. Brandt Commission, *op. cit.*, p. 120.

36. *International Herald Tribune*, 16 February 1982, p, 4.

37. *Ibid.*, p. 4.

38. Christian Conference of Asia, *People Against Domination*, Kuala Lumpur, 24–28 February 1981, Tokyo, Christian Conference of Asia, p. 97.

39. Sewell, *op. cit.*, p. 209.

40. Barnet, *op. cit.*, p. 221.

41. Outline of a programme "Towards a Just, Participatory and Sustainable Society" (unpublished), WCC Unit II meeting at Egham, England, 17–23 April 1977, p. 8.

42. Regehr, *op. cit.*, p. 37.

43. Pavel Oldak, "The Environment and Social Production: a Soviet View," in Paul Abrecht, *Faith, Science and the Future*, Geneva, WCC, 1978, p. 216.

44. Barnet, *op. cit.*, p. 193.

45. *Ibid.*, p. 196.

46. As reported in the 1980 Church World Service study on diminishing worldwide water resources, p. 9.

47. Barnet, *op. cit.*, p. 73.

48. *Ibid.*, p. 73.

49. See, for example, C. T. Kurien, *Poverty, Planning and Social Transformation*, Bombay, Allied Publishers Private, Ltd, 1978.

50. "The Surprises are Coming, and They Aren't All Bad", *Christianity and Crisis*, Vol. 41, No. 4, 16 March 1981, p. 62.

51. Brandt Commission, *op, cit.*, p. 203.

52. Anthony Sampson, *The Money Lenders*, New York, Viking Press, 1981.

53. *Ibid.*, p. 209.

54. The New International Economic Order, first highlighted by the poorer nations at the Sixth Special Session of the UN General Assembly, May 1974, shifted

emphasis from aid to structures of world economic relations. Among the most significant recommendations were increased access to developed country markets for manufacturing goods from poor nations; expanded commodity agreements; indexation of exports and imports; reform of the international monetary system; control of transnational corporations; establishment of a special fund for poor countries in a liquidity crisis; increased transfer of technology. Donald Puchala (ed.), *Issues Before the 35th General Assembly of the United Nations, 1980–81*, UN Association of the USA, 1980, pp. 74–75. See also William Cline (ed.), *Policy Alternatives for a New International Order*, New York, Praeger, 1979.

55. Sewell, *op. cit.*, p. 40.
56. Balance of payments problems are escalating, indicated in the staggering $100 billion dollar current account deficit of poorer countries, as reported by UNCTAD. It was estimated that the annual current account deficit would probably rise to almost $200 billion by the end of the 1980s. *International Herald Tribune*, 16 February 1982, p. 9.

2: The on-going development debate in the "secular" realm

An enumeration of problem areas or dominant forces, such as in the preceding chapter, can be deceptively simple. In a striking analysis of the McBride Report on the power of communications, Nordenstreng contends:

> The report suggests a deceptive way of looking at global problems which should serve as a warning example rather than as a model for the mass media and other promoters of public opinion; an ahistorical, nominalist, and overtly political way to go about it – however convenient it may be in terms of eliminating theoretical and political controversies – does not usually lead us to facing objective reality but on the contrary easily obscures reality by preventing us from seeing the deep interrelationships and the totality of social phenomena.[1]

Similarly, to recapitulate the overarching problems facing the world in the eighties may become a nominalist approach, a way of isolating problems and hiding their inter-relationships, and thus of obscuring reality. The issues we have described above are not discrete and unconnected; they are part of a dynamic and interdependent reality. To treat them otherwise would be to miss the essential, to undercut analysis of causal relationships and to forfeit effective counter-measures. Further, to perceive problems in isolation cuts the nerve of moral endeavour, for every time one turns around there is another huge and complex and unmanageable, yet very important, "problem".

In this chapter we try to contextualize the issues of development by reflecting on differing paradigms of analysis and understanding. Clearly, data pertaining to issues of global justice and development are so complex that they defy clear and simple analysis, but they are not simplified by adding more information. Despite the difficulty of developing adequate paradigms (all subtly and deeply coloured by one's cultural experience and condition), certain conceptual perspectives have emerged. Since this is not an essay on development theory, but an attempt to put the churches' struggle for development-liberation into its proper context, the presentation inevitably will be, and appear, simplistic for specialists in development theory.[2] Above all, however, we want to stress our conviction that development and liberation theories emerge and change not merely on the theoretical level, but through actual engagement in situations of poverty and oppression, and through struggles to overcome them.

The growth paradigm

There are two major development-liberation paradigms, though a third is now coming into greater prominence. Hettne calls the two schools of development theory the "from tradition to modernity" school, and the "dependence and underdevelopment" theory.[3] The dominant paradigm for development, still very influential in its modified forms, is the "growth" model: "Developmentalism is one of the oldest and most powerful of all Western ideas." Hettne summarizes Nisbet thus: "The central idea of this perspective is the metaphor of growth. Thus development is conceived as organic, immanent, directional, cumulative, irreversible and purposive. Furthermore, it implies structural differentiation and increasing complexity."[4] The idea of growth has become linked with the idea of progress.

In caricature form, the essential objectives espoused in this growth model are quantitatively defined, and are measureable in terms of goods consumed and services available. It assumes that standard of living, definable in composite ways through GNP, or per capita consumption of essential commodities, is the goal of development. These general goals are often defined more precisely with reference to such factors as caloric and protein intake, years of schooling, infant mortality, longevity, health professionals per thousand of the population. Some analysts count factors such as energy consumed per person, telephones or radio sets per thousand of the populace, and/or by the movement towards an ever greater prospect of procuring these goods and services.

How will this growth and higher standard of living be achieved? This growth model posits that development towards these objectives can be accomplished best through high productivity, assuming that the best way to achieve justice is through high growth rates, the benefits of which gradually spread from the centre to the periphery, or from the top to the bottom layers of the social and economic pyramid.[5] It assumes that there is an essential, though not always self-evident, harmony of interests between those who occupy positions of political and economic power and those who are poor. There can and should be a "partnership in development".[6] That partnership can be assured best by maintaining stability and order, so that the system is predictable, and rational economic and social planning can occur. Thus the desire for stability and order, often attributed to merely selfish motives on the part of those who hold power, is really linked to the ostensibly larger, and morally-principled, objectives of the development theorists emphasizing this paradigm. This paradigm also tends to emphasize gradualism, evolutionary change, working through existing social structures, with appropriate modifications, from one stage to another. There is considerable scepticism about whether the new economic and political structures advocated by many third world proponents are either necessary or desirable.

Dependency views

A second widely influential paradigm is the dependency view; it stresses the tension and disharmony of interests between the centres of economic and political power and the "periphery" of marginalized persons and nations who are usually in the majority. Rather than a partnership of interests, the powerful exert and extend their power through the further subjugation and dependency of the "powerless". The prosperity of the few is made possible by the oppression of the many. There is a dynamic, but negative, relationship between the growing affluence of the prosperous, and the increasing marginalization of the poor. Economic growth does not automatically achieve just distribution of goods produced. Further, in this paradigm, justice is defined not only by having sufficient goods and services for a dignified human life, but also by the ways in which the poor participate in making decisions concerning the constituents of a good life and how they should be achieved. Justice requires the reduction, if not the complete overcoming, of dependency. Justice is defined less in economic and more in political terms, based upon the belief that enhanced political power will help the poor achieve greater economic benefits.

Operating from this paradigm, Harrington argues that underdevelopment is, to some extent, whether intended or not, a consequence of growth and overdevelopment: "What is critical to underdevelopment is not some physical fact but a world economic structure that perpetuates backwardness."[7] Galtung argues that even our vocabulary tends to hide the reality of structural dependence:

The basic problem of our world is structural, or political. Structural properties like exploitation, penetration, fragmentation, marginalization have to be added to the problematics not only as an expansion of the problems catalogue, but in order to find the tools for causal analysis.[8]

In this same vein, based on his experiences in Cuba, Sergio Arce-Martinez argues that it is incorrect, even impossible, to talk about development before there are fundamental changes in the structures of domination and dependency in society; development can occur only after this domination–dependency relation has been ruptured, and replaced with a system which can generate harmonious partnership in development.[9]

It should be clear that not everyone who insists on a dependency paradigm is a Marxist, even though the Marxist analysis of a class society, and the Leninist doctrine of imperialism, lead naturally to a dependency view of underdevelopment. Thus, the conflictual character of change is stressed; it is assumed that those who currently hold power will do whatever they can to perpetuate their privilege. It is the task of the "underside of history", both within nations and internationally, to struggle actively and in solidarity against this hegemony. History may not be an absolute zero-sum game, where one person or group's gain is automatically another's loss, but it is perceived as generally true that the privilege of the few is purchased at the expense of the impoverishment and marginalization (both) of the many.

During the past decade there has been increasing disenchantment with this second, dependency, thesis. There always has been a vocal group of development theorists who argue that the dependency theory of underdevelopment minimizes such factors as high birth rates, poor natural resources, traditional and inhibiting cultural values, incompetence and corruption, poorly developed economic and political institutions, etc. Added to these more traditional arguments against a one-sided dependency thesis is a growing disenchantment about a theory which seems to underestimate the role of the poor, or the indigenous populace, in the development and liberation process. Granting that dependency theories of underdevelopment contain crucial insights, they also tend to minimize or ignore other critical factors altogether. Indeed, such theories might even subtly encourage dependency itself by exaggerating the importance of external forces and minimizing the importance of self-help or self-reliance as elements in psychic, economic, political and cultural liberation. Kothari contends that:

. . . the "dependencia" theory is very relevant but it becomes an alibi for lack of self-development. You can always put the blame on the door of the exploiters but the exploitation that takes place in your own society is not questioned. There could be no greater slur inflicted upon our capabilities. This itself is neo-colonialism of a sort.[10]

The dependency theory tends to underestimate the importance of the third world communities themselves in the development-liberation process. They certainly are dependent in many respects, but retain critically determinative power over their own situation. Further, some conclude that prospects for structural change are remote and too costly to contemplate. Some feel that structural change without corresponding changes in the values and attitudes of the people will not really bring about a new and better situation.

Recent emphases on the New International Economic Order (NIEO) and on a Basic Needs approach should be seen in the context of these two primary paradigms. The NIEO stresses the need for structural changes in world economic and trading relationships to diminish national dependency. The basic goal of the NIEO is to move from dependent to interdependent economic and political structures. Among major goals of the NIEO are increased aid, new and stable commodity agreements, concessional terms of trade for poorer countries, changes in decision-making procedures in the International Monetary Fund, and review and re-scheduling of poor country indebtedness. These goals call for structural changes in economic relationships, not for more aid or charity alone.

Numerous criticisms have been made of the NIEO, such as the claim that such preferential treatment would further disrupt the natural market mechanisms which, it is argued, should determine patterns of trade. Even many advocates of an NIEO, however, are somewhat sceptical that it would really help the poorest people within the poor countries (often 40% or more of the population) unless there is a corresponding "new national economic order", to circumvent or undermine the privileged national elites (Tarzie Vittachi's "brown sahibs"). Until now there has not been much progress on the development of a NIEO, but some critics believe that the more industrialized countries, until now often opposed to the NIEO, will increasingly recognize the self-interest arguments for adopting several planks of the NIEO platform. Self-interest will dictate loosened and even "concessional" trading patterns: to avoid such frustration among the poor that they will be tempted to retaliatory violence; to keep third world countries within the "market economy" nexus in which powerful nations and corporations still can exert dominant influence; to enable the poorer countries to meet their heavy debt obligations not only to other nations and international organizations, but to commercial lenders; to keep open channels to the scarce resources and cheap labour of poorer nations. Despite meagre progress on the NIEO, a growing perception of self-interest will probably lead industrialized nations to take a more flexible policy in the future.

The Basic Needs approach was first popularized in 1976 by the International Labour Organization, and subsequently given more prominence in other international forums. It has become influential in development policies of some industrialized nations. The Basic Needs approach starts with the recognition that two decades of development efforts have scarcely scratched the surface of the deepest and most persistent levels of poverty – the almost one-half of the population in many poorer countries who eat too few calories and proteins, suffer poor health, and lack education, water and other basic needs of life.

"Basic needs", as defined by the ILO conference, include two kinds of needs. They include certain minimum requirements of a family for private consumption – adequate food, shelter and clothing are obviously included, and certain household equipment and furniture. They include, also, essential services provided by and for the community at large, such as safe drinking water, sanitation, public transport, health, educational and cultural facilities.[11] Because the concept of basic needs is "country-specific" and "dynamic", it "should be placed in the context of a nation's overall economic and social development. It should be placed in the context of national independence, the dignity of peoples and individuals and their freedom to chart their destiny without hindrance."[12] Lack of basic needs characterizes 31 poorest and most vulnerable nations, or the 40 nations on the UN's "most seriously affected" list. The situation of the 31 is worsening in many respects, and even though they form a minority of the population in the third world, the problems are immense. Thus the programme to meet basic needs calls for an all-out assault on deprivation to guarantee basic food, health, shelter and education for the world's poorest people. It is argued that this should be a head-on attack requiring the mobilization of all possible resources.

There are sceptics. Some argue that this is a diversionary "soft-option" for the rich countries who would rather send even increased aid, while keeping the basic structures of control in their own hands – a way of avoiding the harder questions of the NIEO. Others fear that a basic needs approach would be based on needs as defined by external cultures, and would constitute, therefore, another level of cultural imperialism. For example, it has often been assumed that there were "universally" valid points in Maslow's hierarchy of human needs, but recent studies have concluded that these are too culturally parochial to serve as a universal articulation of basic needs.[13]

> Maslow's list of human needs and his ordering of priorities are also particularly ill-suited – because of their underlying naive ethnocentrism – to serve as a conceptual basis for transnational efforts on behalf of the least Westernized groups in non-Westernized societies. The list reflects the values and preferences not of humanity as a whole but of a small sector of academic life in the hegemonic Western country.[14]

Not only *who* decides what basic needs are, and in which hierarchical relationship they stand, but *how* they should be met is a crucial question. Many theorists fear that a shallow emphasis on the provision of basic human needs, despite the moral urgency of doing so, may foil the critically important development of indigenous structures and institutions to meet human needs on a long-term and sustainable basis. In the long run provision of basic needs from outside is both psychically debilitating and physically impossible. For example, even if it were desirable, it would be impossible to meet long-term basic food needs by increasing imports from present food-surplus countries. This is not even desirable. Many studies have demonstrated the subtle but effective manner in which external aid tends to undermine the capacity and will for self-reliant and participatory change. Yet the basic needs orientation has highlighted a persistent failure in development strategies to bring the poorest countries, and the poorest and most marginated peoples of every country, adequately into the development process.

Garcia-Bouza's warning conclusion is important:

> If reduced to a scholarly preoccupation with poverty in non-developed countries and to a – perforce repetitious – exhortation about the need to do something about it, the basic needs approach is bound to lose significance and momentum. [But it need not be.] The future significance of that contribution hinges on its ability to concentrate on social and political changes and not on needs, goods and services, and to progress from general national and international studies to country-specific ones. As a policy framework, basic needs must come to terms with the practical impossibility of a "pure" basic needs strategy.[15]

Towards an alternative paradigm

A number of factors have merged to create the environment for a new paradigm, a fresh way of understanding development and liberation, and the processes through which they may be achieved. The two major old paradigms seem conceptually and practically inadequate. There is also a growing sense that both paradigms are implicitly culturally imperialistic. Both have cultural values in common – such as growth, consumption, similar attitudes towards nature, similar understandings of necessary stages of social transformation (although differing conceptions of what those stages entail). Thirdly, there is increasing disillusionment with strategies for development which are not country- or region-specific, thus tending to be abstract and practically irrelevant. A fourth level of disaffection is that neither of the two paradigms puts local people, and poorer people in particular, at the centre of the development process, either as decision-makers or as beneficiaries of the processes of development. Thus the common people are alienated from the whole development process; they feel like observers rather than participants, lacking control and out of touch. That sense of alienation characterizes not only poor people, but increasingly large segments of the presumedly powerful and well-off. A fifth element is a deepening awareness of the ecological costs incurred by either of the previously dominant paradigms.

A new paradigm is emerging, albeit amorphous and inchoate at the present stage. It is a constellation of experiments and theories around the theme of self-reliance. Of course, the notion of self-reliance is not new; it is the way most societies developed prior to their dependence on transnational economic forces. Gandhi's philosophy of social and economic organization was profoundly self-reliance oriented, as is Schumacher's *Small is Beautiful*, though it started from different pressures and assumptions.[16] India's policy of import substitution to assist the emergence of indigenous industry was an early but contemporary practical expression of a self-reliant economic industrialization policy. At a more extensive level, China's post-1949 development policy was predicted on political, economic and cultural self-reliance: "regeneration through our own efforts", according to Mao Tse-tung.[17] Tanzania has promoted this development policy in an African context. "Intermediate", and later "appropriate", technology movement have been spawned by the same idea of self-reliance.

What does self-reliance mean, at least in its present understanding? It is *not* only an economic concept, but has application to the whole of a society and culture. It is *not* an appeal to autarchy or self-sufficiency, but a way of affirming true interdependence in the long run. More positively, a self-reliance emphasis grows in part out of the negative impact on the cultural psyche of being in a dependent relationship to other, more precisely Western, centres of power. These other centres of power exercise political and economic domination; they also exert insidious cultural imperialism not only overtly, but quietly through the political, economic and technological structures of domination (a dependency often acceded to by sectors of the dominated society).

John Galtung, who has written widely on the notion of self-reliance, focuses his analysis on the "centre-periphery" phenomenon: "the centre-periphery formation is a much deeper phenomenon than political-military colonialism".[18] Seen in the context of a dynamic centre-periphery relationship, "self-reliance is not merely an abstract recipe, a way of organizing the economy with a heavy emphasis on the use of local factors, but a very determined struggle against any kind of centre-periphery formation, with the ultimate goal of arriving at a world in which 'each part is a centre' ".[19] "Self-reliance is a way of resisting centre-periphery formations, including the penetration, fragmentation, marginalization and segmentation of supporting mechanisms." [It is] "the autonomy to set one's goals and to realize them."[20]

This means that, in a modified form of the Roman Catholic principle of subsidiarity, decisions and productivity should be made at the "lowest" or most local level possible. Where a local unit is incapable of meeting all of its needs, it should try at first to have them met by a horizontal rather than a vertical relationship, i.e. with another local community at the same level. This applies to inter-regional collaboration as well. It would not eliminate all vertical dependencies, but these vertical dependencies would be minimized, and agreed to by the local community as something in their own best interests (cf. Rawls' principle that inequalities – not inequities – can be tolerated in society when those with lesser power or authority concede the greater power and authority to some, as being consistent with their own best interests).[21] On the economic level, "the point is to opt for those forms of production which permit local grassroots initiative and innovation yielding results compatible with local conditions, tastes and culture".[22]

It is not our purpose here to discuss all the alleged advantages of the self-reliance paradigm. It is a perspective on development and liberation consistent with other growing emphases in the development process: the need for sustainability; the centrality of people's participation; the importance of concentrating on the specificity of local circumstances rather than assuming that one development strategy is congruent with the needs and possibilities in every place; a growing conviction that the only effective way to challenge increasing concentration of power and subsequent dependency is to make oneself and one's society less vulnerable to external control and manipulation. Perhaps most important, the emphasis on self-reliance helps to defuse the pressures of cultural imperialism implicit in development from the centre, or development based on the assumptions of growth and consumption.

Thus the emerging emphasis on self-reliance, tentative as it is, is fully consistent with a major new emphasis in development theory – the importance of "development from within", and more directly related to contextual factors. "The substitution of a universal development path for a variety of local and national strategies (perhaps coordinated in regional programmes) will necessitate *indigenous* research on the problems of underdevelopment, thereby facilitating the emergence of strategies adapted to varying resource endowments and value systems in particular countries."[23]

Among the most interesting formulations for an "alternative development" has been the one articulated by the Dag Hammarskjold Project on Development and International Cooperation, 1975. According to it, an "alternative development" would possess the following characteristics. It would be:

Need-oriented, that is being geared to meeting human needs, both material and non-material. It begins with the satisfaction of the basic needs of those, dominated and exploited, who constitute the majority of the world's inhabitants, and ensures at the same time the humanization of all human beings by the satisfaction of their needs for expression, creativity, equality and conviviality and to understand and master their own destiny.

Endogenous, that is, stemming from the heart of each society, which defines in sovereignty its values and the vision of its future. Since development is not a linear process, there could be no universal model, and only the plurality of development patterns can answer to the specificity of each situation.

Self-reliant, that is, implying that each society relies primarily on its own strength and resources in terms of its members' energies and its natural and cultural environment. Self-reliance clearly needs to be exercised at national and international (collective self-reliance) levels but it requires its full meaning only if rooted at local level, in the praxis of each community.

Ecologically sound, that is, utilizing rationally the resources of the biosphere in full awareness of the potential of local ecosystems as the global and local outer limits imposed on present and future generations. It implies the equitable access to resources by all as well as careful, socially relevant technologies.

Based on structural transformation: they are required, more often than not, in social relations, in economic activities and in their spatial distribution, as well as in the power structure, so as to realize the conditions of self-management and participation in decision-making by all those affected by it, from the rural or urban community to the world as a whole, without which the above goals could not be achieved.

These five points are organically linked. Taken in isolation from each other, they would not bring about the desired result. For development is seen as a whole, as an integral, cultural process, as the development of every man and woman and the whole of man and woman. Another development means liberation.[24]

Emergent concerns and themes

Contributing to changing development-liberation perceptions have been several concerns or emphases which were less visible in earlier discussions. One is the concern that *people* and their full actualization should be more visibly at the centre of development goals and processes. This concern for the centrality of people emerges from several considerations. One is a recognition of the importance of cultural factors (values, relationships, institutions) in development. Another is the philosophical and theological affirmation of people's right to shape their own goals and the processes to achieve these goals; i.e. to participate not only in the fruits of development, but in the decisions about which fruits to strive for, and how. A third is a healthy reaction against exclusive preoccupation with political and economic structures, and an increasing recognition of the alienating and marginating power of all structures working in mutually reinforcing manners.

People's participation has become a major emphasis in development theory. It grows naturally out of a self-reliant and indigenous value formation and local decision-making. Participation, however, differs from mobilization. The latter is originated, controlled, and manipulated from the power centres of a society. But people's participation raises many ambiguities. It is possible, even probable, that to take seriously participation by all sectors of the populace may create tensions and fissures which might frustrate aspects of development, especially in countries characterized not only by class division, but by a multitude of fissiparous elements, such as religion, race, caste, language, region, occupation.

Further, if one uses the "tradition to modernization" idea of development, either explicitly or implicitly, many traditional values will be advocated even when they impede "modernizing" tendencies or interests. For example, Hettne and Wallensteen argue that "in no country have 'people' opted for industrialization".[25] They assert that the people and the elite usually perceive development in quite different ways: "Those who control the state give priority to values like military, political and economic strength, whereas 'people' think of development in terms of such values as freedom, welfare, security. A responsive political system would therefore have to sacrifice very long-term, costly projects in favour of development activities of more immediate concern to the people at large."[26] Traditional and holistic cultural values, rather than truncated modernized values, would likely be more powerful determinants of development policies. The tensions created would not necessarily be good or bad, but an emphasis on people's participation, so little stressed in traditional development strategy, would pose profound questions about the nature and achievability of development.

Another growing emphasis has been a concern for ecology. In one sense the two predominant paradigms for development-liberation have been, as Hettne and Wallensteen claim, "ecologically blind".[27] In relation to their impact on the environment, both models seemed to assume that "something would turn up" through science and technology, and that development ought to continue to be defined primarily by "sustained increase in real income per head of population".[28] But ecological concerns will have to be more fully reflected in any credible future development model, and this will require the highlighting of several questions in the development process which have not been so prominent in the past. The most obvious consequence of ecological considerations is that issues of justice are made more acute. If there is a limited "pie" instead of a growing pie, what are the rights of present and future generations for equitable shares of that pie? Not only do justice questions concerning current sharing become more sensitive and volatile, but the still more difficult ethical question of the claims of future generations becomes pertinent.

A second implication of the ecological debate is that the adequacy and propriety of growth as the primary development concept is increasingly suspect, especially when coupled with non-Western perspectives on the aims of development (not that they characteristically oppose growth). In this context issues of steady state economy, selective growth, growth in certain geographic regions and not in others, etc. become more germane. These considerations will likely lead to a more nuanced and particularized debate about development within specific geo-cultural environments, with less attention to a "universal" development format. A further consequence may be to intensify questions about the roles of transnational corporations in poorer countries, and the pollution they "import" to these countries.

Until recently the problem of ecological balance has been conspicuous in its absence from all the social sciences with the exception of social anthropology, where the man-environment relationship and its ramifications have been more difficult to hide. Re-thinking has started in several social sciences. Political scientists like Karl Deutsch now speak about eco-politics: the political challenge produced by the growing interplay of man's economic activities and the environment. Environmental interdependence transcends political borders, thereby increasing the importance of international actors and institutions.[29]

A third element emphasized in recent development literature is the actual or potential role of women in the development process. The literature increasingly stresses not only the rights of women, but the enormous contributions which women make and can make, when not systematically marginalized, in the development process.

"A world profile of women reveals that women (a) constitute one-half of the world population and one-third of the official 'labour force,' (b) perform nearly two-thirds of the hours worked, but (c) according to some estimates, receive only one-tenth of the world income and possess less than one-hundredth of world property."[30]

What does this brief glance at women signify in the broadest sense? It suggests that "educational attainment", "participation rates", occupational structure, private and public laws, family planning systems, technological advance and above all socio-cultural attitudes are all weighted against them. Across distance and boundaries in history and society, women have been placed on pedestals as goddesses, but imprisoned within domestic injustice. They have been romanticized in literature and lyrics, but commercialized in life.[31]

For some, issues of women's liberation are perceived as a diversion of energies from what are assumed to be more fundamental issues of poverty, oppression and development. But the broader and more penetrating analyses, of which there is a growing profusion, establish clear linkages between women's liberation issues, and these other questions, though the issues are shaped by particular and differing cultural and institutional environments. For example Krishna Ahooja-Patel mentions that women in industrialized countries are primarily concerned about integration into existing power structures, whereas many women from the third world are more preoccupied with overcoming existing cultural myths and social structures.[32] Some women's liberation efforts seem to ignore broader societal and developmental questions; some efforts seem to ignore issues of the third world in particular. In parallel fashion, much development effort appears to have ignored its impact upon women, even when it has been clearly detrimental to them. Such

were the conclusions of the Mexico City conference (1975) sponsored by the American Association for the Advancement of Science.
Based upon a number of case studies, the conclusion was reached
that:

> development has had a negative effect on women because planning has
> erred in one or more of the following ways:
> a) by *omission* – that is, by failing to notice and utilize the traditional
>   productive roles which women are playing;
> b) by *reinforcement* of values already in existence in society which restrict
>   women's activities to household, child-bearing and child-rearing tasks;
>   and
> c) by *addition* – that is, by superimposing Western values of what is
>   appropriate work for women in modern society on developing
>   societies.[33]

It is argued also that "the efforts of development which have as
their aim the correction of inequalities observed between specific
groups have the tendency to accentuate those which exist between
men and women".[34] Thus, "the hard core of the development problem is constituted by women".[35] Any development strategy for the
future relations within and between nations must take this core
problem into account, not only in the name of justice, but also in
the interests of development. "Self-reliance is a long road as hazard-
ous for women as for nations."[36]

The situation of the poorest poor in the development process also
has become a major focus during the past decade, especially since
1975. This concern is coupled with a new appreciation of the critical
role in development played by rural sectors, where 70% of third
world people still live. Increasingly it is evident that the poorest
sectors and countries are little helped (often they are hurt) by the
traditional development processes. Concentration on the poor is not
only a matter of human rights and justice, but also a strategic
element in holistic development.

One aspect of this discussion is the international community's
increased concern with first meeting the needs of the poorest poor
nations, recognizing that many are least endowed naturally and
geo-politically, that disproportionate aid has gone to a small group
of intermediate level developing countries, and that the poorest
countries are not in a position to derive maximum benefit from
proposed revisions in trading patterns.

Growing attention to the relationship of militarization to
development–liberation has characterized development discussion of
the past several years. Burgeoning military budgets in rich and poor
countries alike, coupled with numerous interventions by the military

in the politics of their countries, have given this issue prominence. Many negative consequences of militarization have been adduced: e.g. deflection of resources into essentially wasteful and non-productive channels, heightening of tensions between countries, suppression of internal opposition, high energy and pollution costs, development of an ethos of secrecy, manipulation and blackmail, constant threat of annihilation which generates psychic distress, erosion of many traditional values including the diminution of democratic participation, and an impact on worldwide inflation.

For some, however, the question of the role of the military in development is more ambiguous, and sometimes perceived in much more positive terms. At the Vasterhaninge conference, for example, several questions were raised about the role of the military that exemplify unanswered issues needing further refinement. While there is broad consensus on the desirability of civilian, as distinguished from military, governments, for some it is not self-evident that interruption of civilian governments by the military is universally undesirable. For instance, it can be argued that "the traditional role of military institutions has been either to maintain the *status quo* or to enlarge the powers of the nation. To this a new role has been added, namely the task of overthrowing the *status quo*; both traditional military organizations and liberation movements may have this ambition."[37] It is argued that the relationship between the military and liberation movements is often more complex than most literature on the subject implies.

Further, in many situations it appears that the military has adopted a developmental role. Without presuming to answer the question, Hettne and Wallensteen refer to the argument that "military institutions can promote development more effectively than civilian ones. Among the virtues ascribed to the military are less corruption, more advanced training, more egalitarian recruitment patterns and more efficient organization."[38]

Perhaps more important for development theory is that military factors be seen as part of the processes of social change. These authors pose four propositions meriting further testing and exploration:

(1) With increasing social contradictions in a society, the role of the military increases to the point where it takes over power, acting either as a neutral arbitrator or as a proponent of one of the contending groups. (2) With the collapse (inefficiency, demoralization) of other institutions in a society military institutions gain in influence. (3) With increasing conflict between nations, military institutions assume increasing roles within nations. (4) With increasing economic and political integration in

the international system, the military increasingly assume the role of stabilizing both internal and international relations.[39]

In short, without arguing for the validity of these theses, or suggesting their implications for development theory, the authors contend that "to allow development theory to operate in an abstract world where militarization does not exist would render its political significance marginal".[40] Yet most development theory to date has paid insufficient attention to the role of the military, and to militarization. That deficiency may now be more adequately addressed.

Two additional emphases have emerged more prominently in development theory during the past decade, neither of which is elaborated here because they are more fully discussed in other parts of this study. One is the "conjunction" and mutual reinforcement of structures of power (economic, technological, informational, political, military, cultural). The other is the erosion (some say collapse), of the world fiscal structure forged at the 1944 Bretton Woods Conference – a breakdown as fateful for the richer as for the poorer countries. Each of these factors is having significant impact on current development theory; both are destined to be far more influential factors in the years just ahead.

In this brief synoptic chapter we have tried to highlight the current development-liberation debate in secular circles as a way of contextualizing the churches' development debate. The churches' debate corresponds in interesting ways with this larger debate, a relationship which has been and continues to be dialectical. Churches have made important conceptual, as well as practical and tactical, contributions, and the churches' development and liberation debate has been greatly enriched by perspectives emanating from quite different social and conceptual contexts. In the next chapter, we turn attention to another aspect of the context of the churches' current development discussions, *vis.* a brief review of some social ethical themes as they have evolved within the ecumenical family since the 1925 Stockholm conference.

NOTES

1. Kaarle Nordenstreng, "The Paradigm of a Totality," in Cees Hamelink, *Communication in the Eighties: a Reader on the McBride Report*, Rome, IDOC International, 1980, p. 12.
2. S. P. Verma, "Theories of Political Development," in Sudesh Sharma (ed.), *Dynamics of Development*, Volume I, Delhi, Concept Publishing Co., 1978. A good example of efforts to make a typology of extant theories of development, and to search for more adequate ones.

3. Björn Hettne, *Current Issues in Development Theory* (SAREC Report #3, 1978), p. 19. SAREC is the Swedish Agency for Research Cooperation with Developing Countries.

4. *Ibid.*, p. 44. Refers to R. A. Nisbet, *Social Change and History*, London, Oxford University Press, 1969, and to J. Bury, *The Idea of Progress*, London, Dover Publications.

5. See, for example, George Gilder, *Wealth and Poverty*, New York, Basic Books, 1981.

6. The theme of the Pearson Commission Report, 1969, referred to in Chapter 1.

7. Michael Harrington, "The Development of Under-development: Why Poor Nations Stay Poor", in *Christianity and Crisis*, October 1977, p. 212.

8. John Galtung, "The New International Order: Implementing Self-Reliance", *Church Alert*, October–December 1978, pp. 6 ff.

9. "Development of People's Participation and Theology", *The Ecumenical Review*, Volume 30, No. 3, July 1978, pp. 266–277.

10. As reported in Hettne, *op. cit.*, p. 20.

11. International Labour Organization, *Employment, Growth and Basic Needs*, New York and London, Praeger, 1977 (a report of the 1976 ILO conference).

12. The annual report of the Overseas Development Council, in the USA, is an excellent reference, as are the reports of the World Survival Situation produced by the United Nations, and the annual World Bank reports.

13. See Jorge Garcia-Bouza, *A Basic Needs Analytical Bibliography*, Paris, OECD, 1980, pp. 16–17.

14. *Ibid.*, p. 17.

15. *Ibid.*, pp. 47–49.

16. E. F. Schumacher, *Small is Beautiful*, New York, Harper & Row, 1973.

17. John Galtung, "Self-Reliance: Concepts, Practices and Rationales", in John Galtung *et al.* (eds.), *Self-Reliance: a Strategy for Development*, Geneva, Institute for Development Studies, 1980, p. 19.

18. *Ibid.*, p. 20.

19. *Ibid.*, p. 20.

20. *Ibid.*, p. 22.

21. John Rawls, *A Theory of Justice*, Cambridge, Massachusetts, Harvard University Press, 1971.

22. Galtung, *op. cit.*, p. 24.

23. Björn Hettne and Peter Wallensteen, *Emerging Trends in Development Theory*, SAREC, report of Vasterhaninge Workshop, August 1977, p. 55.

24. Marc Nerfin (ed.), *Another Development: Approaches and Strategies*, Uppsala, Dag Hammarskjold Foundation, 1977, pp. 10–11.

25. Hettne and Wallensteen, *op. cit.*, p. 59.

26. *Ibid.*, p. 59.

27. *Ibid.*, p. 64.

28. *Ibid.*, p. 63.

29. *Ibid.*, p. 63.

30. "Another Development for Women", in Nerfin (ed.), *op. cit.*, p. 83.

31. *Ibid.*, p. 66.

32. *Ibid.*, p. 70.

33. Irene Tinker and Michele Bo Bramsen (eds.), *Women and World Development*, Washington DC, Overseas Development Council, 1977, p. 5.

34. Winifred Weekes-Vagliani, *Les Femmes dans le Developpement*, Paris, OECD, 1980, p. 7.

35. Ahooja-Patel, *op. cit.*, p. 80.

36. *Ibid.*, p. 80.
37. Hettne and Wallensteen, *op. cit.*, p. 61.
38. *Ibid.*, p. 62.
39. *Ibid.*, pp. 62–63.
40. *Ibid.*, p. 63.

3: Christian ethics in the World Council of Churches arena

Historical overview

Frequently it has been noted that the issues which became visible and crucial in the mission field, expressed in part through the International Missionary Council, have been major catalysts in the formation and vitality of the entire ecumenical movement. Similarly it could be argued that the mission field, and the diverse and problematic experience of the ecumenical Christian community, have generated a complex and profound questioning of the churches' ethical responsibilities in society. Indeed, central to the questions of Christian unity and mission are issues of the nature of the Kingdom, and the churches' responsibilities for witnessing to it. Overlooking or denying this centrality, some critics attack the ecumenical movement for being too preoccupied with social questions, and too little concerned about unity, and faith and order questions. Undoubtedly this is a falsifying bifurcation.

Concern for the churches' ethical responsibility was already evident at the Stockholm, 1925, conference.[1] One after the other, speakers expressed concern to relieve the suffering of the poor and marginated, arguing that the churches have responsibility grounded in faith to do so. However, most assumed that the churches' efforts should be primarily through charity and relief. While some reforms were envisaged, these did not touch the political and economic structures of society. The conference as a whole did not go on record advocating major changes; the mood was reformist at best, if not palliative in many respects. This is not to suggest that palliatives are never necessary or always undesirable, but to indicate that the basic approach in these early stages of the movement was far less critical of basic social structures than it was to become later.

Oxford, 1937,[2] undertook a more basic analysis of both the political and economic orders from theological and biblical perspectives. Thoroughly prepared in advance by prominent theologians and social theorists, the conference led to the formulation of fundamental theological perspectives on the nature of the state and the economic order. The conference's preoccupations were related to the world-wide depression of the 1930s, and to the rising tide of fascism in Europe. But the onslaught of World War II, and the apparent irre-concilability of significantly divergent theological perspectives on the political order (especially), precluded a unified commanding critique of the political and economic orders, or a single command-ing vision of what Christian political and economic perspectives should be. The most fundamental visible difference at Oxford was between Anglo-Saxon pragmatism and relative optimism about natural law and the prospect for the shaping of better societies, and Continental emphases on the "Orders," to avoid natural law cate-gories and to express profound reservations about the potentialities of social institutions and systems. However, the Oxford conference produced rich insights, new ideas, and effectively laid the basis for the post-war discussions of the "responsible society."

Amsterdam, 1948,[3] was beset by a new constellation of forces. The war left its bitter legacy of estrangement and suspicion, though the ecumenical community, which had not been formalized insti-tutionally before the war (at Utrecht, in 1939, the World Council of Churches in Process of Formation was affirmed), remained re-markably intact. Theological perspectives on social institutions which had been left unintegrated at Oxford, remained for the Am-sterdam Assembly to pursue further under the theme "Man's Dis-order and God's Design." The Cold War injected itself into the discussion of economic and political questions, though the discus-sion was to become still more polarized at the Evanston, 1954, Assembly.

In the midst of these pressures, J. H. Oldham's concept of "middle axioms" helped to bridge the significant theological differences which had been manifest at Oxford. Middle axioms already had been lifted up in the official report of the Oxford conference.

> Such "middle axioms" are intermediate between the ultimate basis of Christian action in community, "Thou shalt love they neighbour as thyself" – which though for Christians unassailable, is too general to give much concrete guidance for action – and the unguided intuition of the individual conscience. They are at best provisional and they are never unchallengeable or valid without exception for all time, for it is in a changing world that God's will has to be fulfilled.[4]

At Amsterdam the concept of "the responsible society" helped to provide a common focus for political, economic and social reflection, without becoming identified with any single ideological camp (political, economic, theological).

> A responsible society is one where freedom is the freedom of men who acknowledge responsibility to justice and public order, and where those who hold political authority or economic power are responsible for its exercise to God and the people whose welfare is affected by it. Man must never be made a mere means for political or economic ends. For a society to be responsible under modern conditions, it is required that the people have freedom to control, to criticize and to change their governments, that power be made responsible by law and tradition, and be distributed as widely as possible through the whole community.[5]

This notion of the responsible society highlighted the interplay and balancing of justice, freedom, responsibility and accountability to God and to the people. Through the concept of the responsible society and the formulation of middle axioms, a common ground was prepared for corporate statements on specific social issues and institutions, such as in the critique of both communism and capitalism during the Amsterdam and Evanston assemblies.

Evanston built upon this framework, elaborating still further the idea of the responsible society.[6] Although the Cold War had become, if possible, even more acute, the further delineation of economic and political middle axioms sustained the serviceability of the concept of the responsible society. Yet there were already afoot developments both to reinforce and to challenge that concept. Cold War, East-West consciousness was shifting slowly, but perceptibly, towards greater North-South sensitivity. The mid-fifties saw the ecumenical movement embark on a major study project on the "churches in areas of rapid social change."[7] The 1959 conference in Thessalonika became a symbolic milestone in a new consciousness of the issues of socio-economic development, focusing on areas of rapid social change. This conference began to raise more insistently the structural economic questions which were to become central at the Geneva, 1966, Church and Society conference, and subsequently.[8]

In the late fifties and early sixties, a spate of third world countries were in the midst of independence struggles, and already discovering the hard reality that political independence is but one important phase in the longer, more tedious and more complex struggle for economic and cultural freedom. Increasing numbers of third world churches and their leaders joined the ecumenical caravan. New energies and dynamic perspectives were injected into the Council at the New Delhi Assembly, in 1961, when the International Missionary Council and several major Orthodox communities became partners in the work of the Council.[9] The convergence of these factors helped – even forced – the Council to become much less Western oriented and, some would say, dominated. That the Third Assembly was held in India symbolized how different the Council had become, and how its agenda had changed to make greater room for issues posed most dramatically in third world environments. No wonder that development and global justice questions have come more prominently to the fore during the past two decades.

The 1960s were the first "Development Decade" of the United Nations. The churches, too, searched for innovative and more effective ways to promote development, though they tended to absorb and accept the dominant development concepts of the time, oriented very much towards economic growth and industrialization through capitalization. Emphasis at first was on enlarging the effort – at quantitative changes. Chief among the churches' efforts were attempts to expand project assistance, though changes of emphasis about types of projects began to emerge. Also, there was increasing attention to supporting comprehensive rather than isolated development schemes, and to complement efforts of governments and international agencies. At the same time, new themes began to emerge, in some ways overtaking the churches, or at least initiated from the outside. The Church and Society Geneva conference prophetically highlighted the social and technical revolutions which had been anticipated in the Thessalonika conference. Voices from the third world became louder, and sometimes more strident; theologians were joined by lay experts in economics and politics. Thus the debate became broad and deep – not only between mission and service, between charity and development, but also between development and revolution.

Already some expressed scepticism about the "development" mode of social change. At the same time a deeper understanding of partnership in mission was evolving; third world perspectives became increasingly visible and influential. Some wondered aloud, and eloquently, whether the gradualism implied in the development strategy could be supported amidst the turbulent and revolutionary tides sweeping many poorer countries. Indeed, some appeared to believe that only revolution, with all its moral and ethical ambiguities, was now demanded to overcome injustices – a revolution to counter entrenched power, a revolution for self-defence. Couldn't one develop a notion of "just revolution" built upon the traditional formulations of a just war? One result of this debate was a new ecumenical study and consultation on violence and non-violence, which took place in 1972.[10]

One casualty of the Geneva conference was the idea of the responsible society, which had served as a coalescing vision for approximately fifteen years. Many began to feel that this concept, aside from being amorphous and vague, tended to support the *status quo* in its title and in the way it was formulated – though the definition of the responsible society did stress the accountability of incumbent political and economic leadership to the people, and to God. Still, many felt that order and structure were emphasized to the detriment of change and newness. Some also sensed that the idea of the responsible society needed to be articulated globally rather than only nationally.[11] It is probable that the term fell into disuse in part because it seemed to emphasize political as distinguished from economic factors, while the 1960s was a period of the rediscovery of the vital influence of national and international economic barriers to justice and development. One suspects, as well, that the idea of the responsible society had become too closely identified with previous ecumenical, and dominantly Western, leadership, and the overshadowing of that theme may have been a subtle part of the larger struggle of young, and to some extent non-Western, church leadership for their own conceptual independence.

At the Uppsala Assembly, 1968, the tensions and divisions which were just beneath the surface at Geneva persisted, but "development" was a sufficient common denominator to keep the discussion manageable. There were a few verbal scuffles about the Charter of Algiers,[12] which to many attending the Assembly represented an analysis of structural economic problems which was both alien and threatening. While in some ways the Uppsala Assembly glossed over some of the deeper tensions and fissures which were manifest at Geneva, it did succeed in taking a strong and unifying moral position about the outrageous disparities between rich and poor in the world, and called for responses which moved beyond charitable concern towards structural changes.

The establishment of the Commission on the Churches' Participation in Development, as well as the earlier World Council–Roman Catholic collaboration in the joint establishment of the Society for Development and Peace (SODEPAX), institutionalized more visibly the growing ecumenical concern for development and global justice issues. The Montreux I conference, 1970, solidified the churches' interest in development issues. Coupled with the soon-to-be-established Programme to Combat Racism (stemming from the Notting Hill Consultation of 1969),[13] the development debate within the ecumenical family was given new impetus, but also far greater complexity. The links of poverty and oppression with racism became more evident; international structural impediments to economic development became strikingly apparent; preoccupation of the churches with charity and relief seemed less and less adequate or appropriate.

By Montreux II, 1974, new themes were emerging in the development debate. For one thing, many no longer thought it should be called a "development" debate. "Liberation" seemed to many a more adequate concept than "development" (emphasizing as it did the conflictual character of progress, the structural dimensions of oppression, the psychic values in winning rights and freedom, the people's role in the processes of social change, etc.). Further, poverty was increasingly attributed to structural oppression rather than to the traditionally ascribed shortcomings of the poor. The failures of growth-oriented, consumer-dominated societies became ever more apparent. Development Decade I had been adjudged a failure by many. The intransigence of the powerful seemed confirmed at every point. Thus it was natural, perhaps inevitable, that two new themes, "participation" and "sustainability," should become integral to the evolving ecumenical notion of development. While Montreux I had talked about the triumvirate of social justice, self-reliance and economic growth,[14] by the time of Montreux II, four years later, emphasis had shifted towards "people's participation".

At least four factors were significant in this shift. One was a growing sense that people had been lost in the emphasis on economics, and that people needed to be put front and centre in the development process, "people rather than abstract growth or GNP". Another was an emerging conviction that impoverishment and alienation are at the base of underdevelopment, and that people, especially the poor, need to regain a sense of their own possibilities and identity. A corollary conviction became clearer, that the poor are important not only as beneficiaries of the development process, but that they have unique and creative perspectives to bring to social analysis and social change. Finally, there was a growing weariness and pessimism about the incentives and capacity of the rich to change the systems from which they benefitted so handsomely. Thus the place of the poor in the development process – "people's participation" – was stressed by Itty in 1977.

> Development is essentially a people's struggle in which the poor and oppressed should be the main protagonists, the active agents and immediate beneficiaries. Therefore, the development process must be seen from the point of view of the poor and oppressed masses who are the subjects and not the objects of development. The role of the churches and Christian communities everywhere should be essentially supportive.

In situations where the poor accept their lot of poverty and misery in passive resignation, the churches should assist the masses to recognize the roots of their plight, to acquire a new awareness of themselves and the possibilities for changing their situation. In situations where the poor and oppressed are organizing themselves for the struggle, the churches should manifest their solidarity with them and provide supportive means for the struggle.[15]

In similar manner, and primarily through the work of Church and Society, the emphasis on sustainability became a prominent feature of ecumenical thinking on development. In turn, the issue of sustainability brought to the forefront questions about the nature of the human, and the Christian understanding of non-human nature.[16] This issue is discussed more fully in subsequent chapters.

This cursory review of the highlights of ecumenical thinking on issues of development and liberation provides the backdrop for the Nairobi Assembly, 1975. There was an underlying sense, in Nairobi, that the fissures and tensions within the ecumenical family, perhaps most notably surrounding the issues of the churches' responsibilities for social justice ("not *that* they are responsible for promoting justice, but *how*, and with *what* expectations"), threatened to undermine the unity of the movement. Not only were there differences in understanding the gospel, but some felt that the World Council was being rendered ineffectual through attention to an enormous number of important, but unintegrated, concerns. What was the main vision and purpose of the ecumenical community, anyway? What should it be?

Unwilling to relinquish its solid commitment to social justice concerns, and to theological and biblical study to undergird those concerns, the Assembly nevertheless insisted that these concerns be integrated with more traditional "mission," "evangelical" and "unity" purposes of the churches. Through the Central Committee, it set four main tasks for the years following the 1975 conclave: (a) to express and communicate faith in the Triune God; (b) to search for a just, participatory and sustainable society, (c) to explore the unity of the church and its relation to the unity of humankind, and (d) to relate education and renewal to the search for, and realization of, true community.[17] How these affected the concerns and programmes for global social justice is the task of Part II of this volume.

Constellation of emerging ethical perspectives

A discussion of ecumenical ethics can be organized in any one of several ways. One would be to review the chronological evolution of thinking; another, to review selected topics, such as "appropriate technology"; a third, to try to impose a theological or ethical system on the material, either from the outside, or on the basis of a perceived internal order. Here a fourth approach is used – a description of a cluster or constellation of emergent themes which seem to cut across many ecumenical documents, and which, as yet, do not have explicit coherence. Not all major points are covered, but selected key themes. Such an approach seems faithful to the probing, experimental spirit of the ecumenical community and its understanding of the role of churches in society.

Contextual ethics

During the early years of the ecumenical movement, there was a concerted effort to develop a system of ethics based on biblical and theological foundations. Ethical criteria would be deduced from these sources "deontologically". Increasingly, however, considerable scepticism has developed about the possibility of a deontological ethical system. That scepticism was expressed at the Geneva, 1966, meeting.

> The discernment by Christians of what is just and unjust, human and inhuman in the complexities of political and economic change, is a discipline exercised in continued dialogue with biblical resources, the mind of the church through history and today, and the best insights of social scientific analysis. But it remains a discipline which aims not at a theoretical system of truth but at action in human society.[18]

Such scepticism stems, in part, from a deepened sophistication in the sociology of knowledge (and the socially conditioned character of every perspective) on the theoretical level, and on the practical plane from an acute awareness within the ecumenical family that faithful Christians from differing theological and cultural environments perceive ethical responsibility in quite different, sometimes conflicting, ways.

Without falling into merely positivistic or situationist ethics, the ecumenical movement increasingly has appealed to a "contextual" ethic – one which takes seriously both biblical/theological reflection on the one hand, and concrete historical realities on the other. Oldham's middle axioms were not only an effort to bridge the gap between the ethic of aspiration (ends) and the ethic of inspiration (means), but to bridge the hiatus between the deductive and inductive approaches to ethical decision-making. They also were a bridge between professional theologians and experts in the social and physical sciences.

So, too, the notion of the responsible society was not solely an attempt to steer a course between *laissez-faire* capitalism and socialism–communism in the late forties and early fifties. Nor was it a simple capitulation to those who despaired of ever attaining a theological consensus for grounding Christian social ethics. The responsible society was more than a *modus vivendi* in the ecumenical debate. It was, in part, a growing recognition that while Christian ethics must constantly hold high the ideals of freedom, responsibility and justice (all explicit in the definition), the specific manner in which these goals were to be incarnated in particular social institutions and relations could be defined only in those specific contexts. That contextualism, dangerous and often frustrating, continues to characterize ecumenical ethics. The Zagorsk consultation, 1968, explicitly asked whether the deductive and inductive methods could not be combined through "dialectical interaction" between concrete situations and theological norms.[19]

Perhaps the difficulty of contextual approaches is most evident in ecumenical discussions on violence and non-violence. At a time when traditional doctrines of "just war" are being translated into doctrines of "just revolution," when the traditional rights of self-defence are being appealed to by those victimized by the systemic violence of the *status quo*,[20] when there is heightened consciousness of the psychic as well as institutional modes of violence and oppression,[21] and when there are ever more efficient instruments of violence and oppression available to those in power, the issues of violence and non-violence have become almost hopelessly tangled. Notwithstanding the eloquent witness of absolute pacifists within the ecumenical family, the movement as a whole reflects a much more contextualist approach to violence and non-violence.

The Central Committee concluded, in 1973, that "we have clear evidence that Jesus of Nazareth did not use violence on behalf of the weak, the poor and the suffering against the powerful, even though he identified himself with them."[22] But it admitted that on the meaning of Jesus' example for Christians today there is no agreement. The contextualist approach, however, is clearly supported: "Christians must avoid the trap of seeming to dictate strategies and tactics to people living in distant and different situations. No single one can have universal validity; and those who live outside a particular social conflict do well to be wary of handing out advice."[23] This view follows that of Zagorsk, 1968, which agreed that "we must realize that some Christians find themselves in situations where they must, in all responsibility, participate fully in the revolution with all its inevitable violence."[24]

Leadership of Western churches

Emphasis on contextualism has been deeply influenced by another feature of the ecumenical community which is very important for ecumenical ethics. In the early years the ecumenical family was dominated by Westerners, and theology was judged by its awareness of, and perhaps conformity to, Western – if not Continental – perspectives. Increasingly the *primus inter pares* position of European Christianity, biblical scholarship and theology has been challenged (at Nairobi 40% of the delegates were from the third world, and Eastern Orthodox representatives constituted the third largest "liturgical" family). Increasingly, ecumenical literature manifests a conscious and serious questioning of the normative character of Western culture, Western institutions and Western interpretations of the Christian faith.[25]

But it is not only the churches' Western character which is being questioned; it is also the churches' class character. Often the churches consciously or unwittingly collaborate with the dominant, usually oppressive, social forces and structures which need to be challenged. Western Christendom often reflects or exemplifies Troeltsch's thesis that churches characteristically gradually become accommodated to a culture, develop a perceived vested interest in preserving and extending that culture, and lose their capacity for prophetic witness among the poor.

Within the ecumenical family, largely through the voices of marginalized peoples, the often subtle and unconscious class character (and mentality) of many churches has become more visible. While the class analysis of society and the church may seem disproportionate in some ecumenical documents, it is a basic feature of the churches' life which much recent ecumenical literature has called to attention. The traditional theology and ethics of the churches has been a theology deeply conditioned by Western culture, history and institutions (how could it have been otherwise?). Theology has been for the most part a theology of the "winners" in history. Ecumenical ethics has begun to reveal how partial and incomplete, sometimes unfaithful, have been its understandings of, and response to, the gospel. This is not to disparage Western Christians, but to dispel the illusions (if they still persist) of self-sufficiency and wholeness. This has been a crucial and continuing contribution of ecumenical ethics.[26] The appearance of Latin American liberation theology (deeply influenced by the West), *Minjung*[27] theology, and the theology of base ecclesial communities are carrying on the challenge.

Continuing creation: Christ transforming culture

Another feature of ecumenical ethics is an increasing commitment to a "Christ transforming culture" perspective (to use Niebuhr's classical typology),[28] a view which holds together in dynamic and uneasy tension the convictions that humanity is radically alienated from God, through rebellion, but that the enduring power and presence of the Spirit is able to transform. In the corporate social life of humanity radical alienation and rebellion persist, but society can be transformed (not in a Social Darwinistic, evolutionary, or progressivist manner) through the Spirit. Thus social conditions and structures are always to be judged by, and as far as possible, conformed to the gospel.

At the Oxford conference discussions, but seldom since then, there was considerable evidence of a "Christ and culture in paradox" view, and occasional hints of a "Christ against culture" attitude. Perhaps no one, then or now, took a "Christ of culture" position. It is not so clear, however, that all recent ecumenical literature avoids a "Christ above culture" perspective, as it occasionally appears that an evolutionary rationality is at work – that there is no *fundamental* discontinuity between human aspirations and abilities and God's purposes; that no genuine *metanoia* is required. Some have interpreted (probably mistakenly) some of the Geneva, 1966, materials as so optimistic about human prospects that they fall into unwarranted optimism about human society. Further, some ecumenical documents suggest such a preoccupation with the structural and institutional impediments to justice and human wholeness, that readers could conclude that the Council has lost sight of the fundamental rebellion and alienation in all people, individually and corporately.

Nevertheless, it appears that the ecumenical community has implicitly adopted a "Christ transforming culture" view. While recognizing the importance of order and structure (even for freedom and creativity), ecumenical literature constantly implies that churches have been far too hypnotized with order and stability, and far too little alive to the dynamic pull of the Spirit into the future. Current ecumenical ethics is characterized by a sense of the "draw of the future" to which God is calling us. Creation is perceived as a continuing process, with God at its source; it includes both nature and history.[29] This world is integrally related to the Kingdom of God, though the Kingdom is neither now nor later fully realizable under historical forms and limits. The Kingdom is not some far-off, otherworldly, spiritual reality unconnected with the material hurts and mundane needs and hopes of people.[30] Nor is it fully realizable in human history, or through human efforts. The Kingdom is both present and yet to come, as is described so graphically at the Bangkok, 1973, Assembly, and in the "Just, Participatory and Sustainable Society" document submitted to the Jamaica meeting of the Central Committee, 1979.[31]

Why have the churches so often defended the *status quo*? One reason adduced is that for centuries the churches in Western Europe saw it as their duty to develop and preserve the Graeco-Roman scientific heritage. "This was a heritage of static conceptions of nature and history. The Christian message was thus framed in a static world concept. This situation lasted until the middle of this century."[32] Surely the reasons are more complex than this, but the fact that a major analytical document of the ecumenical movement describes the traditional view in this way indicates how influential today is the "Christ transforming culture" orientation.

"Knowing God" requires action for justice

How are we to discern God's will, to align ourselves with what God is doing in the world? On this point recent ecumenical thinking stresses two elements, each of which will have its profound impact on the way one seeks to act faithfully. The first emphasis is that the God of the Old and New Testaments is a God who acts; what predominantly interests us is not the metaphysical attributes of God ("I am who I am"), but what God has done and is doing among people. Symbolically, Exodus, the story of liberation, was written before Genesis, and even Genesis is primarily concerned with an account of God in action *vis à vis* the world and God's people. Pre-eminently the Incarnation is God-in-action through the Holy Spirit; cross and resurrection are God-in-action through the Spirit; Pentecost is God-in-action through the Spirit; the existence of the church is perceived as God-in-action through the Spirit. Biblical faith is not a new metaphysical system, but a response to God's initiating action, expressing love and requiring justice, in the midst of God's creation. One should not exaggerate the prominence of this in ecumenical literature, but it is an unmistakable theme. It lays the foundation for a second theme, which *is* more explicit in ecumenical documents.

That second point is that to discern God's will, even to know God, requires "following in the way". Knowing God is not something done in the abstract; knowledge of God does not precede ethics, or acts of obedience. Faithfulness is not intellectual assent to formal metaphysical propositions about God or Jesus Christ, nor is it a private mental opinion. To know God requires that one first align oneself with what God is doing, as that is known in part through the Spirit. Concretely that means that we can know God only through (not before) preaching good news to the poor, proclaiming release to the captives, helping the blind to recover their sight, setting at liberty those who are oppressed, and proclaiming the acceptable year of the Lord. In other words we cannot know anything profound about the resurrection (nor experience resurrection ourselves) without the cross – even though traditionally many Christians have built a metaphysics of salvation and even immortality based on a resurrection separated from the cross. To manifest love through justice and compassion is not only a matter of *obeying* God; it is a precondition for *knowing* God as well.

It is not a superficial repetition of Marxist terminology (as some allege) that leads to an ecumenical emphasis on "praxis" as essential to Christian life and thought; nor is it petty moralism. The emphasis on praxis, or dialectical interaction between action and reflection, each constantly challenging, purifying and enriching the other, stems from a basic understanding of the nature of God's relationship to the world. It reflects a basic understanding of the relation of action to reflection, of cross to resurrection, of morality to knowledge and faith, of faith to wholeness and salvation.

Co-creators and subjects of history

Consistent with this emphasis on a God who acts, and who is known through our faithful responses to that action, is an emergent ecumenical stress upon people as subjects rather than objects of history. People are perceived as co-creators with each other, and with God. That is their calling, even when they are prevented from exercising that calling. When people are prevented from realizing their calling by ignorance, or malnourishment, or social structures which stifle their freedom and creativity, God's purposes are violated. Such stifling is an affront to God, a violation of the individual involved, and an impoverishment for all humanity and creation.

This is, in part, the position argued at the Montreux I, 1970, conference and in subsequent World Council literature. It is also one reason for so much attention, on the practical level, to "appropriate," or "appropriable" technology (not "intermediate technology"). Superficially, emphasis on self-reliance would seem to minimize interdependence and the organic connectedness of the whole human family. However, concern for self-reliance is rooted in the conviction that genuine interdependence cannot be experienced until people are relatively equal, until those who have accepted their own inferiority and marginality rebel against such a self-image, until those who have come to accept their superiority have that illusion shattered. It is not possible to talk credibly about interdependence without an interim period of self-reliance, a period when those who have been victimized, and who have accepted their victimization as "natural" or at least tolerable, break the chains of that oppression and self-image. The whole "moratorium" debate in the churches starts here.

Hence the emphasis in ecumenical ethics on people as subjects of their own history, not objects of other's history, is not only a question of expedient social tactics ("people have to take power because it will not be given to them without a fight" – e.g. Pharaoh). It is also grounded in a theological conviction about the identity and meaning of persons as co-creators with God. This emphasis is reflected in the Nairobi Assembly 1975, definition of development: "a liberating process aimed at justice, self-reliance and economic growth. It is essentially a people's struggle in which the poor and oppressed should be the active agents and immediate beneficiaries."[33]

Leitmotif of justice

Throughout ecumenical history the search for justice has been a central theme. Justice is perceived in its double relationship to love – as an expression of love, and as constantly judged by love. Since Stockholm, 1925, at least two aspects of justice have become more explicit. One is that justice pertains not only to fair distribution of the goods and resources of society, but also to participation in determining what goods will be produced, and how. Combined with the stress on subjectivity, above, this explains the recent insistence on the core principle of "people's participation". People have a right not only to *have*, but also to *belong*, that is to share in making decisions which affect them significantly. Consequently, charity and justice are the same thing, even though charity may always be necessary to some degree. Equally important, justice requires changes in those social structures which prevent participation in decision-making. Hence centralization or monopolization of decision-making in society is a major concern of ecumenical ethics. Therefore, present ecumenical thinking envisages far more basic structural change in society than was foreseen even as recently as the Evanston Assembly.

A second aspect of justice which has assumed greater prominence is that it must be conceived in global terms. Today, more than ever, no nation is exempt from the power of other nations, other economic systems and other cultures. Concern for development and liberation has highlighted the complex actual interdependence of the whole *oikumene* – including non-human nature. The world community sees more vividly the ways in which complex economic and political relationships often spell prosperity for some, and concomitant impoverishment for others. It increasingly knows how cultural values flow overtly and subtly across national boundaries, and how they erode or challenge long-cherished traditional values and institutions.

More problematic for ecumenical ethics, however, is the question of Christian responsibility for the future generations of humanity. To what extent does concern for current social justice require us to take into account the needs of future generations? A related question, but with its own range of issues, is "to what extent are we responsible for non-human creation?" Biblically we are told that all of creation is groaning and longing for the glorious liberty of the people of God. How non-human creation must long for real human liberation, subject as it is to our current alienation and rapacity! Creation must not be perceived as a passive object of humanity's whims and appetites. Increasingly we are being pressed to re-think our relationship to our non-human environment.

These questions are part of the larger issue of a "sustainable" society. For sustainability is not an issue of survival and justice for those now living; it involves future generations, and takes into account the place of non-human creation in God's purposes. To date little attention has been given to these aspects of "global justice" within ecumenical ethics, but it is clearly an incipient discussion which requires that the issues be broken open by creative and disciplined minds.

Development towards liberation

No issue has had more far-reaching and profound impact on ecumenical ethics during the past fifteen years than that of "development-liberation". It is the centrifugal force which has spun out into their own orbit numerous other ethical issues, such as limits to growth, development by the people, appropriate technology, violence and non-violence, roles of women in development. The development-liberation debate has challenged many long-held assumptions about the nature of society and the character and purposes of social change: what *is* development? development for what? for whom? what impedes development? development by whom? development by what means?

We have noted the shift which took place in the early 1970s, from "development" to "liberation." That change has not been universally and unequivocally accepted. This was not a mere terminological shift, nor a whimsical one. It was rooted in some fundamental questions about the nature and meaning of "development," and the inadequacy of the development paradigm for biblical faith. "Liberation" was thought to express more adequately the following elements:

a) that historical change is not a slow evolutionary working out of a natural law inherent in the universe. Rather social change and justice exemplified in the biblical account come about by *metanoia*, through divine initiative and human responses to fight against injustices, through conflict;

b) that history is conflictual – a struggle among various power centres. A "partners in development" emphasis idealizes partnership, but often masks the reality of power struggles beneath the surface or veneer of cooperation. There is a symbiotic relationship between overdevelopment and underdevelopment; the poverty of the masses is to some degree a product of the affluence of a few. The affluent are called upon not only for greater charity (which may only perpetuate injustices), nor only to help the poor develop their own self-reliance. The rich must reshape their own institutions and life styles from a preoccupation with having and controlling. The problem of poverty is not only "out there" among the poor, but also among the rich who are possessed by their possessions and slaves to their own power;[34]

c) that the Western notion of development, stressing capital-intensive economic growth, competition, consumerism, industrialization through concentration of wealth and power, is called into question – especially when it is linked to *laissez-faire* capitalism. Trickle-down doesn't work effectively;

d) that development is not simply a matter of economics, nor only a question of having more *per capita* income, calories, or even education and health, important as these are. Development is also a matter of human dignity, self-reliance and participation of the people in determining their own destiny. Development should be people-centred, "as if people mattered".[35] People's participation is thwarted by big bureaucratic governments, as well as by concentrated business;

e) that sin is expressed not only in one-to-one personal relationships, but poisons and is reinforced by the structures of society, which give the powerful greater sense of self-righteousness as well as greater manipulative control over the weak;

f) that development tends to maintain the power of the elite, as gradualism serves the *status quo*. Liberation is often significantly discontinuous with the past. In this process the poor and marginalized are the *chief* actors in challenging the existing system and forging a new one.

Thus the transition from "development" to "liberation" was not a simple adoption of fashionable Marxist doctrines; it was more basically a result of the effort to reread the biblical materials and to see Christian theology with new eyes, from the angle of vision of the poor and oppressed, "from the underside of history" (to use Gutierrez's felicitous phrase). Emphasis on liberation has spawned a whole corpus of creative biblical exegesis, and is increasingly influencing Christological and ecclesiological perspectives.[36] Emphasis on "liberation" has been one of the most significant, if not *the* most significant, catalysts in recent biblical and theological scholarship, and at the same time has posed a tremendous challenge to the life of the churches at the institutional, ideational and action levels.

Conflictual character of society and history

As stated above, ecumenical thinking has come to stress the conflictual character of society and history. It is the arena "where tomorrow struggles to be born".[37] It is the arena where righteousness struggles against the principalities and powers – principalities and powers which may be of a supernatural origin, but which certainly are manifest in flesh and blood principalities and powers. Power in society is not neutral, since it is always exercised by sinful people with their vain struggle to overcome alienation by expanding their power and control over others. Is that not why the Jubilee Year provides for a radical disruption of accumulated privilege,[38] and the restoration of property and freedom to the poor? As we have argued above, modern society concentrates power in the hands of relatively few decision-makers – through technological advances, through rationalized social and political organization, through control mechanisms for the populace, etc. Technological developments are ambivalent – bearers of good and evil; and development, especially if it is perceived primarily in economic and technological terms, often becomes a vehicle for exploitation. Technological developments, therefore, are not challenges only to sustainability (important as this is), but also to social justice.

Ecumenical ethics contends that it is utopian to expect that, given personal and corporate sin, social justice can be achieved through an emphasis on reconciliation alone. It is not prepared to romanticize history. It is not prepared to ask the exploited to endure their exploitation in docile self-abnegation. Ecumenical ethics is not prepared to let the arrogance and power of the rich go uncontested. While harmony and cooperation are the ideal, they cannot be realized without struggle and justice, and history shows that justice is seldom voluntarily practised by the rich. This "realistic" assessment of sinful humanity, and of the conflictual nature of society, has helped to justify the controversial support given by the World Council to liberation movements, through the Programme to Combat Racism, and to accept the proposition that in some circumstances Christians find it justified in faith to take overt violent action against an already violent social system. It may be romantic to believe that conflict can achieve justice (often it increases oppression); but it may be even more romantic to believe that justice can be achieved without struggle and elements of conflict.

Central role of the poor

In the struggle for justice, the poor have a privileged role to play. "We urge the member churches to plan their participation in development primarily in support of the poorest of the poor, the rural sector and its spillover into urban squatters and slums."[39] Top-down development seems problematic at best. On one level, the prophetic tradition of the Bible urges that the rich and powerful have a special concern for the poor. The poor are to be protected, not trampled on. Woe to the rich who are impervious to the plight of the poor! But there is also another level at which the Bible sees the poor (and not only the poor in *spirit*). It sees the poor as those who are most open to the transforming power of the Spirit; it sees the poor (read "powerless in society") as the potential bearers of a transformed, turned-around society. Thus there are three main reasons why recent ecumenical literature stresses the "people" or the poor.

The first is that the poor have a special need for justice. As children of God they have basic human rights which are being denied by those who could help, but refuse. And these basic rights are not only to have a fair share in material prosperity, but to participate in setting society's direction.

The second is a strategic reason. One cannot expect the powerful to voluntarily yield power; moral appeals to the rich often fall on deaf ears. Moral suasion produces extremely modest results. Power has to be taken ("while both oppressors and oppressed are equally in need of liberation and God's forgiving love, it is far more likely that the will and strength to end oppression will come from those who bear the brunt of it in their own lives rather than from privileged persons, groups or nations").[40] And in the very process of taking power, it is frequently contended that the poor discover their true identity; they discover their potential to be actors in history ("the real importance of people's power is related to the process of creation of self-reliance, as a fundamental element in the struggle against poverty and for development").[41] This is the lesson of Exodus. Despite repeated promises under duress to let the Hebrew people go, Pharaoh could never quite bring himself to do it when pressures were relaxed. The People had to take it upon themselves, empowered by God.

The third reason is that the poor have a unique contribution to make to human history, especially in achieving justice. Again, the biblical witness is compelling. God called an obscure and sometime slave people to covenant; the new covenant was initiated through a "messiah" who identified with the poor and outcast; Jesus' disciples were social nobodies; faith has been revealed not to the wise and prudent, but to babes in the things of this world. The Bible does not argue the efficacy of poverty only in terms of an eternal, spiritual life, but in terms of a living witness for social justice and transforming righteousness among the people of earth. The poor are not extolled because some day they will reap the after-life reward of simple living, but because they have a special role to play in God's redemptive work upon earth. Their special role is not in spite of their poverty, but because the poor are more open to God's power working through them to transform society.[42]

While some ecumenical documents may come close to romantic idealization of "the poor", this emphasis on the poor as the primary agents of development and liberation has become a central feature of ecumenical ethics, and has opened up both new insights and creative tensions within the churches.

A "social" ethics

Ecumenical ethics are, by and large, a social ethics; they are primarily concerned with how faithfulness may be more fully manifested in the corporate life of humanity. They are concerned primarily with structural and systemic justice.[43] Without underestimating the importance of private morality, ecumenical ethics are more attentive to how faithfulness applies to political, economic and social institutions. This attention to macro-level issues may seem incongruous with the emergent emphasis on the role of people's movements, and would be, were there exclusive attention to top-down social change.

Ecumenical ethics are "social" partly as a reaction to the privatization and other-worldliness of much of nineteenth and twentieth century Protestant thought. Ethics often has been reduced to private morality, whereas the biblical witness is that corporate life and history are fundamentally important in God's purposes. The Hebrew people are called to be a righteous nation, and not only righteous individuals within a nation. Persons are fully persons only in community, and the systems in which people live have a tremendous impact on the quality and potential of people's lives ("natural calamities frequently result in food scarcity, but the problem of hunger in the world is essentially man-made. The many are hungry because the few own the land, control trade, and determine crucial policies pertaining to the production of food").[44]

This concern for systemic issues and public policy has had direct influences on the churches' own social engagements. Traditionally the churches have paid more attention to helping people adjust to existing systems than to calling those systems themselves into account. Charity approaches implied the basic legitimacy or tolerability of the system; it could not be changed basically. For example, the wide range of educational programmes sponsored by the churches in mission lands were concerned primarily with elevating promising individuals to positions of leadership within the system, but these leaders often became alienated from the very communities which had nurtured them. Thus social structures remained intact, and with them social injustices. Recent ecumenical ethics stresses community-based change – social organization more than social service. A basic task of solidarity with the poor is to "join hands with those engaged in organizing the poor in their fight against poverty and injustice".[45] Implied in that community organization approach is a commitment to systemic changes. Development and liberation, then, require not an accommodation to existing social structures but a re-shaping of them to more fully incorporate justice.

Churches as "sign" communities, in solidarity

Finally, ecumenical ethics has moved to a much deeper awareness of the corporate churches' role as agents of social justice. It has become increasingly evident how much the churches, in their internal life as well as in the "public policy", often have supported the *status quo*.[46] The long-standing tradition of churches which stand in Olympian fashion, objectively above the struggles and playing a "reconciling" role, is suspect. It does not describe either what the churches actually do, nor what they ought to do.

Recent ecumenical literature urges churches to become partisan in favour of the poor,[47] to be in solidarity with the poor – as the ecumenical community by-and-large believes that biblical witness shows that God took sides on behalf of the poor (the churches' "most telling power resides in their vulnerability, their willingness to risk their reputation, their wealth, their status, even their life for the sake of the needy and the poor"). The church is called to be a "sign" community – a community of faith, hope and struggle for justice which makes visible to the world its commitment to a God who is making all things new. That "sign" can be visible when the church, in its own life, evidences the scars of the struggle in its own body.[48]

One recent ecumenical document calls for a church not only in solidarity with the poor, but "towards a church *of* the poor". Interpreting this document, one ecumenical leader goes on to suggest that for the poor the dichotomy between mission and service does not exist, because service *is* mission! Occasionally one hears that wherever people are struggling for justice, there *is* the church – defined essentially by the struggle itself. Whether or not one can accept this position, ecumenical documents reject the view that service to the poor is secondary, either chronologically or in importance. Indeed, Christian faith is nurtured and strengthened, even discovered afresh, by participating in the struggles of the poor for justice and liberation. So also real Christian unity.

Thus the ecumenical discussion about development and global justice is not mere speculation; it confronts the churches directly in their internal life. It raises profound ecclesiological, as well as biblical, theological and ethical questions. It upsets many traditional assumptions about the nature of the church, and the character of obedience and faithfulness. It is increasingly apparent that the Stockholm dictum that "doctrine divides, but service unites" may be wholly inappropriate to express the reality of the present debate. The social thinking of the ecumenical movement is forged out of the divergences of culture, race, sex, age, class, theology and ecclesiology. It is affected by differences between Protestants, Catholics and Orthodox; between East and West, and North and South. It is influenced by differences between theologians and lay persons, between the powerful and the victims of the powerful, between Christians living in minority and majority situations, between Christians enjoying broad civil and religious rights and those having almost no scope for socially unconventional expression of their faith. Thus, in a fundamental sense, ecumenical ethics has become a divisive and tension-generating force within the search for Christian unity. As Lukas Vischer indicated at the Accra Faith and Order Commission, 1974:

What does it mean to be the church in the contemporary world? Conflicting opinions emerge on spiritual as well as political issues, and new movements appear, frequently beyond the frontiers of the existing churches. The ecumenical movement itself reflects the tensions in the churches and is, therefore, at least at first sight, not so much a place of growing unity as the scene or new controversies.[49]

Despite these tensions, and to a certain extent because of them, fresh faith, energy and hope are emerging in the midst of this struggle for justice, unity and wholeness.

NOTES

1. G. K. A. Bell (ed.), *The Stockholm Conference, 1925*, London, Oxford University Press, 1926.
2. J. H. Oldham (ed.), *The Oxford Conference, Official Report*, Chicago and New York, Willett, Clark & Company, 1937.
3. W. A. Visser 't Hooft (ed.), *Man's Disorder and God's Design*, report of the First Assembly of the WCC in Amsterdam 1948, London, SCM Press, 1949.
4. Oldham, *op. cit.*, p. 219.
5. *Man's Disorder and God's Design, op cit.*, pp. 192–193.
6. W. A. Visser 't Hooft (ed.), *The Evanston Report*, New York, Harper & Bros, 1955.
7. In anticipation of the Thessalonika Conference (1959), two books were prepared: Egbert deVries, *Man in Rapid Social Change*, New York, Doubleday & Co., Inc., 1961; Paul Abrecht, *The Churches and Rapid Social Change*, New York, Doubleday & Co., Inc., 1961. The Thessalonika Report is *Dilemmas and Opportunities*, Geneva, WCC, 1959.
8. M. M. Thomas and Paul Abrecht (eds.), *World Conference on Church and Society, Official Report*, Geneva, WCC, 1967.
9. Joining the Council at this time were four Orthodox communities from Eastern Europe: Bulgaria, Poland, Romania and Russia.
10. "Violence, Non-Violence and the Struggle for Social Justice" (the Cardiff consultation, 1972), *The Ecumenical Review*, October 1973, pp. 430–446.
11. Paul Bock, *In Search of a Responsible World Society*, Philadelphia, Westminster Press, 1974, pp. 181–182.
12. These questions were raised primarily in Section III of the Assembly, generally prior to the submission of the section report to the plenary.
13. WCC consultation on racism, Notting Hill, London, 19–24 May 1969.
14. Pamela Gruber (ed.), *Fetters of Injustice*, Geneva, WCC, 1970.
15. "The Director's Report" (to the 1977 meeting of the CCPD).
16. See, for example, "The Humanum Studies" under the direction of David Jenkins; the Faith and Order report from Bristol, 1967, "God, Nature, and History"; preparatory papers for the MIT conference on "Faith, Science and the Future" (especially the book by Bishop Paulos Gregorios, *The Human Presence*, Geneva, WCC, 1978).
17. Central Committee, *Minutes of Twenty-Ninth Meeting*, Geneva, 10–18 August 1976, p. 95.
18. *World Conference on Church and Society, Official Report, op. cit.*, p. 201.

19. "Theological Issues of Church and Society", Zagorsk consultation 1968, pp. 2–3.

20. Cardiff, *op. cit.*, pp. 5–9.

21. Central Committee, "Violence, Non-Violence and the Struggle for Social Justice", 1973, pp. 16–17.

22. *Ibid.*, p. 12.

23. *Ibid.*, p. 17.

24. Zagorsk, *op. cit.*, p. 8.

25. For example, "particularly restrictive has been reliance upon Western models of theology and the adoption in other places of Western models of theological education" (p. 91). Startling in its ramifications is the affirmation that "Christian experience affirms that no culture is closer to Jesus Christ than any other culture" (p. 88). Equally challenging is the statement that "we cannot allow our faith to add to the tensions and suspicions and hatreds that threaten to tear apart the one family of humanity" (p. 74). David Paton (ed.), *Breaking Barriers*, London, SPCK, 1976.

26. This hegemony of the West and of the dominators is not only at the theological level. Ecumenical ethics challenges the concrete economic myths which support the dominance of the West, *viz.*
    – "economic growth must be a prelude to social justice, and not *vice versa*;
    – inequality is needed to produce savings and capital formation;
    – economic growth itself promotes equitable redistribution;
    – rationalization means mechanization;
    – stabilization and the absence of inflation are to be preferred to the inevitable uncertainties associated with dynamic change;
    – economic development in the developing countries should be modelled on that of the industrialized countries;
    – the chances of development of underdeveloped countries are dependent upon, or even optimally secured by, a continued rapid economic growth in the rich Western countries."
    Zurich Consultation, 1978 "Consultation on Political Economy, Ethics and Theology", *Anticipation*, No. 26, June, 1979, p. 29.

27. Kim Yong Bock (ed.), *Minjung Theology: People as Subjects of History*, Singapore, Christian Conference of Asia, 1981.

28. H. Richard Niebuhr, *Christ and Culture*, New York, Harper & Row, 1951.

29. Undoubtedly one of the most challenging and creative arenas of ecumenical reflection and debate pertains to the relationship between nature and history. To what extent is "nature" a biblical concept? What is man's relationship to nature? Are process theologians correct in their emphasis on God's creativity *with* nature, rather than "in" or "to" nature? Does non-human nature have an intrinsic, or merely instrumental (in relationship to humanity) value? How is non-human nature related to the salvific work of God, and the consummation of the Kingdom? The Bristol statement, 1967, provides a coherent statement on these issues, thus catalyzing an already incipient discussion. That discussion was deepened and sharpened in the Church and Society deliberation on technology and science, especially in the Zurich, 1977 Consultation, "Humanity, Nature and God". Further, the preparatory materials for the MIT conference, 1979, enrich the discussion. This is an immensely fertile and promising conversation.

30. In 1973 the Central Committee articulated some of the concrete hopes: "We believe that for our time the goal of social change is a society in which all people participate in the fruits and the decision-making process, in which the centres of power are limited and accountable, in which human rights are truly affirmed

for all, and which acts responsibly towards the whole human community of mankind, and towards coming generations. Such a society would not be the Kingdom of God, but it might reflect within the conditions of our time that subjection of the powers of this world to the service of justice and love, which reflect God's purposes for man." "Violence, Non-Violence and the Struggle for Social Justice", *op. cit.*, p. 9.

31. "As Christians we are called to search for the Kingdom of God and his justice. We call this Kingdom 'messianic' because we believe that Jesus, as the Christ, the Messiah, has brought, lived out, and inaugurated the Kingdom on earth, within time and space. Without this Christological manifestation the Kingdom would be an abstract utopia. In speaking of a messianic Kingdom we also make two other affirmations: it is already at work, and therefore not futuristic or spiritual escape, but it is not yet fulfilled, indeed [it is] beyond historical achievement. It is operative in human reality and still we are waiting for it. Waiting without action would be a denial of the historical coming of Christ. But action without waiting would be a denial of the second coming of Christ. History derives its inner power and strength from this active and waiting presence between the two comings – one historical and the other eschatological." "Report of the Advisory Committee on 'The Search for a Just, Participatory and Sustainable Society", Jamaica Central Committee meeting, 1979, p. 5.

32. (Bristol) "God, Nature and History," *op. cit.*, p. 16.

33. Paton, *op. cit.*, p. 125. This principle of participation is applied to several concrete circumstances, such as "the community must be given the opportunity to share in the planning of safeguards and in the ultimate choice between technologies" (p. 125).

34. This is spelled out in Section VI of the Uppsala Report, and reiterated at the Nairobi Assembly: "We as Christians must recognize that the ultimate test of the quality of life on earth is the obedient sacrifice of costly Christian discipleship. As such, Christians live according to an ethic of self-giving and self-limiting, as fully exemplified by our Lord Jesus Christ who is both divine and human." Paton, *op. cit.*, p. 136. See also pp. 133ff.

35. A major preoccupation of CCPD over the past eight years has been to reflect directly and correctly on the experiences of "the people," and to enhance the identity and energies of "the people," as at the core of development – liberation strategies.

36. Note, for example, Jon Sobrino, *Christology at the Crossroads*, Maryknoll, New York, Orbis Books, 1978. See also the CCPD trilogy by Julio de Santa Ana, *Good News to the Poor* (1977), *Separation Without Hope* (1978), and *Towards a Church of the Poor* (1979), all published by the WCC.

37. Apt title of Thomas J. Liggett's study on Latin America, New York, Friendship Press, 1970.

38. See for example the discussion of the Jubilee Year in John Yoder, *The Politics of Jesus*, Grand Rapids, Michigan, Eerdmans, 1972.

39. Paton, *op. cit.*, p. 137.

40. *Ibid.*, p. 102.

41. *Ibid.*, p. 133. For a more explicit and controversial discussion of this point, refer to de Santa Ana, *Good News, op. cit.*

42. A thesis cogently developed in de Santa Ana, *Towards a Church of the Poor.*

43. "Poverty, we are learning, is caused primarily by unjust structures that leave resources and power to make decisions about the utilization of resources in the hands of the few within nations and among nations. Therefore one of the main

tasks of the Church . . . is to oppose these structures at all levels." Paton, *op. cit.*, p. 123.

44. *Ibid.*, p. 122.
45 *Ibid.*, p. 123.
46. "We call the churches to a serious self-criticism of their economic, political and ideological role in their own societies. We ask all Christians to take costly and exemplary actions to show by deeds and words their solidarity with and concern for those who are deprived of adequate quality of life." *Ibid.*, pp. 139–140.
47. "Where mutually exclusive interests are at stake, the church must take sides on the basis of the criteria of justice and love. Participation in the struggle means understanding reality on the basis of commitment [as distinguished from objectivity], a fundamental option for the poor. The basic criterion for a Christian methodology [of action] is love, not as an emotion, but as action." "The Search for a Just, Participatory and Sustainable Society," pp. 9–11.
48. Abrecht, *World Conference, op. cit.*, p. 209. The Nairobi Assembly referred to the "Christian community as a sign of liberation," and called to foretell in its own life and witness the unity to which all fractured and divided creation is called. Paton, *op. cit.*, pp. 61, 90–91.
49. "Uniting in Hope," Accra Commission Report, 1974, p. 13.

Part Two:
Towards a church
in solidarity with the poor:
five models

Introduction

As indicated above, the Nairobi Assembly affirmed that "the development process should be understood as a liberating process aimed at justice, self-reliance and economic growth. It is essentially a people's struggle in which the poor and oppressed are and should be active agents and immediate beneficiaries. The role of the churches is to support the struggle of the poor and oppressed towards justice and self-reliance."[1] Since Nairobi the theme of "the church in solidarity with the poor" has come into greater prominence and importance.[2] The poor are perceived to be of special significance in salvation history, not only because of their moral claim on us and on the churches, but because they are in a distinctive way agents of transformation in history through their openness to the vision of a more just society, their relative freedom from established ways of doing things, and their experience of the oppression of existing systems which gives them insight into the failure of these systems to attain justice. It has frequently been affirmed that God has made a special option for the poor; God is not neutral.[3] The germane issue for the years ahead is not *whether* churches should be in solidarity with the poor, but *how*.[4]

Chin and Benne argue that there are three basic strategies for social change: the empirical-rational strategy, the normative re-education strategy, and the application of power strategy.[5] The first strategy, dominant among intellectuals in Europe and America, assumes human rationality, and that people will follow their rational self-interest. Thus the fundamental strategy for social change from this perspective is to assist people to see their self-interest in new and sharper fashion. The second strategy does not deny rationality, but sees it as conditional and modified by subjective norms and values, especially coming from the community. "Change in a pattern of practice or action will occur only as the persons involved are brought to change their normative orientation to old patterns and to develop commitments to new ones."[6] Such normative changes require not only new information, knowledge or intellectual rationales, but "changes in values, skills and relationships". The third strategy is far more activist, and less reliant on intellectual or moral processes. It involves the mobilization and application of either legitimate or illegitimate power to bring about changes.

Traditionally the churches have relied heavily on the second of the above strategies, although the second has usually been closely linked to the first. More recently the churches, and the World Council, have explored strategies of the third type, the exertion of power, legitimized through existing constitutional or other provisions, or legitimized by appeals to a higher morality (as in support of select freedom movements). Increasingly the question of the justifiability of this third strategy is coming to the fore in ecumenical discussions, particularly in the context of what it means to be in solidarity with the poor.

Despite this leitmotif of "solidarity" over the past several years, the meaning of what solidarity implies and requires is not yet fully clear; there are differing interpretations and emphases. There is not even complete unanimity on what it means to speak of "the poor", or what it means to claim that God has made a special option for the poor. What is clear, however, is that there are numerous ways of thinking about what the churches' solidarity should mean.

As the CCPD programme on "Towards a church in solidarity with the poor" indicated, the struggle of the poor is marked by four interlocking goals and processes: (1) to become aware of their dependent situation, and to struggle to overcome the attitudes and structures which suppress them; (2) to develop greater self-reliance, not only as a political or economic objective, but for the realization of more self-conscious personal and corporate identity, and their potential for exerting power; (3) to change structures in the direction of justice, at least to guarantee the minimum needs of all; and (4) to create a society in which all people participate in decisions which will directly affect their lives and their future.[7]

Within their own programme sectors, several parts of the ecumenical family, and various offices within the World Council, are struggling to manifest more fully and more faithfully this basic affirmation of solidarity with the poor. Without pretending to be exhaustive, we have selected five "modes" of being in solidarity with the poor which are evident in the work of the Council.[8] None of these expressions of solidarity has a monopoly on the full meaning of the word, though one sometimes detects a sense that too often people feel that being in solidarity *their* way is the only way to be truly Christian and faithful!

As we see them, five modes of "solidarity" manifest in the programmes of the Council are the following.

1. Through the transfer or sharing of human and material resources, solidarity is expressed by helping needy people meet their immediate needs, and by helping them develop the base for longer term self-reliance. This is pursued most visibly through the Project system, covering several of the "desks" of the World Council.

2. A second mode of solidarity is through development education, conceived not only as learning information about need and oppression in some distant environment, but sharpening an awareness of the structural relations and interdependencies which bind the whole world (or the "three" or "four" worlds) together, often to the disadvantage of the poorer nations. Development education today often includes an action component, not only as a way to overcome particular objective problems, but as an integral element in the educational and analytical task. This mode of solidarity is perhaps most evident in the work of the Commission on the Churches' Participation in Development, and in the Education department, but is an element in several other programmes of the Council as well.

3. A third way of being in solidarity with the poor is through systemic analyses of basic social systems, assessing how they promote or impede prospects for global justice. Not content with palliative or piecemeal approaches, systemic analyses make a critique of existing social, political and economic institutions and relationships. This is done in part through a demythologizing of existing relationships, and in part through a projection of possible alternatives for the future. Two examples will be cited in particular, albeit cursorily: the work of the Christian Medical Commission, and the special inter-unit study on transnational business and a New International Economic Order.

4. A fourth approach to solidarity with the poor is through critical reflection on major cultural values and myths which govern societies, especially influential societies. In one sense this is the theological-ethical task of churches. This mode of solidarity requires fundamental reflection on the nature of the gospel, and on the call of the Christian community in the light of that reflection. Obviously this mode is integrally connected with other styles of solidarity, but overarches them as well. Three expressions of this kind of solidarity are the CCPD studies on "solidarity with the poor", the continuing reflection on a "just, participatory and sustainable society", and the reflections on the implications of the rise of base ecclesial communities. Chapter seven uses these latter two as illustrations.

5. A fifth style of being in solidarity with the poor is identification with groups of the poor on local levels who are in some ways confronting the power of the system with their own awakening power. To some extent this mode of solidarity is expressed through the Urban Rural Mission, the Programme to Combat Racism, and through the Commission on the Churches' Participation in Development. The basic characteristic of this approach is to discover where groups of the poor and oppressed are struggling actively to confront a patently unjust circumstance, and to become a partner in that struggle. Emphasis is not on creating groups, but in joining existing struggles, working under the leadership and animation of the oppressed.

In the chapters which follow in Part II, these five differing modes of solidarity will be exemplified and discussed as a way of illustrating the diversity of the understanding of solidarity,[9] of posing issues about solidarity in their concrete settings, and with the hope that through this survey a keener appreciation of both the complexity of solidarity issues, and the unity and mutually enriching character of the struggle for faithfulness, will be forthcoming. It is also hoped that, though the work of the Council often is perceived as scattered and unintegrated, this perception is belied by a common vision of unity as based on faithfulness expressed, in part, through commitment to global justice. This is part of our spiritual nourishment for the continuing combat against injustice and oppression.

NOTES

1. As quoted in Julio de Santa Ana, *Good News, op. cit.*, p. 114.
2. This focus on solidarity is evident in several complementary programmes of the Council: "Empty Hands", the CCPD studies on "Towards a Church in Solidarity with the Poor", the Melbourne conference on "Thy Kingdom Come", and "Racism in the Eighties".
3. This theme was strongly argued at the Puebla, 1978, meeting of Roman Catholic leaders, following in the spirit of the Medellin Conference, 1968.
4. Several persons, commenting on the first draft of this manuscript, argued that the member churches of the World Council are not fully committed to solidarity with the poor, even though it may be an increasingly prominent theme in ecumenical organizations.
5. Robert Chin and Kenneth Benne, "General Strategies for Effecting Changes in Human Systems", in Warren Bennis, *et al.*, *The Planning of Change*, 3rd edition, New York, Holt, Rinehart & Winston, 1976, p. 34.
6. *Ibid.*, p. 34.
7. de Santa Ana, *Towards a Church, op. cit.*, pp. 14–15.
8. It is not argued here that these five modes are the only ones exhibited through the Council. For example, a major feature of the World Council, through

Assemblies, Central Committees and Executive Committees, has been the issuance of significant statements on key issues of social policy and justice. Another has been as liaison and/or interpreter between factions in disputes or tensions. These additional modes may be as significant as the five spelled out in Part II of this essay.

9. In this discussion it will be evident that not all prominent programmes of the Council are referred to, even when they may be closely related to solidarity issues. For example, there is little reference to the Programme to Combat Racism, the Commission of the Churches on International Affairs, the programme on Women and Men in the Church, Faith and Order studies, or the programme on Dialogue with People of Other Faiths and Ideologies. We have not tried to give "equal time" to each part of the Council, as if this were a political game where everyone had a measure of commendation. The whole programme of the Council is important, as we have pointed out when using other illustrations in previous volumes. Efforts cited here are simply to lift up examples.

4: Relief and modified project assistance

Perhaps the kind of "solidarity with the poor" which first comes to mind for most Christians is that represented in relief and development agencies, like the Commission on Interchurch Aid, Refugee and World Service. Since the early post-Second World War years a prominent feature of the ecumenical family has been this branch of the Council whose major work has been the channelling of material resources to needy persons and communities. During the early years its primary attention was to bring relief to war-torn Europe, for the rebuilding of churches and church institutions, and for the Palestine refugees. During the past two-plus decades its focus has shifted, as well as its processes for achieving its tasks. Gradually CICARWS has taken on more and more developmental type projects and programmes, has moved much more fully into "third world" situations, and has experimented with ways to bring genuine partnership into the decision-making processes of the Commission.

The project system

The major instrument in this effort has been the Project List, defined in changing stages of evolution in differing ways, but always having as its basic purpose the sharing of human and physical resources between more materially affluent parts of the church and others. Historically, funds for strictly interchurch assistance (e.g. refurbishing or building of churches, supporting local pastors, providing modest pensions for retirees) have been associated more with some geographic areas than others, and the long-term trend has been a gradual reduction in both absolute and relative amounts of money made available through the project system for strictly interchurch aid. By comparison, funds for burgeoning refugee populations (now about 15–18 million worldwide) have increased dramatically. In 1980, about $43 million was channelled through CICARWS for refugee work, in addition to major contributions through material resources (actual material resources such as medicines or blankets, as distinguished from money). Such increases in refugee assistance result not only from a growing number of refugees, but from a changing perception of the churches' responsibilities for refugees: after relief efforts to find a more permanent home and livelihood; continuing care for the psychic wounds and displacement felt by many even in a new environment where physical needs are met; and advocacy on behalf of refugees, so that their needs and rights are protected by official government policies.

Because the sharing of resources is fraught with hazards, to both the so-called donor and the so-called recipients, the project system has been under constant criticism and review. A brief recapitulation of major changes over the past decade-and-a-half highlights changing perceptions:
- from isolated projects to more comprehensive programmes;
- from bricks and mortar to investment in people;
- from individuals to more emphasis on communities of people;
- from remedial measures to preventative efforts;
- from dependency inculcation to self-reliance;
- from centralized decision-making to local and regional decisions;
- from priorities established in "donor" countries and churches, to articulation of priorities on a local level;
- from emphasis on trickle-down change to more concentration on the poorest sectors of society as agents of change;
- from social service to enhancing organization of local aspirations and initiatives (social welfare to community organization);
- from one-way transfer of physical resources to sharing of a variety of resources in which all parties have important contributions to make;
- from naivete about self-sufficiency of the affluent to deeper appreciation of the poverty of the rich, through development education or consciousness raising.

Despite these significant shifts of emphasis (shifts still in process, and often ambiguous), no one believes that a suitable or optimum system for the sharing of resources, material and spiritual, has yet been forged.

The moratorium debate of the last decade emanating from the African context, but relevant to most others,[1] was rooted in the problems of domination and dependency, and centred on the question whether there should be a temporary interruption of financial and personnel support from churches in the materially richer, traditionally mission-sending, nations, to enhance freedom and self-reliance of third world communities of Christians. Only thus could genuine interdependence be ultimately achieved. While the moratorium discussion has subsided, many of the basic concerns which prompted that debate in the first place are still on the churches' agendas, and manifest in all Project List reviews (probably 90% of financial sharing from one church to another is still through bilateral denominational transfers).

One major attempt to revise the Project List system occurred in the early 1970s, and aimed to bring about more local and regional decision-making about specific project priorities. The now-familiar three categories evolved, replacing the previous system of simple listing of project needs without attempts by the regions to indicate priorities. With this change, projects listed in Category I were priority projects as determined by the region in question (Africa, Latin America, the Middle East, and Asia) and these were accorded highest priority by those seeking to channel funds. Additional requests were listed in Category II and Category III. While these did not enjoy priority endorsement, they were listed as of interest and value by the potential recipient communities.

> Category I consists of a group of projects with a 100% guarantee of financing. In every country [or region] it is up to the local churches to decide together which projects to list in Category I, with a certain ceiling. Category II comprises projects initiated locally and presented to donors and have no guarantee of financing. Category III projects are those not usually presented by a country but are part of a worldwide network.[2]

Thus the emphasis since the early 1970s has been on support for Category I projects as a way of responding directly and more fully to the perceived priorities of local Christian communities. For the first several years Category I projects were fully subscribed (in 1980, the total for Category I requests was about $3.5 million), but beginning in 1979, and subsequently, the picture has been less satisfying. In those years Category I projects have not been fully subscribed, and special measures were taken to make up the shortfall. One consequence of this approach to decision-making about projects has been the growth of block grants to certain national and regional church groups, rather than funding for a multitude of specific, sometimes isolated, projects.

The shift towards local decision-making also has highlighted the importance of the network of relationships evolving between churches and Christian groups in both "North" and "South", and has provided the institutional context for deeper sharing of ideas and convictions. Naturally enough, the perspectives and expertise of the local actors have become far more influential, even determinative, in the total decision-making process. Another consequence has been significantly increased interaction among church leaders in the local and regional levels, and the mutual enrichment which such sharing often promotes.

A further consequence is that fewer projects are proposed and listed, with some of the weaker proposals having been eliminated early if they did not enjoy the confidence of a local screening group. As a by-product of fewer isolated projects and a greater number of block grants, it has been possible to give greater attention to selected projects, and often a more rapid response from "donors" has resulted. Another result has been greater effort to develop complementary projects, often lasting over a longer period of time, so that strategic planning becomes an increasing part of the process. While the elements of paternalism and domination have not been eliminated totally (paternalism, domination, tensions and rivalries persist at the local and regional levels) some of their worst effects have been reduced.

Despite these improvements, certain dissatisfactions persist. The director highlighted some persisting problems in his 1980–81 report to his Commission, advocating a further review and alteration of the project system.

> It has tended to focus attention on the transfer of funds. The decision-making process as to how resources shall be allocated is not truly participatory. In addition, there is little evidence that the projects supported encourage increased self-reliance. Nor are the churches encouraged to discover and use their own resources. In summary, the Project List does little to encourage true dialogue between churches or the linking of service with mission.[3]

This criticism of the Project List was amplified in the basic document for the Glion, Switzerland, "Consultation on a New Resource Sharing System", convened by the Commission on World Mission and Evangelism, the Commission on Interchurch Aid, Refugee and World Service, and the Commission on the Churches' Participation in Development.

> The problems and inadequacies of the project system became more and more obvious. It perpetuated the dependence of the receivers and entertained a piecemeal approach to the needs of the churches. The procedures were lengthy, without providing sufficient certainty of funding. Some partners disregarded the Project List because in their opinion it offered no vision or they found it too "churchy". Others, on the contrary, wished to see more emphasis on the building up of churches and evangelism. Others again insisted that the List was indispensable for ecumenical cooperation in service and development.[4]

Corroborating this conclusion, a review of projects over several years in one of the geographic areas revealed several persisting weaknesses, a failure to attain certain key objectives.[5] While some countries were favoured, this favouritism did not follow the pattern of supporting the poorest and most needy countries. Minority churches enjoyed comparatively little support, and most projects were not ecumenical in endorsement or implementation. Despite strenuous efforts over many years to move away from bricks and mortar, a large number of projects were for buildings and/or running of services. Projects tended to be traditional rather than aimed at fundamental structural changes.

In brief, major shortcomings of the current project system persist. (1) Churches and groups of the poor at the genuinely local level do not adequately exercise leadership in the initiation of projects, in decisions about their shaping and priority, or in their actual implementation. (2) Many projects are traditional and meliorative rather than developmental. Many perpetuate traditional social relationships, and actually undermine self-reliance. (3) Projects continue to be isolated rather than complementary, occasional rather than strategic. (4) Frictions and tensions exist between decision-makers at the local and regional levels, and these factors are often more determinative of project decisions than emerging common understandings of what the churches should be promoting in socio-economic development. (5) The project system tends to perpetuate the dominance of an emphasis on physical sharing of resources, rather than on openness to and exploration of alternative styles of sharing which stress mutuality of gifts rather than a flow of gifts from affluent donors to needy recipients. (6) In the stress upon projects and development, concern is often expressed that insufficient attention is given to interchurch aid, and mutuality in mission. (7) The structures of the WCC itself are insufficiently integrated to facilitate efficient and effective deployment of project assistance resources. (8) Currently the project system does not highlight the significance of human networks, or relationships, which ultimately constitute the core of successful self-reliance, participation and development. (9) The present pattern of project assistance does not adequately challenge "donor" churches or agencies to take seriously structural factors of domination and dependency from which they themselves benefit, as individuals, churches and nations; the project system does not require or include elements of consciousness-raising and development education as it applies to the rich. (10) Finally, the project system by stressing local and regional decision-making, by focusing on often isolated projects, by emphasizing the transfer of financial resources, and thus implicitly reducing the role of the "donor" to that of sending money, undermines the pressures for a mutual effort to probe the deeper theological, ecclesiological, ethical, socio-political and cultural implications and rationale of the project approach as an agent of social change.

These shortcomings of the project system have stimulated, in the late 1970s, still further efforts to reshape the entire project system. The Newby Report[6] stressed the need for far-reaching structural change within the World Council of Churches, as well as within the project system itself. Less sweeping has been the recent effort of CICARWS, along with other parts of the Council, to make alterations designed to bring churches at the local levels more fully into conversations about priorities for projects; to reduce the number of projects so that listings would be more realistic and each project could receive more concentrated analysis and evaluation; to enhance the prospect that proposed projects would be viewed more comprehensively and strategically on the local scene; and to increase the coordination among various branches of the World Council, each now tending to have its own network of contacts in the poorer countries.

In the summer of 1981 CICARWS proposed, and the Central Committee meeting in Dresden confirmed, new policies and procedures to govern the project list, based on "the calling of Christ's Church to be the Servant Church summoned to free human beings from all forms of captivity"[7] (a formulation which some may find utopian insofar as it ignores, among other things, human beings' captivity to themselves as well as to other people and structures). The new Project List would attempt to move from preoccupation with material sharing to greater stress on personal and spiritual sharing as well.

A new Project List would consist of two parts: (1) "Priority projects", including those of a composite nature, proposed by national groups and endorsed as priority projects by one of the (currently six) regional review committees. An effort would be made to guarantee funding for such projects, up to a predetermined but gradually expanding ceiling. These projects would constitute the bulk and main thrust of the project system. (2) A second listing service would complement the first. Such a listing, perhaps appearing biannually, would list projects screened by national or regional committees, but not endorsed by them as priority projects. Complementing these new screening and administrative measures would be an emphasis on enlarging the Project List to include, more prominently, "activities related to the development of human resources, ecumenical dialogue on witness and service, new forms of solidarity where the emphasis is expressed not in money but in common commitment to issues of justice and human fulfilment, communication and mutual support".[8]

Emerging from this overall review has been a new commitment that the Project List (or "Resource Sharing System", as the Glion consultation called it) should be perceived and developed in a much more theologically grounded understanding of the nature and mission of the churches; should promote a holistic idea of the witness and ministry of the churches; and should strengthen the commitment and capacity of churches, on the local level and in regions, to manifest their solidarity with each other and with the poor. Each region is urged to develop its own set of guidelines and priorities in light of this fundamental commitment to one another and to the poor. De Santa Ana has suggested the importance of regional perspectives when he argues that different geographic areas in the network system have developed differing ways of defining their priorities.

> The activities of the Latin American Network are focused on programmes for cadre formation and Christian participation in development; in Africa the regional network has defined its priorities as theological education in development, women in development, youth in development, and churches and TNCs in Africa. The Asian network is deeply concerned with people's mobilization and people's organizations for development. Groups related to the Commission for the Churches' Participation in Development in North America, Western Europe, socialist countries of Europe and Australia are giving highest priority to development education.[9]

In the years ahead, it is anticipated that there will be an expanded role for local, national and regional groups in the articulation of priorities, and in the selection of certain projects for priority listing. This practice should open up a fresh and deeper dialogue among networks, and establish new patterns of partnership not only in the so-called "receiving" regions, but with "funding" partners as well. It is hoped that such mutual reflection on the whole range of church responsibilities for global justice will quicken the internal life of partner churches as a consequence of their growing commitment to the poor. These regional and national groups are asked, further, to "open ways for more interaction with non-institutional groups" (e.g. the base ecclesial communities, or groups of the poor not necessarily related to the churches) and "to promote new and innovative ways of sharing".[10]

Modified conceptions of projects would be enhanced by much

closer cooperation between various units of the World Council. To this end the Central Committee concurred with the recommendation that there should be a merger of the CELAP (Latin America) and CCPD networks, and collaboration with the Commission on World Mission and Evangelism. This closer integration of work in Latin America also would be pursued in the Africa and Asia regions, pending agreement in principle from those regional groups themselves.[11] Movement in this direction would require the strengthened internal channels of communication and cooperation within the WCC itself, and might lead to an all-WCC project listing to replace the (currently) eight different funding channels within the Council. More coordination and homogeneity of perspective are clearly desirable, not only for the sake of efficiency and better mutual reflection, but also to reduce the confusion of, and burden on, the colleague or partner groups in the poorer countries trying to work through the WCC.

Even as presently constituted, however, the function of the World Council and Project List should not be discounted. "Of the $56 million requested in 1980, $32 million was raised and channelled through the WCC. Some of the remainder was channelled directly from donors to the projects."[12] It should also be noted that material aid from Protestant churches to countries in all parts of the world totalled $76 million in 1980, an increase of 44% over 1979 ($53 million).[13] The WCC Material Aid office itself purchased or channelled $11.3 million worth of goods such as clothing, footwear, agricultural equipment, tools, seeds, medicines, food, shelter, blankets and transport vehicles. While poor countries in practically all continents have benefited from these material resources, the main country recipients have been Kampuchea and India. For the first time it appears that Africa is becoming the major continental recipient of material aid. One of the main concerns for the future is to discover how to use material resources from third world countries more fully, because of generally lower costs, as a way to foster solidarity among third world countries, and to make a small effort to increase exports of poorer nations.

Partner groups

The Project List of CICARWS has not been the only WCC instrument for the channelling of material and financial resources. Another significant and pioneering effort has been made through the Commission on the Churches' Participation in Development. With funds allocated in the Ecumenical Development Fund, established after the Montreux I (1970) conference, a major element in the CCPD programme has been block grant support of partner groups in selected countries and regions (six at the beginning). These block grants have become important new initiatives towards solidarity, incorporating a number of features which seem to move beyond a project approach. Block grants have been allocated to groups rather than for specific projects, thus putting at the centre of the entire process a relationship of trust in the capacities and competencies of the beneficiary groups. Block grants also permit a more integrated and holistic effort at development programmes, and underwrite longer-term efforts not dependent upon whims of potential funders from year to year. Counterpart groups which have been funded through these block grants, renewed on an annual basis, are in much deeper and sustained dialogue with the whole CCPD network than is the case of projects, thus enriching the reflection process in a very significant manner.

Where continued Ecumenical Development Funding has seemed undesirable (in order not to undermine self-reliance, or to release resources for other programmes), consortia for alternative funding have been formed. A chief benefit of such consortia is that they provide an ongoing framework for continued ecumenical collaboration, and also an important base for continued analysis of the role of the churches in the development and liberation process. Several groups once supported through Ecumenical Development Fund grants have now been moved into a consortium category, while others are in process of forming new consortia. Though there are shortcomings in the consortium and block-grant approach (one is the persisting danger that recipient groups will become too dependent upon outside resources, underestimating the innovative ways that local resources can be generated), they continue to prove to be important alternatives to projects for development assistance.

One striking example of the success of such block grants through CCPD's administration of the Ecumenical Development Fund has been the "motivators' " training programme in Indonesia. The Indonesian partner group receiving EDF funds struck upon a distinctive style of engagement in solidarity with the poor. It was based upon the selection and training of young volunteers to live and work in exceptionally poor villages in various parts of the archipelago. The basic philosophy was to enable young motivators assist poor villages to discover and mobilize their own resources for self-reliance, to make themselves less vulnerable to decisions made outside of their village. With very modest expenditure, hundreds of such motivators have been trained, and assigned, usually for two years, to work in specific villages. Over 120 villages have had motivators in their midst.

The story of Waisika exemplifies the approach and achievements of the programme. In 1972 the programme committee in Indonesia decided to select this village near Timor to receive two motivators. A joint expatriate-Indonesia evaluation team has written the following account.[14]

Waisika was almost a dying village. There were only forty families, the remnant of a large community who over a period of years migrated to nearby mountains for fear of death, sickness and famine. The forty families earned their livelihood from twelve hectares of cultivable land. They hardly had any good drinking water supply. Their food was mainly corn with very little vegetables. The village had not seen a cow. Their only intake of animal protein was an occasional catch of fish from a nearby swamp. Incidence of malaria and other forms of tropical disease was such that many spoke of Waisika as a haunted village to be feared or shunned. They had little access to educational institutions or even informal influence from the outside world. The nearest road was forty km away, a distance which could be covered only by walking. The villagers hardly bathed, as they believed that a dirty body would attract fewer mosquitoes.

What is the situation nine years afterward? Waisika now has 536 families and a new nearby village of seven families. From where did these 500 families come – about 5,000 people? They are people whose forefathers belonged to Waisika. They had migrated to the mountains, but had an agriculture based on shifting agriculture on small burned plots of mountain land. Their life was exceptionally poor, not much better than that of the people who stayed in Waisika, though they thought otherwise. They too were having a hand-to-mouth existence. But how and why did they come down from the mountains? The answer is the slow and steady efforts of the young motivators.

What kind of life do they have in Waisika now? There are now 350 hectares of land under cultivation; they plant mainly paddy and corn, more than adequate for their consumption. In fact, paddy has become a cash crop for additional income for most families. With the introduction of irrigation by the villages, a good part of the cultivated land yields two crops per year. The villages are also using new seeds, better fertilizer and better forms of cultivation. For example, in 1972 when the first motivator tilled a piece of water-covered land it was a big joke. At another stage the motivator introduced cow and plough, both previously unknown in the village. Now there are six cows and three ploughs in the village, and with local government support many more are on their way. Waisika today is a different village. Its face has changed. Wet and marshy lands have become fields rich with paddy and corn. Most families have vegetable gardens, including vegetables unknown before 1972. The nearby mountains which were periodically burned down by nomadic people, which were deforested and denuded, are becoming green. The village today has an adequate number of schools to provide primary education for all school going children, and they are there studying. With the initiative of the people, and with the support of local government a road has been built over forty km linking the village to Kalabahi. The villagers have learned to make bricks to improve their houses. Waisika has entered a money economy. A good market is being built and their surplus products are finding their way not only to the rest of the island but to the outside. The new road, and services of the lorry provided through the church, help to ensure that the villagers are not at the mercy of the prices of the occasional visiting trader when they have surplus products. Most families have begun to rear goats and pigs, and some have started cultivating fish.

The situation of drinking water has improved considerably. In many parts wells have been dug or local streams diverted. In the centre of the village the water table is too deep for a well, so a bamboo pipe over seven km long has been constructed to secure fresh water from a mountain spring. There is today a health officer in the village; the overall health situation has improved considerably. The village has four well constructed Protestant churches and one Roman Catholic Church, all of which serve as community centres for social gatherings.

The village people are fairly well organized in small groups. There are farmers' organizations for collective farming. There is an organization of women, undertaking educational programmes, handicrafts, etc. There is even an orphanage for thirty children (a development that the evaluation team thought questionable). Another aspect needs to be mentioned. This process of development was a collective improvement. The village still remains an egalitarian society, with fairly equal land opportunities for each family. Most of the farming and other efforts are conducted on a collective basis. Most of the common facilities have been constructed by people working together ("gotong royong").

The people of Waisika are still poor. Children are still malnourished. The general health of the population is not good. Women walk long distances for water and still have the tiring task of hulling the rice without mechanical help. They have never seen a rice mill. But the fact is that they have come a long way in this short span of time. More importantly, they have the collective will to go on improving themselves, their land and their water. According to them another 600 hectares of land are waiting for their spades and ploughs to turn them into grain fields within the next few years.

The key to this development story is the community motivation provided by a group of young motivators, usually a pair working at one time over a period of two or three years, replaced by another pair for a subsequent period. These motivators are men and women of an average age of 22 to 23. Their education is usually not more than secondary school. However, they had the six-month training session at Cicembar, provided by the Development Commission. The method they used included living in the village, working on a plot of land, and demonstrating through their life and work a better way of village living. The investment that the Development Centre made in the programme is very little. Average annual input did not exceed $1200 (two motivators' salaries, and seed money).

With so little expense so much has been achieved. But more important is the fact that in this development process the people were the main agents and the motivators were only catalysts. The results are enduring and pregnant with long-term results. The motivators can soon be removed without adverse effects. The people of Waisika are on the move, using their own will and resources. The story of Waisika is the story of a people – a people who were not a people ten years ago.

This thrilling story could be repeated with accounts from many villages across Indonesia which have been influenced by the motivator programme. It illustrates one effort and approach by a WCC branch to be in solidarity with the poor by experimenting with new forms of resource transfers and the sharing of power. The evaluation team noted that the programme is people-centred and comprehensive. "The base is not a methodology of outside capital, but a drawing out of the people themselves."[15] Not least important, of course, is the impact of the programme on the motivators themselves. "We have seen ex-motivators at work in strategic places – in government agricultural schemes, in theological colleges, as village pastors. They are all a core of future leadership in church and society."[16]

Another significant aspect of CCPD work has been the transfer of more modest amounts of "seed money," or programme assistance for small-scale local groups working on specific social justice and awareness-building efforts. Working often at the very margins of society, and frequently under the threat of persecution or repression, these groups are enabled to exist and witness because of the usually meagre (often less than $5,000 US) transfers that CCPD has been able to make. In any one year perhaps 25–40 of such efforts have been assisted.

Loans and investment programmes

Grants for projects, or block grants, and programme assistance are not the only means used to transfer material and fiscal resources. For many years the Ecumenical Loan Fund (ECLOF) has made available comparatively small loans to church agencies on a low interest, relatively long-term repayment basis. Money for these loans, made available to national ECLOF committees to apply to projects those committees select, is received from various grants of church agencies, but replenished through repayments.

The repayments record is astonishingly good, and the programme continues to expand steadily. This expansion is evident in the number and total amount of loans from 1979 to 1980 (89 to 118 loans, $1.4 to $1.9 million), or an overall growth rate of 33%.[17] The average loan through ECLOF is about $16,000, demonstrating that most loans are for comparatively small enterprises. This confirms the principle of making loans to small-scale operations. Most loans carry low interest rates – between 3 and 10%, with most of them at the lower edge of the range. While in the past many loans were made for capital projects of churches and social services, an increasing number of ECLOF loans are now pointed towards development objectives, though in 1980 six of every ten loans were still for general capital loans of the more traditional type. The reduction of loans for real estate development, and their expansion for small-scale rural artisanal, animal husbandry and agricultural projects reflect the changing priorities of the ECLOF programme.[18]

In many ways comparable to ECLOF, but focusing more exclusively on development block loans of a larger and more comprehensive nature, is the work of the newly-formed Ecumenical Development Cooperative Society (EDCS), founded in 1975 and now operating with share capital of over $5 million. EDCS is funded through share capital rather than through outright grants. At some later stage of maturation a modest rate of return can be expected, perhaps 6%. It is hoped that through EDCS, money now deposited in such large portfolios as church pension funds can be invested responsibly for global justice through development. Among the more salient criteria for projects (selected by the ecumenical and diverse board of directors) are the following:[19]

> The poor and powerless should be the beneficiaries participating in indigenous projects/programmes which provide basic needs, or for improved conditions required for them to meet those needs.
>
> Such persons organized in cooperative efforts should be directly engaged in operating the project/programme for their own benefit.
>
> The ownership of the project/programme should reside in these people.
>
> There should be potential for achieving self-sustaining activity and growth in reasonable measurable time frames.
>
> Overall development strategies should be seen in the light of the people and their efforts to attain basic human rights within their community and nation.

The project/programme should contribute to the social, economic and political advancement not only of those who are directly engaged in it but also for the larger community surrounding it – avoiding also unsustainable uses of non-renewable resources and unsustainable impacts upon ecological systems.

Examples of loans made include: $100,000 to a Roman Catholic group in Ecuador for an agricultural credit programme designed primarily for impoverished Andean Indians; $200,000 for lowest grade employees at Vellore Christian Medical College for the construction of their first homes; $325,000 for a poultry feed mill in the Camerouns; $350,000 for eleven weaving cooperatives of alpaca garments in Peru, run by Indian communities; $350,000 for thousands of small-scale bee farmers in Turkey; $500,000 for a mariculture project to be run by the Hong-Kong Kowloon Worker's Mutual Benefit, since in Chinese culture fishermen are among the lowest in social standing.[20]

At the present time there are 142 members or shareholders in the EDCS, most of the money having been contributed by church groups, which have also made some outright grants for the administration of EDCS so that share money is not spent for administrative costs. Recent legal rulings have opened up the opportunity for shareholder membership to individuals, and to individual churches. Designated funds also have been allocated by some German churches to make it possible for certain third world communities to become members, even when they do not have the initial approximately $250 required for membership.

In short, EDCS, along with the longer term ECLOF and CCPD counterpart and programme assistance funds, complement in very significant and innovative ways the traditional transfer of financial and material resources through the project system. Each of them has a peculiar institutional character, but all are struggling to find more adequate ways of making the sharing of financial resources more effective, efficient, and expressive of true ecumenical sharing.

Forms of ecumenical sharing

This leads naturally to the final point of this chapter. Driven by a commitment to discover new forms of sharing within and among the churches, CICARWS, in conjunction with other units and sub-units of the Council, undertook in the late 1970s a three-year study on the "ecumenical sharing of resources". This study culminated in the publication of a discussion and study guide for the churches entitled *Empty Hands*,[21] emphasizing a mutuality of gifts among rich and poor – not a one-way street from the materially affluent. The theme of this study and message was the "practice of solidarity" within the churches, to be achieved through an attitude of empty hands, for hands that are full – even full of gifts – cannot embrace the other.

In recommending the study guide to member churches, the 1980 Central Committee noted that the general secretary already had observed that what was needed was not more discussion about the importance of sharing and mutuality, but the need to put these into practice in interchurch and intrachurch relationships.[22] Particularly acute were relationships between former mission churches and the mission-sending bodies, and between the materially less affluent and powerful churches. "Some parts of the church consider themselves to be poor, while others think of themselves as rich, perpetuating the blockages which prevent true sharing."[23] In making this assessment the churches tend to conform to the standards and values of this world, measuring riches not by the churches' wealth as a people of God, but by material standards. Poverty and wealth are to be measured "according to the intention of God and his purpose of sharing".[24] Subject to special questioning are the material assets of the churches: land, investments, financial resources, buildings, because from a Christian point of view riches cannot be thought of in these terms primarily.

In this study the concept of "solidarity" itself was spelled out more precisely, and several possible implications for the churches were suggested.

> Solidarity signifies mutual dependence or interdependence, where the wellbeing of some is dependent on that of others. It also signifies a moral duty of mutual aid among members of a group who consider themselves one. The first question is not what we can give or what we can receive, but how we can enter into the needs and lives of others. It is unlikely that solidarity can really be expressed by giving alone; the sharing of information, of intercession, of personal visits, of experience, will have priority. Solidarity calls for a change of attitude and for new ways of behaving, individually and collectively. It makes us question our ways of being and acting, our life-style, our systems of values. Solidarity implies a commitment to change structures which allow exploitation, domination and oppression. We earn the right to be partners with others only by dealing with the problems at home in our own society [as well]. Verbal solidarity is not enough.[25]

It is this vision of solidarity which is held out before the Council and the churches, especially in those relationships involving transfer of fiscal and material resources which are so often the occasion for poisoned relationships. The document on the ecumenical sharing of resources does not specify concrete new actions which the churches must undertake. That is a frustrating part of the document; one would have hoped for more concrete suggestions for practical sharing of resources, especially within the context of World Council of Churches programmes. Rather, the document is an invitation to member churches to explore the meaning and implementation of sharing still further. But *Empty Hands* does lift up the issue of sharing in a way which may compel churches to face more seriously their own failure to achieve real mutuality in sharing, their own imprisonment in a transfer of resources mentality which overlooks the deeper human aspects of sharing. That document keeps before the Council a somewhat amorphous yet convincing vision by which to appraise the adequacy of all "transfer of resources" projects and programmes designed to be in solidarity with the poor.

NOTES

1. CCPD/CICARWS Latin American Consultation, "The Churches' Participation in Development Programmes and Projects in Latin America", Itaici, Brazil, September, 1980.
2. Willem Schot, "Do We Project Ourselves in Projects?", Geneva, CICARWS/ WCC, 1977, pp. 17–18.
3. Jean Fischer, "Activities Report, 1980–81", p. 23.
4. Basic document, p. 2. The consultation was held 3–6 February 1982.
5. Ghassan Rubeiz, "Funding Patterns of the Middle East Desk of WCC: 1974– 1979", 1980, p. 14.
6. Donald Newby, "Toward a New Process for Mission and Service", a report on the Project List Review, 1979.
7. "Project List Review", Dresden Central Committee Meeting, 1981, p. 3.
8. *Ibid.*, p. 3. The final recommendations of the Glion consultation were not available at the time of writing this study, but the preparatory documents developed suggested priorities. "The promotion of priority projects will reflect the selective emphasis on areas of priority: (a) *ecumenical* projects fostering new ecumenical initiatives or dealing with situations where it is strategically, technically or politically important that support be given through a multilateral, ecumenical agency such as the WCC; (b) *comprehensive* projects, where there is an attempt to bring together in a local situation the whole life of the church, evangelism, theological education in unity, development, service to society, etc.; (c) *solidarity* projects, where the expression of ecumenical support and solidarity is more important than the financial need expressed. This would require or make possible the involvement by others in the struggle and suffering of people, in the midst of which churches seek to witness and serve; (d) *minority church* projects, especially those which seek to link these churches and their special needs with other churches; (e) *relationships* projects, for churches without traditional or historical links with others in the ecumenical fellowship, and among churches within the third world."
9. Julio de Santa Ana, "Network", 11, p. 12.

10. "Project List Review", *op. cit.*, p. 5.
11. *Ibid.*, p. 5.
12. Fischer, *op. cit.*, p. 27.
13. Helmut Reuschle, "Material Aid Statistics, 1980", p. 1.
14. "Preliminary Summary Report of the Evaluation Team", presented at CCPD Commission meeting at Salatiga, 21–28 June 1981, p. 7.
15. *Ibid.*, p. 8.
16. *Ibid.*, p. 3.
17. "Ecumenical Church Loan Fund: Report 1980", p. 4.
18. *Ibid.*, p. 5.
19. Fred Bronkema, "Ecumenical Development Cooperative Society: a Model for Action in Development Cooperation", pp. 3–4.
20. *Ibid.*, p. 4; and "Board Circular No. PT6" (which describes the rationale and mechanics of the mariculture project).
21. *Empty Hands: an Agenda for the Churches*, Geneva, WCC, 1980.
22. *Ibid.*, p. 4.
23. *Ibid.*, p. 6.
24. *Ibid.*, p. 7.
25. *Ibid.*, pp. 26–27.

5: Development education

Changing perceptions about development education

Though "development education" (perhaps better termed "consciousness-raising for global justice") is one response to trying to affirm solidarity with the poor, it has to be noted that there are many different perceptions about the purposes, contents, and modes appropriate for this task.[1] Hence, while in one sense "development education" is a very old enterprise, in some respects it is quite new, in view of the diverse and changing perspectives of the last fifteen years. The experience of the World Council is instructive for understanding the issues of "development education".

When the Montreux Consultation (1970) advocated that 25% of "development project" funds of the churches be assigned for development education, it signalled a new level of understanding of the problems of development.[2] It suggested that greater public support in the industrialized countries was required to improve and intensify church, government and intergovernment development efforts. Also, Montreux conversations were a preliminary stage in exploring a connection between affluence and underdevelopment. However, for most people the 25% goal was seen primarily as a new quantitative objective; it was not a new way of perceiving the dynamic relationship between enrichment and impoverishment, and for many the assumptions regarding stages of economic growth remained intact. Poverty was not perceived dynamically, but as a condition which could be overcome by greater partnership issuing from leading centres of industrial strength. Development education itself was perceived primarily as sharing of information about the plight of the poor. It was assumed that the problems were "out there" and that if good people knew about the problems they would try to correct them.

Within the churches, the early 1970s were formative years for development education. Though few, perhaps no, churches attained Montreux's 25% goal, a consciousness of the relation between domination and dependency became more prominent. Poverty was linked more directly to oppression by, rather than partnership with, centres of power. "Liberation" came to be regarded as a more suitable goal than "development", as the latter obscured the historically conflictual character of progress towards global justice. Gradually poverty became perceived in much more systemic, structural and dynamic terms. Consequently many churches in the industrialized world began to understand more clearly their own, and their governments', connection with, and partial responsibility for, continuing underdevelopment and oppression.

Thus development education moved beyond the mere sharing of information, to analyses of why people are poor, why nations are poor, and why the situation for the poor remains so bleak. Development education began to explore the links between the poverty "out there" and the material "affluence which a few are privileged to enjoy". Affluence became a moral question, not only in the abstract sense that "it is easier for a camel to pass through the eye of a needle than for a rich man to enter the kingdom of heaven", but in the concrete realization that affluence could too often be traced to injustice, or be connected with the inability of millions of poor people to get enough food or medical attention for themselves and their children. Affluence itself, as well as poverty, became more consciously morally problematic.

Thus, by 1974 development education had evolved significantly from information sharing and appeals for more charity, towards structural analysis and greater attention to the need for changes not only in poor countries, but in richer countries as well. People were increasingly encouraged not only to increase their charity (though some argued that charity should be terminated altogether because, it was alleged, it simply reinforced the forces of oppression, or reduced pressures for structural change), but to question the inadequacy and injustice of their own social values and institutions. Development education increasingly came to involve efforts to influence a broad range of government policies in the rich countries, particularly those pertaining to trade with, and aid to, the third world.

An increasingly important component of development education in the 1970s became a commitment to "new life-styles". New life-styles were designed to move development education beyond a mere "head trip" of either information or analysis, to personal engagement and witness ("personal" not to be confused with private or individualistic). Some criticized the "new life-styles" approach as being too sentimental, too dissipated, too individualistic, too ephemeral; could they impact the entrenched unjust social policies and systems? Some felt that life-style emphases moralized the issues in a shallow way, rather than contributing to the more basic ethical and systemic reflection. Yet the new life-styles movement persisted and significantly expanded, in part, one imagines, because people refuse to be paralyzed or immobilized by the belief that they are powerless. The experience of the 1960s was perhaps important also. The tumultuous 1960s and early 1970s indicated that direct confrontation with the "system" tended to heighten and strengthen its opposition. Confrontation heightened oppressions.

Finally, for many people life-style changes by individuals or groups also *include* vigorous efforts to bring about systemic change.[3] There was also a growing conviction that "new life-styles" were important whether or not they had a measurable influence on, or a direct connection with, subverting or changing existing systems. Altering one's life-style, though apparently insignificant and ineffectual in the face of the powers of this world, could influence others and ultimately the corporate consciousness. Praxis – the dialectical relation between practice and theory – could lead on to possibly more adequate and effective action and analyses.

To avoid the trap of merely intellectualizing the consciousness-raising process, two additional features of development education, beyond changing life-styles came to prominence. One was a concerted effort to examine the connections between local problems and national or global problems (e.g. the parallels between issues posed by agribusiness in central Canada and in central Colombia, or cheap labour policies in Greenfield, USA, and cheap labour policies in Seoul, South Korea). Efforts were made to discover ways of getting people actively engaged in a palpable local struggle as part of their life-style and education in order to understand more concretely the issues of global injustice. More conventional, but often influential, have been in-depth study and action trips to third world countries, or to third world environments within first world countries.

A further stage in this not neatly chronological evolution was a deepening conviction that development education might be most effective when clustered around certain issues (nuclear energy, disarmament, TNCs, water shortages, civil rights violations, human rights, etc.), rather than thinking of development issues as an undifferentiated cluster. Development education as a global project was perceived as too massive, too abstract, too complex and insufficiently related to the reality of differing local contexts, to provide a sound pedagogical basis.

Thus development education became more and more a process of forming, or responding to, study or action groups around specialized themes or problems. Yet this emphasis on selected issues of development education posed the danger of fragmentation and isolation. Would the connections between phenomena be overlooked or underestimated? One way to escape too much fragmentation has been the forging of networks of persons and groups. These networks are formed around issues, but connect people with diverse but kindred interests, and from many places. Today there exist many networks, e.g. on disarmament, nuclear energy, human rights, transnational corporations, community action programmes, communications, and development education itself. Many of these have specific church connections; many do not.

In addition to these issue or subject-centred networks, numerous geographically-concentrated networks also are taking shape, usually to focus in a more comprehensive way on a variety of issues affecting a certain region, such as Central America. Many such groups are related to churches and/or religious communities which serve as a common denominator. The functions and parameters of such networks are defined by the participating groups themselves, but in addition to sharing information, strategies, experiences, and analyses, a significant purpose is to sustain and strengthen the commitment of others in the network who are constantly challenged by the almost overwhelming magnitude of their task. One of the most common features of most *ad hoc* social change movements is their transitory character, both in personnel and overall programmes. The building of networks, then, has as one major purpose to coalesce and sustain moral energies for the battle – what CCPD has called "strengthened spirituality for combat".[4]

Growing in complementary fashion with a new life-styles approach, and the formation of networks of like-minded groups, has been a broadened and deepened awareness of the structural and systemic impediments to development. New factors have had to be taken into account. For example, insistence on people's participation has made the development process far more complex conceptually and organizationally. In the past few years the concept of sustainability has complicated the debate still further. In particular, the injection of sustainability criteria intensifies justice questions, undermines some of the deepest and untested assumptions about traditional development models, and reveals that the development-liberation debate applies equally, though in different ways, to the first, second and third worlds. These newly emphasized aspects of development naturally influence and complicate the character of development education. To recognize the complexity of development and liberation issues may lead to atomization, but also to a keener perception of common elements, common configurations, conjunctions of interdependent factors. As the development education task force of CCPD indicated:

> Today we watch a convergence of the various issues (such as racism, militarism, TNCs, human rights, questions of sustainability, etc.) with a cumulative effect. This convergence is characterized by a tremendous increase of power, military power, corporate power, bureaucratic power, which is seemingly anonymous and difficult to locate, difficult to attack. This convergence of issues which naturally influence and reinforce each other could have important consequences for the organization of development education programmes – [including the need to] identify the vulnerable point of access. The other important urgent point of access is militarism and the struggle against the arms race.[5]

Growing awareness of the convergence of issues and their interdependence entails both dangers and possibilities for greater effectiveness. These dangers and opportunities centre around the question of the role of "ideology" in promoting social change. For many, "ideology" is a general conceptual frame of analysis and perspective for looking at and analyzing data, and not a preshaped and unwavering view of reality (the latter being a connotation which the word in English often carries). There are obvious dangers in an ideological and structural analysis (dangers against which pragmatic, problem-solving Anglo-Saxon culture traditionally has fought). Principal dangers in the structural analysis and "ideological" approach are perceived as a tendency to exaggerate certain factors as determinative or causal (even to the point of single causation); an insistence on interpreting all new data in the context of already shaped expectations or analyses (leading to insufficient nuance and openness to genuinely new factors); a predisposition to exaggerate structural features of a society as distinguished from more human elements personified in individuals or groups; and a proclivity to insist upon wholesale, perhaps culture-wide, radical change rather than on a more piece-meal gradualist problem-solving approach. Practically speaking insistence on wholesale changes may deter and postpone significant improvements which could have been made, or may serve to stiffen and reinforce the existing "system" rather than to renovate it at strategic pressure points.

Conversely an inordinately pragmatic approach may prove inept simply because the whole fabric of inter-related issues is not perceived. A problem-solving approach often does not attack key causal factors. Often, in the absence of a structural analysis, the solution to one problem seems to open a Pandora's box of additional and unexpected new ones. Can a problem-oriented approach bring sufficient sustained pressure to bear on key structural and institutional actors which are so dominant in the world? Both ideologues and pragmatists have their strengths and liabilities; is it possible to promote a dialectical interaction of both modes? The point here, however, is that the more development and global justice issues are perceived as converging and inter-related, the more intense will be the pressure for clearer (and perhaps simpler) ideological perspectives – while at the same time many education and action groups are not prepared, psychologically or intellectually, for that level of systemic reflection. In the future, development education almost certainly will be even more profoundly challenged by the potential tension between these two approaches to social analysis and change.

Recovered theological emphases

Experience in development education over the past several years has naturally influenced theological reflection. That does not imply a *new* theology, but does suggest that diverse contemporary experience has sharpened or helped us to appropriate again, or emphasize, elements in the gospel which were dormant, hidden or not existentially critical. It is only natural that the struggle for justice, development and liberation has shaped theological insights and emphases. "It has helped us to recover neglected aspects of the gospel heritage not as a way of justifying radical commitments to doubting churches, but as a serious attempt to faithfully and obediently understand and work for justice and liberation which are so central in biblical testimony."[6] A short enumeration of several key points illustrates this fact.

1. There is a challenge to the nature of theological reflection itself. Is it possible to engage in sound theological reflection without being immersed first in "what God is doing in the world" – participating in the struggles for justice, liberation and wholeness? Some argue that without actual engagement in solidarity with the poor, theological reflection is mere intellectual abstraction; authentic Christian theology has to take shape in the soil of struggles for justice. This point is made eloquently in the literature growing in the context of liberation theology, with its emphasis on praxis – "one cannot know God without being engaged in what God is doing in this world".

2. The contextual (limited to a specific cultural milieu) character of all theology has become more self-evident; the inherent limitations of theological perspectives from any one cultural tradition, including Western or Eastern, is obvious. At the same time the

richness of theological reflection organically connected with differing cultural soils and climates is more fully appreciated.

3. The role of the poor, not only in social change, but also in theological reflection, has become more widely valued. This special role of the poor, often open to God's word and power in particular ways, has been important in the whole panorama of church history, but characteristically is underestimated by the powerful as naive. Innumerable testimonies to the power of biblical study in the context of base communities illustrate the direct and vital way that the poor creatively shape theological meanings of the gospel for their own communities.

4. The struggle for global justice has again put the question of the nature of power near the centre of theological reflection. "Our experience of the 1970s has been a constant reminder of the intransigence of power, its demonic side, its tendency to corrupt and poison even the most altruistic motives and efforts. We have seen that seduction by power in individuals, in political groups, and in religious communities. And yet it is evident that power is not only negative, but a necessity which is positive for individuals and communities. There is the power of love, of hope, of vision, as well as the power of domination and coercion."[7]

5. Theological views of non-human nature, too, have been deeply influenced by the issues of development, and efforts in development education. Recent recognition of the natural limits to unbridled growth has encouraged a fresh look at biblical understanding of humanity's relation to non-human creation. Taking more seriously the perspectives of Christians from differing cultural traditions, and attempting to listen more openly to persons committed to other (non-Christian) faiths and ideologies, has challenged traditional theology to new sensitivities and brought new insights.[8] These questions were brought into clearer focus at the MIT conference on "Faith, Science and the Future".[9]

6. Finally, development education has been dynamically related to new conceptions of mission. Traditionally, development-liberation issues have been ambiguously related to mission. Despite clear assertions about the relation of mission to justice and salvation, such as those of the Bangkok Assembly (1973), development education as an essential element in that debate is "rooted in the conviction that the Kingdom is at least integrally connected with righteousness and justice on earth".[11] Thus the debate about the character of development has required new attention to a Christian understanding of the relation of mission to the Kingdom of God. An enormous amount of theological work is still needed in this area.

Given the cost of development education, and given the potentially divisive character of effective education for global justice, it is appropriate to ask whether the Montreux I proposal was sound in advocating that a quarter of church development project resources should be spent on development education. Couldn't scarce resources and energies be spent better on actual projects to help sick, hungry, uneducated or oppressed people? There is an understandable impatience to "get on with the urgent task" right now of feeding the hungry, curing the sick, hoping that at a later stage, after urgent needs have been met, there will be time and resources for development education.

Probably all of us feel the attraction of this argument, especially when confronted by actual human beings in practically hopeless conditions. Admittedly there is a trade-off, at least in the short run. Yet such an argument tends not to take seriously enough the goals of self-reliance and people's participation, and tends to underestimate the ways in which existing structures of power and decision-making in the richer countries adversely impact prospects for sustained development and liberation in the materially poorer countries. In short, such arguments tend to underestimate the fact that much poverty results from oppression and injustice, and cannot be overcome with simple charity, important as charity is in many cases.

Churches in development education

For these reasons the World Council of Churches continues to advocate a strong role for the churches, in particular, in development education, in order to raise the consciousness of their constituencies about global injustice and its implications for corporate life in the churches, as well as outside. Admittedly, the churches suffer many liabilities in promoting development education: they are relatively small and poor in comparison with the total population; people spend relatively little time directly relating to church-sponsored programmes, in comparison with their other activities and concerns; churches frequently align themselves, intentionally or not, with the *status quo*, and many members have traditionalist attitudes and values (studies on prejudice);[12] churches are generally identified with the values and institutions of Western society, including their political and economic assumptions; etc.).

Notwithstanding these liabilities, churches possess significant assets for development education efforts.

1. Not least important is the ethos of the churches and the inherent unambiguous and persistent demands of the gospel for justice, for wholeness, for transcendence over the parochial idolatries of any

culture, for a sensitive and caring attitude and relationship to non-human nature – for God so loves the world that God gives Self for its redemption. Though this ethos is constantly eroded, masked, overlaid, those communities seeking to bear witness to the gospel are judged, nourished and confirmed by these central affirmations – convictions which emancipate individual Christians and communities and enable them to risk new visions and new faithful actions for justice in a global society.

2. Coupled with this central ethos is the fact that Christian communities are rooted not only in the gospel, but in a variety of cultural environments, and profoundly influenced by those differing cultural contexts. That the church is called to be one, yet experiences its diversity, requires that the implications of this diversity have to be taken seriously. Others' experiences of the gospel, even when radically different from our own, must be listened to, even when not fully accepted. That pluralism of perspectives, not washed away in relativism or vapid "tolerance", ensures that the churches can provide a compelling challenge to superficial or narrow interpretations of the gospel as seen from only one cultural context. We have in mind not only diverse cultures of differing geographic territories, but differing cultures of class, religion, language, ethnicity, sex, age, within the same geographic area. Here we refer not primarily to liturgical and other practices of the church (though these differences also are illuminating and important), but to fundamental theological, biblical and ethical reflection. Development education, animated by the churches, can draw upon this rich resource in many ways, but especially through the ecumenical community and its efforts to speak and to be faithful together.

3. Similarly, the long history of Christian mission has afforded contact with other cultures and religions which, while often a source of friction and misunderstanding, has helped to shape a philosophy and style of intercultural and inter-religious relationships marked by serious attention to the other (an *expectation* that one can learn and grow through the other) without capitulating to relativism or syncretism. This kind of critical and appreciative distance, combined with interaction, provides a sound basis for promoting development education. We are not arguing here that the long history of mission has heightened scholarship about other cultures and religions, though numerous missionaries have pioneered anthropological, linguistic and cultural studies of great importance. What seems equally important is the emerging style of relationship of Christians with other people from differing cultural contexts. While continuing to struggle for an authentic and more effective style of relationship, in

the midst of persisting tensions, mission efforts historically have forced the Christian community to think about such issues in ways which enhance their capacity for significant development education. Further, we are convinced that in the years immediately ahead this kind of experience will become still more important, as the world increasingly perceives development and liberation issues as not only political and economic, but also as profoundly cultural and religious.

4. A fourth advantage of church-sponsored development education closely relates to this historic experience in mission. In many places the Christian community is small and struggling, often experiencing in its own life oppression and marginalization by the larger society – sometimes marginalization or oppression from sister religions or even sister churches. Members of the Christian community often are marginated socially, politically and economically. They experience injustice issues personally and inescapably.[13] They often are not only identified with the poor and oppressed; they *are* the poor and oppressed. The need for "solidarity" is not a moral imperative, but an existential reality. When the experience of such Christian communities is taken seriously by the larger ecumenical Christian family, the reality and urgency of their situation cannot be ignored. While the larger ecumenical community ought not, from a moral point of view, to take the experiences of injustice suffered by Christians more seriously than those of other people, the special and sustained relationship with sister Christian communities makes them a unique source of concern and understanding.

5. A fifth asset of the churches in development education is long experience in, and commitment to, projects for social betterment. It is true that such projects sometimes have reinforced dependency relationships, or have inculcated values and attitudes which today seem anachronistic. Without judging the past with the presumed better wisdom of today, it is still true that projects, programmes and other efforts at social betterment have provided a rich fund of practical human skills and relationships, and a vast amount of day-to-day experience about what does and does not work in development.[14] These practical involvements, coupled with theorizing, make possible the kind of praxis which is essential for the purification of both theory and practice. Not only does the multiplicity of church-sponsored social betterment projects provide a rich array of case studies and intriguing information for development education studies; it also provides something far more important – actual records of the struggles of the churches to be more faithful, with all of the lessons learned in that engagement-reflection process. Development education, centring on such experiences and struggles (suc-

cesses and failures), has much to teach about the nature of development-liberation and how it might be realized.

6. A further advantage of the churches as agents of development education is the number of formal institutions through which they may work. Often such church institutions are described as albatrosses, preventing real experimentation and conserving traditional values. That is a danger, and an undeniable part of the current picture. However, across the world there are schools, colleges, theological institutions, and other centres of a less-formal educational nature (clinics, hospitals, community organization centres, cooperatives, etc.) where new perspectives on development and liberation can be animated. In addition, the regular liturgical and teaching life of the local church community can be instruments of consciousness-raising; indeed, it seems critically important to experiment vigorously with new ways of injecting the development-liberation motif into the normal patterns of church life and worship, particularly.

In short, many institutions and programmes already exist; new ones need not always be created, even though old ways of thinking and acting often need to be transformed. One example is theological education. One of the main concerns in theological education over the next decade should be to inculcate in future church leadership an awareness of, and commitment to, a vision of the gospel and of the church which requires vigorous witness for global justice. Education for development does not require a complete rejection of institutions and programmes of the past, but a re-thinking of their tasks and programmes, and a re-deployment of energies and resources consistent with that differently shaped vision.

A way ahead

These arguments would seem to suggest that most development education should be done in the context of existing denominational and church structures, partly because of the communication and educational patterns and channels already available, partly because development education should be done in the context of general theological and faith formation, and partly because development education needs to be concretized and contextualized for differing audiences, and existing church channels seem most likely to accomplish this. Does that mean that the World Council and other ecumenical agencies have nothing to do in development education? Certainly not, for bodies like the Council can bring a breadth of experience and perspective from many cultures and ecclesiastical traditions which are necessary to overcome provincial understandings of global justice. Further, there are particular innovative tasks in which ecumenical agencies like the Council can take a lead.

Four main lines seem important at this juncture. One main line of action is to help catalyze churches to stress the need for development education in their existing channels of communication, and especially in their educational institutions, including those of theological education. A major contribution of the Council could be the sharing of educational materials, bibliographies, innovative experiments such as unique kinds of "exposure" programmes in "third world" environments in the first and second worlds. Perhaps "institutionalitis" has been stressed too much. Much emphasis has been put on the static and negative aspects of church institutions. Rather than dismissing them as elitist, traditionalist, formalistic, privatistic, perhaps there are new ways of reviving a prophetic orientation in them – a propheticism which characterized many of these institutions in the past, and of which there are important examples today. What, for instance, do the recent emphases on, and experiments with, non-formal education imply for more formal educational efforts of the churches as they strive for global justice?

A second main line, consistent with much recent work of the Council, is to bring third world experiences in development education more fully into contact and interaction with educational efforts in the more industrially advanced countries and regions, perhaps through networks of development educators. It has often been observed that most development education has been centred in the more materially affluent nations, with little being done in the poorer nations. Perhaps this is true, but the observation may be based on the fact that we tend to look for the same kinds of development education in third world environments (in the same way that development itself tends to be defined by the way the rich perceive it) as exist in Western Europe and North America. In the third world, development education exists, but may not be readily recognized as such. Perhaps development education is happening in a very basic and effective manner in base communities, or in community development programmes among the oppressed, or through the traditional emphasis on personal identity and wholeness in some of the more evangelically oriented churches. If so, it ought to be identified and put into dynamic contact with development education efforts in the materially rich countries.

Where education for global justice is not happening in third world churches, much greater attention could be given to this aspect of church witness in those countries. It should never be assumed, of course, that the location of a church in a materially poor nation makes it a church of the poor, materially, psychologically or morally, any more than it can be automatically assumed that churches in the affluent parts of the world are never in solidarity with the poor. Though an obvious point, the literature on churches and development (perhaps this essay as well) abounds with simple polarization of churches in rich and poor countries, and a too-easy assumption that the lines are clearly drawn between them.

A third task ahead in development education, and one which the Council could foster, is the linking of global and local issues in development-liberation. Experience shows that much effort is spent on macro-level generalizations, and little attempt is made to illuminate the links between general macro-level phenomena and what is happening in parallel form on the local level. It is critically important to see the larger and global picture; traditionally that has been ignored. What is needed, however, is a conscious effort to see the links between, for example, issues of global food policy and the problems of capitalization, salination, marketing, etc. of local farmers; or the problems of vulnerability of local workers, or consumers, at the hands of even local businesses (e.g. when a plant is moved to another section of the country, or to another country altogether because labour costs are cheaper there). Perhaps no significant development education can occur without helping people at the local level get existentially involved in local social justice movements which have their counterparts or larger manifestations on a global level. Efforts to make the connections will not only be sounder and more effective pedagogically, but will also provide means for testing global development perspectives.

A fourth task ahead is sometimes called "spirituality for combat". In recommending this as an area for major concentration, the CCPD evaluation team noted that "the increasing tensions, conflicts, contradictions and frustrations which people are experiencing as they get involved in efforts and struggles for justice demand their price. The patience and strength of many people is wearing thin. Many have just begun to understand that they have embarked on a long range struggle and are groping for the spiritual resources necessary to sustain a long and oftentimes costly commitment."[15]

This "spirituality" is not to be understood in a merely pietistic way, though it is not without elements of piety! Spirituality includes the more traditional notions of prayer, meditation, biblical reflection; it also includes ongoing theological reflection on the meaning of issues facing humanity in new shapes and forms. It includes, indeed, "a deeper exploration of 'Christian modes of resistance' to the powers of oppression, destruction and death".[16] It includes involvement in a community of faith and hope, a place where experiences of the struggle and experiences of faith can be shared, and where the community of faith can transcend itself through a deeper awareness of the cosmic struggles in which God is engaged. It includes action as well as reflection – action which is rooted in learning how to live in the context of different sets of values and expectations.

Such practical spirituality is not only a consequence of new levels of spirituality, but a contribution to them as well. One dimension of deeper spirituality through new life-styles comes for many through a new sense of powerlessness and vulnerability, by which, however, greater resources for wholeness may be revealed. We are convinced that one of the greatest contributions which the churches can make to development-liberation, through development education, is creative exploration of new and more effective ways to help people experience the spiritual strength and power which often comes through new levels of identification with the poor, with each other, and with the Lord of history. Whereas the CCPD study referred to this as "spirituality for combat", we perceive it not only as useful *for* combat, but new spirituality discovered *in* combat for justice and wholeness. This change of wording will help overcome the erroneous notion that chronologically spirituality precedes combat.

To sum up, in the thinking of the World Council, development education has several main features. (1) It is not merely intellectual, but requires a significant level of engagement and commitment to be in solidarity with the poor. (2) It is informed in large measure by the interpretations of reality which the poor themselves give. (3) It assumes that the problems of global injustice and mal-development are not only personal, but structural, and that poverty is a consequence of oppression more than a result of the inability of people or nature to provide the necessities of life. (4) It assumes that all peoples are in need of development, and not just the poor, or just the rich. (5) It assumes that development and liberation are not only political, economic and cultural issues (though they are that), but also moral, ethical and spiritual ones as well. (6) It assumes that issues of development are integral to the gospel, and that concerns for global justice should permeate the life and witness (liturgical, diaconal ministries) of the worshipping community.

Conceived in these ways, efforts at development education are not only crucial to the inner vitality of the churches, but constitute a significant mode of practising solidarity with the poor.

NOTES

1. Dan Force, development education staff person for Church World Service, reported that it has been practically impossible to find a term acceptable to all persons working in this field, not only because of different styles and philosophies of work, but because every term conveys different meanings to different theorists and workers. The term "development education" is used here since that is what has been used most consistently in ecumenical discussions.
2. Gruber, *op. cit.*, p. 126.
3. An example of how personal life-style changes consciously include attention to systemic issues is the Shakertown Pledge, in Adam D. Finnerty, *No More Plastic Jesus*, Maryknoll, New York, Orbis Books, 1977, pp. 199–203.
4. "Preliminary Summary Report", *op. cit.*, pp. 15ff. (unpublished).
5. *Ibid.*, pp. 11–12.
6. *Ibid.*, p. 3.
7. "Preliminary Summary Report", *op. cit.*, pp. 4–5.
8. Recognizing with appreciation the efforts being made to open up the development-liberation discussion to persons of other faiths and ideologies, and with particular appreciation for the dialogue programme under Stanley Samartha's leadership, the development education review task force highlighted the importance of this component in development education. This is particularly important in view of the increasing awareness of cultural dimensions of the development debate, as distinguished from its political and economic aspects.
9. Roger Shinn (ed.), *Faith and Science in an Unjust World (Volume I)*, Geneva, WCC, 1980; and Paul Abrecht (ed.), *Faith and Science in an Unjust World (Volume II)*, Geneva, WCC, 1980; Paul Abrecht (ed.), *Faith, Science and the Future*, Philadelphia, Fortress Press, 1978.
10. "Salvation Today", Bangkok (1973) assembly of the Commission on World Mission and Evangelism.
11. "Preliminary Summary Report", *op. cit.*, p. 5.
12. Many studies show that church members are often more apt to hold traditional and prejudiced attitudes (e.g. anti-semitism, racism) than persons not belonging to churches.
13. In this connection the experience of base ecclesial communities is often exhilarating – such as the scriptural passage studies reported by Ernesto Cardenal, *The Gospel in Solentiname*, Maryknoll, New York, Orbis Books, 1979.
14. This feature has been lifted up as a main reason for Church World Service (USA) involvement in its new pilot development education programme. See unpublished "CWS Global Education Task Report and Recommendations", p. 2, report dated 10/80.
15. "Preliminary Summary Report", *op. cit.*, p. 15.
16. *Ibid.*, p. 15.

6: Structural analyses

Changing perceptions of the health care system

Health has been a major concern of the churches for many years. Hospitals, clinics, medical personnel training, and modern medicines have been prominent features of church-supported efforts to upgrade the living conditions of people, at first in mission lands and more recently in the third world. Hundreds of millions of dollars have been made available by Christian communities to provide health services where there were none, or where they were not available for deprived sectors of the populace. Even today health care is second only to direct educational programmes of the churches in third world countries. Until quite recently a large number of the projects supported through the World Council Project List, as well as the much larger number of projects and programmes under the auspices of denominations, were in the field of health. It is no exaggeration to claim that the Christian churches have played a prominent role in the extension of Western style health care to poorer countries, and had a significant impact on the emerging vision of health care possibilities and responsibilities within poorer nations.[1]

Despite this impressive effort in the field of health, or perhaps partly because of it, the churches have used their experience and involvement to raise fundamental questions about the effectiveness of much of the traditional health care they have been instrumental in generating. They have contributed to a demythologizing of the efficacy of popular approaches to health care characteristic of much church mission and government health development programmes of the 1950s and 1960s, and still current in many poorer countries. They have expanded and sharpened the concept of health itself. They have participated actively in analyzing and proposing alternative health delivery systems. They have helped to illuminate and highlight the non-medical aspects of health care, such as the connection between health care and general developmental objectives and conditions. The changing programme emphases of the Christian Medical Commission illustrate these changing perceptions and practices in the work of the World Council. That the Commission focuses its attention on solidarity with the poor is evident in its 1980 report to the Central Committee, entitled "Health Care and the Church in Solidarity with the Poor", stressing the social justice aspects of health care.[2]

One contribution has been the CMC's role in demythologizing the efficacy of many aspects of modern health care. Paradoxically, the main cause of population explosion has been the introduction of the benefits of modern medicine and health care into populations that formerly suffered from relatively high premature death rates and low life expectancy. It was progress which opened up new issues. The Physical Quality of Life Index (PQLI) developed by the Overseas Development Council shows dramatic improvements in quality of life brought about by the introduction of modern medicine. In spite of these dramatic successes, it is necessary to note the failure of modern health care to remedy the ill-health of the masses of the poor, or to prevent ill-health in the first place. As the Commission argues, there are rampant but preventable diseases like tetanus (killing 1 million per year), lack of vitamin A (100,000 children go blind each year, with between 15 and 30 million blind people in the world), malaria (taking the lives of 1 million children per year).[3]

In addition, there is a scandalous maldistribution of health resources; the rural populace, the poor, and females receive relatively little attention. Kingma argues that 20–25 million "under-fives" die annually, with a large number of these deaths due to diarrhoea and polluted water.[4] And WHO studies (1981) "show that developing countries have still only been able to provide reasonable access to an acceptable level of care to 15–35% of their populations, and the rural population is served only to the 10–14% level".[5] Feuerstein contends that "in some countries 80–90% of the total health budget is spent in services in the larger population centres where only 10–20% of the population live".[6] Fendall, professor of tropical community health, has stated the case graphically: "If I were to compose an epitaph on medicine through the twentieth century, it would read: brilliant in its discoveries, superb in its technological breakthroughs, but woefully inept in its application to those most in need."[7]

What are the reasons for this "failure" of health care? Kingma, currently Director of the Christian Medical Commission, adduces three main causes. "Over the years, a number of unhealthy views have been creeping into the popular conception of health, and the role that the medical professions play in its preservation."[8] These are *professionalization* (leaving responsibility for health to doctors and nurses); *institutionalization* (caring for sickness in hospitals and away from families and friends); and *pharmaceuticalization* ("we feel cheated if a doctor says that no medicine is required").[9]

To these Western and "modern" emphases in medicine, which have helped to cause distortions in health priorities in the poorer countries, could be added other causes, perhaps equally important for the "failure" of today's health care systems. Perhaps the most pernicious of these, and one which has not yet received due attention in the Commission's work, or in the churches' work generally, is the free-enterprise, profit-centred nature of many health care systems, even in the poorer countries. Health care is big and profitable business for those who control the health system – from doctors, to hospitals, to manufacturers and distributors of pharmaceuticals. Power over a scarce and highly desirable commodity (health) is concentrated in relatively few hands, and it is small wonder that the poor, who live at the margins of the money economy, receive disproportionately little health care. Health care run as a free enterprise business leads to injustice. An inter-religious task force in the USA recently made this point vigorously. Noting the widespread inequities in health care in the country which spends perhaps the largest percentage of its GNP (10%) on health, the report stated that

> Access to appropriate health care is one of those basic necessities [of life]. Our economic system alone cannot guarantee this right, because it rations health according to ability to pay. Hence the necessity of social intervention through government to correct the injustices of the market place. This means, at the very least, the repudiating of any social view asserting or implying that health care services are due only to those who can afford them, leaving the poor and the powerless at the mercy of the charitable impulses of the wealthy and powerful. Any person or group alleging loyalty to biblical religion must be in unequivocal opposition to any system of delivering health care services which tolerates barriers to the access of anyone needing those services.[10]

The Commission also has participated in a more adequate emerging notion of health. For instance, increasingly it has been recognized that although Western/modern medicine has achieved significant advances, there has been a growing tendency to narrow the conception of health to the absence of diseases, or to define health as related to only those things which medical professionals are able to define, work on and possibly control. The ecumenical community, however, has been led to consider health in its religious context, and in differing cultural environments. For example, Kofi Appiah-Kubi from Ghana argues that "most Africans think that health is symptomatic of a correct relationship between a people and their environment, which includes their fellow beings; the natural as well as the supernatural world. Concepts of health within the framework of African culture are far more social than biological. Health is not an isolated [physical] phenomenon."[11] The tendency to understand health as the "absence of disease" has been commented on frequently. Health is not the absence of disease, any more than peace is adequately definable as the absence of war. The National Council of Churches of Christ in the USA adopted a statement in 1976 attacking such a narrow conception of health.

> In the public mind, health has been equated with the absence of disease. But as we increase our ability to discover defects in the human body and in human behaviour, the complexity of disease grows. Therefore, in our present way of looking at things, the problem of illness has no solution. A way of medicining or doctoring based upon knowledge of disease does not produce health.[12]

The World Health Organization has sought to base its work on a larger notion of health. It recognizes the psychic and social dimensions of health, as well as mental and physical ones. Health is defined as "a state of complete physical, mental and social wellbeing and not merely absence of disease or infirmity", and WHO calls upon nations to recognize that all citizens of a state have a right to health. WHO calls upon all nations to ensure, by the year 2000, a national level of health which will make it possible for all their citizens to lead socially and economically productive lives.[13] While utopian in its insistence on a "complete" state of health, and in charging the state with responsibility for providing this high level of health, the definition does open up vistas of the meaning of health often obscured in recent emphases on health as the absence of disease.

The concept of health enunciated by Kingma, and endorsed by the Christian Medical Commission, is more modest in its view, and does justice to the dynamic aspects of health. Health is perceived not as a static condition, but far more in terms of relationships. Health is seen as wholeness: "a dynamic state of wellbeing of the individual and society; of physical, mental, spiritual, economic, political and social wellbeing; of being in harmony with each other, with the natural environment, and with God".[14] As Kingma points out, this dynamic and holistic view of health "permits a new look at what contributes to the healing process. Healing depends, in the first place, on the innate capacity of the body, mind and spirit to heal themselves."[15]

The demythologizing of health, and the articulation of new and more complete understandings of health, have led to a third area in which the Christian Medical Commission has participated in an analysis of existing social structures from the point of view of justice. It is a new and emerging vision of what strategies are most likely to promote individual and communitarian health. Perhaps most important is the growing realization that health is integrally connected with a wide range of other factors in the development/ liberation process. It has been estimated that only between 5 and 10% of a person's general health can be attributed to formal health care; far more crucial and determinative are genetic and environmental factors.[16] Investments in safe drinking water, hygienic cooking habits and conditions, adequate diet, proper waste disposal, for example, are far more important for the general health of the populace than strictly medical factors, though the significance of these latter should not be ignored or underestimated. Studies on the improvement of health in the more industrialized countries demonstrate the primacy of improved environmental factors in the historic decline of disease and the increase in general health.[17] Therefore ecological issues (rapid deforestation of the world, desertification and salination of arable land, provision of fresh and safe water, etc.) are clearly linked to the possibilities of a healthy life among the poorest of the poor. The argument that concern for ecology and sustainability is a luxury of the rich, but which the poor cannot afford, is belied by the vulnerability of the poor, for health and survival itself, to the healthiness of their environment.

Another significant strategic lesson pertains to who is responsible for health care. We are not raising here the question of who should pay for health care. Modern medicine has tended to increase the alienation of the patient from her or his own health care, coupled with a growing unilateralism of the medical professionals in defining the shape of health care and health policy. Health care often is referred to as the "health delivery system", a phrase which suggests that medical professionals *deliver* health to predominantly passive recipients. Increasingly in the popular view health is perceived as something delivered, supplied from the outside, packaged and applied, by medical professionals. Health is viewed as something done *for* patients, and not *by* patients for themselves. Patients tend to become and to think of themselves as objects to be worked upon. In McKnight's view, the increasing professionalization and specialization of the health worker inculcates in both the professional and the patient a sense that the patient is deficient in something which the doctor can provide, that the problem is with the patient, who really has a collection of problems.[18] Therefore, patients become alienated from their own potential restorative processes and experience a growing psychological need for health professionals to take care of them. Patients need to recover a sense of responsibility for their own health.

This need for increased responsibility for one's own health has its counterpart in community health. Increasingly the community is perceived as responsible for its own health, congruent with developmental emphases on self-determination, self-reliance and people's participation. This is more than an effort to mobilize people at the "grassroots" to take advantage of health care proffered from the outside. It is an attempt to enable communities to shape their own health expectations, and to organize their own resources (as much from the local scene as possible) for health care. There are many reasons for this emphasis, such as a decreased reliance on outside forces, and a greater likelihood of health care at the local level. However, not the least important reason for community based primary health care is this: given the communitarian and psychological aspects of health and wellbeing, the required corporate struggle of the total community can enhance the sense of participation of all those engaged in the process.

The World Health Organization has enunciated seven basic principles in support of primary health care based on local communities' aspirations and organization. These have been endorsed by the Christian Medical Commission, and become a more integral part of its thinking and work.

> Primary health care should be shaped around the life patterns of the population it should serve; it should be designed in support of the needs of the peripheral level [the most marginated peoples]; it should be fully integrated with the other sectors involved in community development; "the local population should be actively involved"; it should "place a maximum reliance on available community resources"; it should "use an integrated approach to preventive, promotive, curative and rehabilitative services for the individual, family and community"; and "the majority of health interventions should be undertaken at the most peripheral level".[19]

In his usual challenging manner, Charles Elliott warns against too much romanticism about primary health care, for several reasons. A "primary health care strategy *alone* does not deliver us from the kind of professional domination we all associate with hospital-based curative services".[20] On the pragmatic level he notes that (1) local communities tend to give health care low priority; (2) they do not necessarily accept medical equality as a goal of the health delivery system; (3) front-line health workers rapidly become professionalized; (4) while more people may have access to health care, the level of that care is usually relatively low; and (5) the adverse impact of diseases on communities probably has been exaggerated, without adequate attention to the ways people adapt to diseases.[21]

At a deeper, theological, level, Elliott urges the avoidance of naivete about primary health care. Primary health care is as likely as any other system to become dominated by those who have power within the system. "Because one is up against people as they are, one is also up against institutions as they are, mirrors and magnifying glasses of humanity's moral and cultural ambiguities."[22]

> We all are looking for ways in which the delivery of health care does not become subverted into the protection of a profession; and for ways in which the receiving of health care does not become distorted into a process by which the neighbour is robbed.[23]

Thus in the past two decades the churches, in part through the pioneering and analytical work of the Christian Medical Commission, have modified their emphases in the health care field in fundamental ways. While there continue to be over 2000 church-sponsored hospitals throughout the world, and while there persist major efforts in training health professionals, questions of justice and continuing poor health care for large segments of the populace, mostly the poor, have forced increasing attention to new visions of health, and new strategies for health care. The major shifts can be recapitulated briefly.

1. There is growing recognition of the crucial importance of environmental factors in health, and in the relationship between general socio-economic development (diet, safe water, employment, justice for women, population pressures, ecological health, etc.) and progress in physical health.
2. Increased attention is being paid to the social and psychic dimensions of health and wholeness, rather than isolating the physical from other aspects of health. This emphasis has been shaped, in part, by a renewed appreciation of the health of the community which is the context for the individual's health, and of some of the communitarian and psychic/religious aspects of what had been ignored or belittled as "traditional healing".
3. Emphasis has shifted from professionalized, institutionalized and pharmaceuticalized – basically curative – health care, to preventive and promotive measures to foster health. There has been a corresponding diminution of "brick and mortar" investments, and far greater attention to investments in people.
4. A new appreciation of self-reliance and self-determination in health

care has emerged. This emphasis is rooted in a belief in the need to overcome a sense of alienation of people from their own health, as individuals and communities, and a strategic concern for the most effective development and deployment of health resources. This implies that local resources and local people, acting in concert on the local level, should be major determinants of health care policies. In part the campaign against Nestle's infant formula, which the churches and the Christian Medical Commission have promoted actively, has to be understood in the framework of more self-reliant, less dependent, health care.

5. Increasingly justice for the poorest sectors of the population is seen as a primary plank of the churches' health care efforts. In the past this often led to attempts to serve the victimized and the poor through clinics, hospitals, etc. Today the Christian Medical Commission has adopted advocacy strategies. Not content with "picking up the pieces" of broken and unfulfilled lives, the Commission is now engaged in questioning the social and medical structures which dominate health care — such as the domination of the medical profession by a laissez-faire, profit motivation; the role of transnational corporations in controlling certain aspects of health care, e.g. through pharmaceuticals; or the adverse impact on health of government policies which ignore the devastation of the environment and the way the poor are particularly vulnerable to this destruction.

In short, the work of the Christian Medical Commission, in concert with the churches generally, and with associations like the World Health Organization, has shown itself in solidarity with the poor, in large measure through its critical analysis of the social, cultural, political and economic factors which impede or promote health. While some critics may argue that this systemic analysis diverts resources from more pressing immediate health needs, the Commission has proved free and imaginative enough to explore new levels of solidarity with the poor which are instructive for work not only in the health field, but in other arenas of socio-economic development and justice as well.

Critique of transnational corporations

A second topic which represents the Council's effort to be in solidarity with the poor through analysis of existing social structures and systems is its assessment of the role of transnational corporations in development-liberation. As a specific issue, this is of recent vintage in the ecumenical movement. One could argue that, to a certain extent, the discussion of the TNCs should be put in the larger WCC debate about technology. While the issue is integrally related to technology and the ways in which a technological ethos and technological capacities enhance centralization of power, it has seemed best to focus on the narrower, but still complex and controversial, issue of TNCs, especially in view of the recent special inter-unit programme on TNCs. To focus on TNCs also highlights the fact that the deepest justice issues in society are rooted in how societies organize themselves; they are political more than technical questions.

Since its inception, the World Council has taken a keen interest in economic issues, an interest which already was manifest at the Oxford conference (1937). Amsterdam (1948) offered a balanced critique of both capitalism and communism, and Evanston (1954) continued that critique with, as some believe, a less critical judgment on capitalism. As experiences of the third world became increasingly influential in World Council discussions, first in the rapid social change studies culminating in Thessalonika (1959) and then at New Delhi (1961), the problems of free market presuppositions and relationships came to the fore. By the Geneva, 1966, Church and Society conference, issues of economic development became more prominent, and reflection on differing macro-economic models more sustained. That conference, coupled with the Beirut (1968) discussions, followed by the Uppsala Assembly (1968), began to highlight some of the structural problems impeding economic and social development in the poorer countries.

Yet even at Uppsala primary attention was given to modifications of the free market system, though some delegates did call for wide-ranging and profound changes in economic relationships between countries. Sections II and IV called for vastly expanded aid, and new channels of assistance, but also lifted up the importance of new structural relationships in the economic sphere, pertaining not only to charity and concessions, but to justice in trade and in the exploitation of natural resources. In the official reports there is much criticism of certain features and practices of the free market system, but no outright condemnation of that system.

In subsequent years the criticisms of capitalism and the free market have become more sustained, more strident and more closely reasoned. By the time of the Nairobi Assembly (1975) the critique of a free market system had become more specific; references to new structures of international economic relationships began to be focused more directly on curtailing or eliminating some of the basic features of the free enterprise system. "Growth in an economic order based on the so-called 'free market' system has a built-in exploitative tendency, where resources are unevenly distributed."[24] More specifically, "transnational corporations are a typical example of the ways in which capitalist forces in the national and international spheres join together to oppress the poor and keep them under domination".[25] The same report alleged that "some churches are landowners, related to feudal, capitalist or neo-capitalist structures":[26] and the final recommendations urged that the World Council help member churches to continue dialogue and research on the "role of transnational corporations".[27] This has been carried on in the World Council over the past several years, as an inter-unit enterprise, but under the aegis of CCPD.[28]

In that continued exploration of the role of TNCs, criticism has become even more vigorous and explicit. "The growth of oligopolistic power and the increase in the profits of TNCs in the 70s seem to have a positive correlation with the growing difficulties with which nations and people are confronted. In general, global corporations have tended to aggravate, not to solve, the world's greatest problems."[29] "The Bad Boll International Consultation (1981) stated that the only legitimate relationship between the prophetic church and TNCs is 'one of struggle and conflict. TNCs cannot be converted to ecumenism. Their economistic, exclusive and hierarchical logic makes this impossible.' "[30]

The Advisory Group on Economic Matters, working parallel to the transnational study, acknowledges that though technological growth over the past two centuries has brought many advantages, technological changes now taking place are not only quantitatively, but also qualitatively, different. These qualitative differences in current technological changes, enhanced by and often under the control of TNCs, can be exemplified as follows.[31] (1) "The pace of technological development has accelerated. The expansion of knowledge has become cumulative and exponential, rather than cyclical, and repetitive and comparatively slow." (2) The technology is unicentric, Eurocentric (including the North Atlantic community). (3) "The links between knowledge generation in science, knowledge application through technology, and knowledge utilization for systematically articulated social and political economic ends by both TNCs and states have increased not merely quantitatively but qualitatively." (4) Knowledge and communications have enabled TNCs to integrate vertically, from the control of raw material production through final processing. (5) "The increased scope and spread of technological change has often created widening inequalities in status, power, and income between and within nations." To these qualitative differences have been added enormous new capacities for concentration through four recent developments: *bio-technology, micro-electronics, telecommunications,* and *nuclear power.*[32]

As one who was originally sceptical about the importance of the

World Council duplicating studies on TNCs already being done by many others, and believing that the meagre resources available to the Council might be deployed more profitably in other areas, this writer has come to appreciate the peculiar contributions made by the churches to the discussion of transnationals. Those contributions, almost universally critical of transnationals, have not been in the area of additional technical or economic information; they have been primarily in the clarification of criteria for the evaluation of the impact of TNCs on poorer nations. They have brought unorthodox and non-economic criteria of assessment into the centre of the discussion. They have tried to listen to the experience of oppressed communities as they are impacted by TNCs. Instead of concentrating on the claimed advantages of transnationals (capital transfer and formation; transfer of technical and marketing skills; job creation; connection with an international economic interdependence beneficial for all parties, etc.), the ecumenical debate on transnationals in particular, and the market economy in a more general way, has followed along two revealing lines: (1) whether the alleged positive contributions to the poorer countries actually are realized, and (2) whether the criteria used to evaluate TNC contributions are right or even adequate.

While many studies challenge the alleged benefits to the poor claimed by TNC advocates (e.g. 85–90% of the capital for many TNC ventures in poorer countries originates in those poor nations themselves: the number of new jobs created often is far fewer than projected), we intend to focus on the second point – the criteria used to assess the benefit or liability of TNCs for the poor countries. There are several such criteria frequently mentioned in ecumenical circles which implicitly or explicitly challenge the view that TNCs are advantageous for poorer countries or, as some enthusiastic advocates of TNCs claim, "they represent the only realistic hope for building a truly harmonious, interdependent global community"! The seven following criteria, prominent in ecumenical literature, are not completely absent from more sanguine assessments of the role of TNCs, but in ecumenical circles the importance of these criteria is far more explicit and more heavily emphasized.

One major criterion used in ecumenical circles is that policies or social systems need to be tested against what they do to the poor, or more specifically, how the poor themselves assess those policies or systems. How do the poor experience TNCs? How do the workers experience TNCs? Recent ecumenical efforts have not been content to repeat the theoretical analyses of technical economists and social scientists, important as they are, but to make audible the voices of the poor. Thus, for example, two recent publications highlight such experiences.[33] This is not to suggest that exclusive attention is given to the direct experiences of the poor, and no thought paid to macro-analysis by technically trained economists and social scientists. Indeed, the perspectives of technical elites have played a major role in the work of Church and Society in most of its recent meetings, have been an important part of the just-concluded four-year inter-unit study on transnationals, and have been prominent in the Advisory Group on Economic Matters, a high level task force convened by CCPD on three recent occasions to reflect on international economic conditions and objectives. Nevertheless, a major contribution of the ecumenical family continues to be its serious attempts to hear and amplify the voices of the poor in their direct experience of how TNCs affect their own lives.

A serious criticism of TNCs centres on their tendency to concentrate economic and political power. They connect poorer nations, and their leadership, with world economic systems in ways which, while opening up new possibilities for economic growth, also leave the poorer nations more vulnerable to decisions taken outside their borders. This concentration of power is manifest not only in production-oriented TNCs, but also in banking and finance. Sampson, for example, has shown that in recent years private banking has taken up the slack of public lending to the poorer countries, and that many poorer nations are more indebted to private commercial interests than to government and intergovernment agencies. While such loans have enabled many nations to cope with huge balance of payments deficits, they have greatly increased the vulnerability and dependence of poorer countries on the more industrially developed nations – and at the same time increased the fragility of the world economic system.[34]

A symbol of this increasing dependency may be the purchase of military hardware from industrialized nations. The new hardware is claimed to have many advantages for the poor purchasing nation: strengthening it in relation to surrounding nations, increasing internal security against potential dissidents, enhancing the image of the nation abroad and at home, developing a core of more technically trained people who operate and work with the hardware, etc. But the decision to purchase this equipment also entails costs, and the more technically sophisticated the equipment, the higher the costs are likely to become. Aside from the initial direct fiscal cost of such hardware, for which a country may heavily mortgage its resources, the decision to buy from a particular supplier creates dependence upon that supplier. Parts must be made available; expertise for maintenance and replacement is necessary; the hardware must mesh with other equipment. Dependence soon passes from the technical level to a vulnerability on the political level, where the political interests of the supplier country may become more determinative of the relationship than those of the receiving nation. That may be "realpolitik", but it is a system which perpetuates and deepens the dependence of poorer nations.

This increasing vulnerability and dependence, fostered by TNCs, either unconsciously and unwittingly, or consciously and overtly (as when a company interferes in the internal politics of a nation to maintain a stable climate for investment and productivity) contradicts two main concerns in ecumenical understandings of the development-liberation process: self-reliance and people's participation. To the extent that TNCs magnify the process of centralization of decision-making and the consequent vulnerability of the poor or peripheral sectors of the world, they threaten the very possibilities of genuine human development.

If one argues that vulnerability is the necessary price for growth and interdependence, as those who stress the positive role of TNCs often do, the Advisory Group on Economic Matters warns that interdependence between grossly unequal "partners" is a euphemism for the perpetuation and growth of gross imbalances and inequities.[35] While some talk grandly about an "international division of labour", it is often assumed that the poor will always be the hewers of wood and bearers of water. "All recent evidence indicates [that] poverty and marginality in the third world cannot be overcome by integrating parts of developing nations into the Western-dominated international economic system."[36] In short, the tendency for TNCs to extend, to accumulate and to concentrate economic and political power is a fundamental contradiction to the goal of self-reliance and participation.[37]

A third ecumenical criterion for development pertains to renewability, sustainability and the carrying capacity of the bio- and socio-spheres. It is argued that TNCs show little appreciation of sustainability questions, that, in the interests of profitability or strategic corporate and national interest, they have been willing to denude poorer nations of raw materials, and export pollution to them. Four-fifths of TNC production in third world countries is in production of energy and raw materials.[38]

> When competition, accumulation and the quest for profit orient the administration of science and technology, the result is the exploitation of natural resources (the material environment) within the short-time horizon of return on capital, be it private or public, rather than within the

long-time horizon appropriate to the interests of humanity and the whole of society.[39]

It is argued that TNCs pursue exploitation and pollution practices in poor countries which have been banned in their home countries. Proposed copper mining in Puerto Rico, which would eviscerate the land and displace a comparatively prosperous farming population, opposed by church groups in the late 1960s and early 70s, is but one example of how little ecological considerations typically are taken into account in TNC policies.

A main reason for an ecumenical emphasis on appropriate technology (technology based upon local conditions and supplies) is that such technology tends not only to diminish reliance on outsiders, but also to be more ecologically harmonious. Appropriate technology also is often less costly in the use of non-renewable energy, and thus more ecologically tolerable. Technology imported by TNCs is usually technically sophisticated, increasing the reliance of the poorer nation on outside knowledge, equipment and often people.

In more subtle, but significant, ways reliance on TNCs exacerbates the ecological question. For example, while it is important to seek economies of scale, it is also important to recognize that production for export, which is the goal of a great deal of TNC production, is often extremely costly in energy for transportation and packaging. Studies on energy consumption in the USA indicate that a very large amount of energy is expended on packaging, processing and transportation.[40] For the poorer countries, production directed towards local consumption, to meet basic needs locally, should reduce appreciably this high level of energy consumption. Perhaps this energy saving is most evident in food production, where emphasis on local food production to meet basic local needs is often preferable, even from an energy conservation point of view, to the introduction of export crop agri-business.

> However, technological progress in contemporary society has evolved alongside an increasing number of major problems. There is evidence to prove that these are related, not parallel, processes. Use of capital and input-intensive agricultural technology requires increasing amounts of energy to obtain a constant – and often a decreasing – output. The environmental problems of vastly expanded production of both goods and waste, and of the unconstrained use of limited natural resources are obvious.[41]

Another prominent criterion in ecumenical literature is the question of TNC impact on employment, qualitatively and quantitatively. This is a critical question, given tragic statistics on under-

and unemployment already cited in Chapter One. Under- and unemployment are major obstacles to development, as well as fundamental issues of human rights. Do TNCs promote employment?
And if so, what kind of employment? Such a large and complex
question is beyond the scope of this brief reflection. However, the
ecumenical literature remains sceptical about the capacity of generally high-technology, capital intensive, industry to produce a large
number of new jobs (presently the number of people in poorer
countries employed in TNC operations is small, and perhaps no
more than 2% of the work force.)[42] It is also sceptical about the
validity of claims to have upgraded local working conditions by
setting a good example in pay, environment, working hours, etc.

There is a concern also, not only about the *number* of jobs, but
the *kinds* of jobs, generated by high technology.

> The present technological wave of electronic devices, including robots
> and computers, places unprecedented numbers of jobs at risk. Whether
> or not it eventually creates new jobs, the transitional levels of unem-
> ployment and the individual human tragedies involved are a challenge to
> anyone concerned with social justice and human development. Modern
> technology has increased the numbers of professional and skilled jobs.
> However, it has tended to break up and reduce the requisite skill levels
> for many existing skilled jobs. Increasing polarization between relatively
> well paid, interesting, high status skilled jobs, and ill-paid, deadening
> and low status jobs is discernible in many economies.[43]

As primary agents of the extension of the power, hegemony, institutions and ideology (growth, productivity, efficiency, profitability,
free market, etc.) of the developed world, TNCs may have a
long-term beneficial effect on employment opportunities in the
poorer countries, but it is not yet clear that the number of jobs,
short-term or long-term, will increase. Nor is it clear that the kinds
of jobs which they make available will benefit the masses.

A related criterion and question is whether equity and justice are
promoted through TNCs. A pervasive theme in recent ecumenical
literature is that TNCs, while perhaps marginally improving the lot
of many people, and significantly raising the living standards of a
few, aggravate rather than reduce disparities and inequities. This is
evident in the area of human rights, where some governments re-
press their own peoples in the name of economic growth and national unity.[44] More fundamentally and pervasively, however,
market mechanisms distort production priorities to favour the affluent (who have effective purchasing power) and tend to minimize the
importance of meeting basic human needs. They also enhance the
power of the already powerful, unless countervailing power is

brought to bear. When local leaders in poorer nations accept the "development" ideology of the world's elites, and themselves profit from such collusion, the countervailing power has to be mobilized from among the poor.[45]

The Zurich consultation argued that traditional views of economic development (e.g. growth before justice; inequities tolerated to encourage savings; growth promoting more equitable distribution; stability and absence of inflation as preferable to the uncertainties of change; etc.) needed to be deeply questioned. However, the consultation also argued that certain emerging new theories also needed to be tested thoroughly. These are such ideas as the following: "(1) modernization (in the form of rationalization, maximization and centralization of technical and economic power) leads to increasing domination and not automatically to justice and participation; (2) in the present system economic growth generally leads to injustice; (3) at present, technological advance tends to enhance the power of the powerful."[46] Two years later the Advisory Group was less equivocal:

> It is the excluded, the oppressed and the exploited who have paid the highest price for the prosperity and power of the affluent and might, domestically and internationally. A just international order in the 1980s will only come about through a worldwide recognition of the right of the poor and the oppressed to set their own agenda in the light of their socio-cultural experience and social biography, in the context of human solidarity.[47]

And, it was argued, "it is no accident that in the Punjab and the Philippines increased grain production, increased concentration of land holding, increased modernization, increased unemployment and increased absolute numbers of malnourished human beings have gone hand in hand."[48] Fr Theo Mathias argues, however, that unemployment and malnourishment have *not* been increased in the Punjab.[49]

In brief, in current ecumenical opinion, TNCs are generally thought to exacerbate, rather than reduce, inequities; they are given little hope of contributing directly to the achievement of justice.

Finally, ecumenical discussions are increasingly concerned with the need to at least slow down the erosion and disintegration of traditional values in the face of the onslaught of a Euro-centred technological and consumerist society. While the baby-formula issue is perhaps the most celebrated case of a dangerous and disruptive imposition of alien values on traditional and vulnerable societies, it is clear that on a much broader, more pervasive and often subtler basis, the values of technological societies are introduced and assiduously cultivated through transnational corporations. The decades of the 1980s and 1990s almost certainly will be characterized by much greater attention to religio-cultural "imperialisms"; issues of the relation between "religion" and the state, already so evident in many countries (Iran, Pakistan, Ireland, Cuba, Ethiopia, Israel, South Africa) will become more central to discussions about development and liberation. A revival or reassertion of traditional values (e.g. communitarian rather than atomistic emphases in society; an organic rather than a competitive view of the relationship between humankind and non-human nature; a "needs" orientation rather than an accumulation and consumption ethos) is likely, desirable, and even in the interests of already highly technologized and industrialized societies which are marked by increasing stresses, tensions, violence and alienation. Technology is not value neutral; it is based upon and carries its own value assumptions, some of which are inimical to traditional values and practices.[50] Recognizing this process, recent ecumenical literature emphasizes the role of the poor as the legitimate shapers of values and priorities in determining what kinds of technology are appropriate to their needs and to their common aspirations.[51] "If they (new technologies) are to meet their needs or be popular and democratic, these articulations must be based on the perceptions of the poor."[52]

Without further labouring the point that TNCs are bearers of alien values in most poorer and more traditional societies, thus frequently threatening the coherence and health of those host societies, let us cite one eloquent – if complex (!) – paragraph from the Advisory Group which captures the concern and advances the argument. It serves as a suitable conclusion to this brief discussion of criteria emphasized in recent ecumenical literature which help to provide a new framework for a structural analysis of one of the most powerful and controversial institutions in modern society, the transnational corporation.

> Ultimately, when the nature, destiny and unique worldview of a people are considered from the larger perspective of time and history, it will be seen that the modern transmitters of cybernetics, capital, resources and know-how do not provide those positive historical references which define a nation's image and identity and gather up those inner reserves of power that can release forces for massive social transformation encompassing social, cultural, economic and political levels, and produce self-reliance. Self-reliance, e.g. the resurgence of self-strength, is indeed possible when a people are made to fall back on their historical antecedents as discerned from their own indigenous perceptions or reality. These internal forces and the directions they indicate for people's long future

are alien to the technocratic prescriptions of transnational corporations, in spite of their magnificent promises of scientific achievement.[53]

NOTES

1. It is instructive to note that this major investment in health is diminishing, and changing its focus, but it is still sizeable. For example, the Association of the Churches' Development Services, in the Federal Republic of Germany, expended approximately 250 million Deutschmarks in 1980, with 33.5 DM (13.6%) allocated to health. It should be clear, however, that some of the other categories supported, such as "comprehensive programmes", may have included a health component. "Annual Report of the Association of the Churches' Development Services, 1980", p. 49.
2. Document 7, Central Committee, 14–22 August 1980, 7 pp.
3. Kingma, *op. cit.*, pp. 4–5.
4. *Ibid.*, p. 5.
5. *Ibid.*, p. 5.
6. Marie-Thérèse Feuerstein, "Rural Health Problems in Developing Countries: the Need for a Comprehensive Approach", *Contact*, Special Series No. 3, June 1980, p. 34.
7. Susan Rifkin, "Community Participation, A Planner's Approach", *Contact*, Special Series No. 3, p. 2.
8. Kingma, *op. cit.*, p. 6.
9. *Ibid.*, p. 6.
10. "The Health Care Crisis in the USA: Analysis and Recommendations for Public Policy", *National Impact*, August 1980, p. 7.
11. "The Churches' Healing Ministry in Africa", *Contact*, No. 29, October 1975, p. 3.
12. "Crucial Issues in a Philosophy of Health Care", *Consultation on Emerging Issues and Future Directions in Health Care*, March 1977, sponsored by the NCCCUSA, p. 1.
13. "Declaration of Alma-Ata", International Conference on Primary Health Care, at Alma-Ata, USSR, 6–12 September 1978, co-sponsored by WHO and UNICEF, found in *Contact*, Special Series No. 1, April 1979, p. 111.
14. Kingma, *op. cit.*, p. 7.
15. *Ibid.*, p. 7.
16. "Available evidence, both theoretical and empirical, suggests that medical and biological factors account for approximately 10% of the pie, Health. The other three – environmental, socio-cultural and behavioural [account for about 90%]. Yet we tend to spend almost all of our money on medical care. Our traditional approach to health, through a sophisticated medical care system, has been to emphasize, with a relative neglect of improving the environment and strengthening the host, the identification and consequent destruction of disease agents." Rick Carlson, "Toward a New Understanding of Health Within the Limits of Medicine", in *Consultation on, op. cit.*, p. 13.
17. Oscar Gish, "Towards an Appropriate Health Care Technology", *Contact*, Special Series No. 1, April 1979.
18. John McKnight, "Professionalized Service and Disabling Help", in *Consultation on, op. cit.*, p. 19.
19. Kingma, *op. cit.*, p. 9. Essentially these points are taken from the Alma-Ata conference referred to above.

20. "Is Primary Health Care the New Priority? Yes, But. . . ." *Contact*, Special Series No. 1, April 1979, p. 71.
21. *Ibid.*, p. 71.
22. *Ibid.*, p. 72.
23. *Ibid.*, p. 72.
24. Paton, *op. cit.*, p. 123.
25. *Ibid.*, p. 131.
26. *Ibid.*, p. 133.
27. *Ibid.*, p. 139.
28. A recapitulation of the Inter-Unit Study process has been given by Marcos Arruda in "The WCC Programme on TNC's: Some Lessons and Challenges", Geneva, WCC, 1982.
29. Marcos Arruda (ed.), *Transnational Corporations, Technology and Human Development*, Geneva, WCC, 1981, pp. 25–26.
30. As quoted in Arruda, "The WCC Programme on TNCs", *op. cit.*, p. 14.
31. Marcos Arruda (ed.), *Transnational Corporations, op. cit.*, Geneva, WCC, 1981, pp. 25–26.
32. *Ibid.*, pp. 44–49.
33. Christian Conference of Asia, *People Against Domination*, Tokyo, 1981; and Christian Conference of Asia, *Minangkabau: Story of the People vs. TNCs in Asia*, Hong Kong, 1981.
34. The advisory group referred to the "collapse of Bretton Woods", concluding that this collapse is manifest not only in the enormous debt owed by poorer nations, but in a number of areas affecting rich nations as well. It called the present monetary "order" really a "disorder", requiring structural changes not unlike those suggested by the Group of 77. Arruda, *Ecumenism, op. cit.*, p. 33, and 71ff. For commercial lending discussions, see Anthony Sampson, *op. cit.*
35. Arruda, *Ecumenism, op. cit.*, p. 71.
36. *Ibid.*, p. 82.
37. We insist on speaking of how TNCs foster political as well as economic concentration because, as the advisory committee pointed out, there is a mutuality of interests and support between TNCs and local political elites, a major factor in local repression and denial of basic human rights. Thus TNCs may have a major impact on the denial or suppression of human rights, in poor countries especially. *Ibid.*, pp. 76–77.
38. Arruda, *Transnational, op. cit.*, p. 33.
39. Arruda, *Ecumenism, op. cit.*, p. 14 (report of the Zurich 1978 consultation.)
40. See, for example, Carol and John Steinhart, *The Fires of Culture*, North Scituate, Massachusetts, Duxbury Press, 1974.
41. Arruda, *Transnational, op. cit.*, p. 14.
42. *Ibid.*, p. 34.
43. *Ibid.*, pp. 17–18.
44. Arruda, *Ecumenism, op. cit.*, p. 64.
45. *Ibid.*, p. 75.
46. *Ibid.*, p. 20.
47. *Ibid.*, p. 60.
48. Arruda, *Transnational, op. cit.*, p. 51.
49. In private conversation in spring 1982.
50. *Ibid.*, p. 50.
51. *Ibid.*, p. 50.
52. *Ibid.*, p. 51.
53. Arruda, *Ecumenism, op. cit.*, p. 6.

7: Theological and ethical reflection

It may seem trite to describe one form of witness in solidarity with the poor as biblical and theological reflection on contemporary experience. Yet such reflection is both integral to the calling of the churches, and an important element in the struggle for global justice. It is set forth here as a fourth mode (rather than first or last) of solidarity to suggest that theological and biblical reflection is done best in the midst of the solidarity process, dialectically shaped in the midst of lively interaction between action and reflection. Theological and biblical reflection is not chronologically prior to engagement; it is most fruitful in the actual historical struggle of people.

Further, to have put biblical and theological reflection as the first mode of solidarity might have conveyed the impression that the churches are characteristically the source of creativity for social and ethical visions, or typically the pioneers of social reform. History often suggests the contrary. Churches often have been late-comers to movements for social transformation, having been pushed or drawn there by pressures from others – of the suffering and oppressed. Based on his experience in Cuba, and his more general reflections on the usual roles of churches in society, Prof. Arce challenges the common assumption made by many church leaders that the Christian community often is champion of social change and social justice. His view, perhaps too one-sided, is an important corrective to the more frequent and equally one-sided and romantic view that the churches are the vanguards of justice.

> Our present theological task consists primarily in "interpreting" today's revolutionary world to the church, and not *vice versa*. It is not a matter of "interceding" on behalf of the Christian faith to its "cultural detractors", but rather of mediating the revolutionary culture to its Christian detractors.[1]

Within the World Council of Churches, this mode of being in solidarity with the poor through biblical, theological and ecclesiological reflection occurs in many ways and in several areas of its work. It could be argued that in practically every one of the Council's programmes there is a sharpening of aspects of biblical and theological issues, whether speaking of the "Humanum Study", Church and Society's explorations into relationships with non-human nature and into bio-technology, Urban Rural Mission's conceptions of morally responsible and strategically effective social change, Faith and Order's studies on the nature of the church and Christian unity, or the lively but complex discussions in the programme on Dialogue with People of Living Faiths and Ideologies.

While it would be possible to discuss the mode of solidarity from a large number of Council initiatives, two specific efforts will be cited here: the recent programme emphasis in Unit II on a "Just, Participatory and Sustainable Society", and the Commission on World Mission and Evangelism's Melbourne conference on the theme "Your Kingdom Come". The first helps to focus on the churches' vision of the relation between social conditions and the Kingdom, while the second centres on ecclesiological questions.

Towards a just, participatory and sustainable society

Adopted as a programme emphasis for the post-Nairobi period, the "Just, Participatory and Sustainable Society" study cuts across units and commissions of the Council, though it is animated through Unit II, Justice and Service. It is important to be clear about what the concept of a "Just, Participatory and Sustainable Society" (JPSS) is and what it is not.[2] If one keeps in mind the purposes of the JPSS study, some of the widespread confusion about, and opposition to, that effort might be eliminated or at least moderated. The JPSS is not a secular version of the Kingdom of God! It is an effort to paint a broad-stroked picture of the kind of society towards which Christians can aspire, without being trapped in the "either-or" alternative of capitalism or communism – and indeed without being trapped into identification with any extant social order. One could speak of a search for a "third way", were that phrase not already identified with specific political movements in some countries.

Ever since the idea of "The Responsible Society" lost favour (see chapter 3), there has been a need to develop a common vision of the kind of society towards which the Christian community might aspire. Despite the dangers of confusing any proximate social system with a Christian society, such a common vision would require attention to systemic and structural questions, and not only to occasional problems, or to simple pragmatism or problem-solving. It would require an emerging positive formulation and not only a "prophetic" negativism.

While the Kingdom cannot be identified with any existing or imagined socio-political construct, and despite a current prevalent temptation towards a utopianism which disregards or minimizes human frailty and sin, it has become increasingly uncomfortable and unprofitable for the churches only to criticize all existing social systems. Such indictments are made on the basis of often hidden, usually undeveloped, assumptions. Shouldn't they become more explicit, more coherent, more open to challenge, and more consciously rooted in the ethos of the larger Christian community?

More practically, even if the churches do not want to be identified with existing political-economic systems, they constantly are being stereotyped and categorized. If they criticize capitalism, they are presumed to be socialist or Marxist. If they raise questions about the adequacy of socialism or Marxism, they often are included in the capitalist or "free market" camp. In the world of development theory there seems to be little room for alternatives between or aside from the poles! Is there an alternative vision which can be differentiated from the two dominant extant socio-political systems? A major task in the JPSS discussion is to demythologize existing paradigms of development and liberation and to point to new possibilities emerging from the experience, especially the experience of those struggling for justice. The JPSS discussion provides an emergent, still fluid, conception which offers a framework for creative reflection cutting across stereotyped positions. The concepts of "justice", "participation", and "sustainability" appear as dominant concerns in ecumenical debates about the social order – "justice" having been long a central feature in ecumenical ethics (though not always understood precisely as it is today), while the emphases on "participation" and "sustainability" have come to prominence only in the 1970s.

Further, JPSS is not conceived as a finally formulated idea; it is an invitation to further exploration on the basis of already clear proximate, core convictions. It is *not* a fully integrated and developed doctrine, nor are its component parts harmoniously articulated. It is not a conception fully grounded, at this stage, in biblical and theological reflections. It is not a blueprint for analysis, or for setting up a new social order, presumably applicable to diverse socio-cultural and political situations.

Professor Miguez-Bonino, chairman of the JPSS working team which reported to the Kingston meeting of the Central Committee in 1979, noted two temptations which the drafting team sought to avoid: "that of trying to elaborate a blueprint or to establish pro-grammatic decisions, and that of flying off into pseudo-theological abstractions."[3] Pursuing the same line of argument, the function and utility of the JPSS conception has been defined cogently by Raiser, who played a key role in preparing the working team's document presented to the Central Committee. Speaking before church leaders in Norway in 1980, Raiser argued that we have arrived at a stage in the evolution of development-liberation ex-perience and theory where the old notions no longer seem adequate. The present complex and volatile historical reality is shattering per-ceptions of development which for years seemed so persuasive and adequate. Today's world situation poses basic questions to Christ-ians about their understanding of a just and good society; the ques-tions are not only moral, but theological and religious. The issues are more complex than during the earlier discussions of the "re-sponsible society". Borrowing from Kuhn's description of devel-opmental stages in science, Raiser posits a parallel process in Christian thinking about social justice issues.

> Most processes of social and historical change can be understood in terms of a sequence of relatively stable periods where there are predominant paradigms for explaining the facts, questions, issues posed, problems arising (during which time there is a paradigm which solves the existing riddles), and the periods of major crisis where the paradigm doesn't cover the facts any more, where the paradigm disintegrates into its component parts. Slowly, through a process of innovation, new paradigms come into being. A new paradigm is valid only if it succeeds in integrating the continuing validity of the former paradigm into a new set of explanations.[4]

Raiser contends that the JPSS discussion revives the "middle ax-iom" approach to Christian social ethics, so important in the history of ecumenical ethics. At a time when there is a "disintegration of traditional paradigms", a time when theory-building is very diffi-cult, if not impossible, the appeal for new and compelling middle axioms may open up the way ahead. The middle axiom approach "does not pretend to offer a coherent system of teaching, nor simply an escape into the relativization of all norms and values; it aims at agreement on essential criteria for ethical judgment and guiding principles".[5]

It is this critically important role which the emerging ideas of a JPSS can play in ecumenical ethics. JPSS provides a common frame-work for corporate reflection on a generally agreed upon constella-tion of values. It does not absolutize those values or imply that no other values will become prominent as the constellation comes more clearly into focus. It does not so neatly and tightly define the concepts of justice, participation and sustainability that they become strait-jackets inhibiting reflection and action in unique historical-cultural situations. Ironically, however, the utility of the JPSS idea is closely linked to efforts to spell out the adequacy of such middle axioms, their inter-relationships, and their applicability to particular social situations. One of the most urgent needs at present is to define more carefully the meaning of the three notions of justice, sustainability and participation, and to highlight their ambiguities and inter-relationships. But this "spelling out" must be done in the context of genuine struggles for justice. In this respect the Cyprus consultation also was helpful in showing that perceptions of churches' engagements in political ethics are deeply influenced by the social positions of Christians and of churches making the assessment. It noted "church-centred" (where churches are socially powerful), "politics-centred" (where social situations are fluid and churches often minorities), and "people-centred" (where the aspirations of the poor and oppressed are central) perceptions.[6]

Important aspects of the concepts already have been articulated. For example, the 1974 Bucharest conference (Church and Society) first used the phrase "a sustainable society", defining it to include the following considerations.

First, social stability cannot be obtained without an equitable distribution of what is in scarce supply or without common opportunity to participate in social decisions. Second, a robust global society will not be sustainable unless the need for food is at any time below the global capacity to supply it, and unless the emissions of pollutants are well below the capacity of the ecosystem to absorb them. Third, the new social organization will be sustainable only as long as the rate of use of non-renewable resources does not outrun the increase in resources made available through technological innovation. Finally, a sustainable society requires a level of human activity which is not adversely influenced by the never-ending, large and frequent natural variation in the global climate.[7]

The notion of participation is also being gradually clarified. For instance, a CCPD consultation of 19 people, gathered in Geneva in early 1982, and focusing on "The Churches and People's Participation", described "participation" thus:

People's participation is the people's initiative to assert themselves as subjects of history. When we speak of people as the subject of people's participation we are referring to particular groups in society, namely the poor, the oppressed, the marginal groups, the working class. People's movements do not aim to develop participation within existing oppressive structures. The aim is rather for people's movements which lead oppressed groups to power so that they can control their lives and their economy, creating just and participatory structures. In that sense people's participation is both a means and an end.[8]

While the meaning of each of the three key concepts in JPSS needs to be more fully spelled out, the relationship among them is also a key task for the years ahead. The relationship of justice and participation to sustainability was highlighted in Birch's address at the Nairobi Assembly, and the Assembly itself called for "a deliberate transition to a sustainable global society in which science and technology will be mobilized to meet the basic physical and spiritual needs of people".[9] And the Church and Society working group, encouraged by the Central Committee meeting of 1976, noted that "the twin issues around which the world's future revolves are justice and ecology", adding that "a sustainable society which is unjust can hardly be worth sustaining. A just society that is unsustainable is self-defeating. Humanity now has the responsibility to make a deliberate transition to a just and sustainable global society so organized that man and other living creatures on which his life depends [an anthropocentrism which was soon to be moderated!] can be sustained indefinitely within the limits of the earth."[10]

A helpful effort to spell out the implications of the JPSS vision was a chapter on the "Criteria for Quality of Life", in the preparatory volume for the MIT conference on "Faith, Science and the Future", in 1979. The Overseas Development Council (Washington, USA) had developed a "Physical Quality of Life Index", measuring literacy, life expectancy and infant mortality as major objective indices of quality of life. To this the Overseas Development Council added the "Disparity Reduction Ratio", attempting to provide a measurement of improvements in quality of life over time.[11] The longitudinal measurement was itself perceived as an important aspect of the development process. The pre-MIT essay called for application of the following criteria, which, while less precise and quantifiable, begin to flesh out the JPSS goals.

1. The quality of goods and services produced, taking into account the relation between production of basic needs (food, clothing, housing, transportation, health care, education, culture) on the one hand, and luxury goods on the other.
2. Distribution pattern, including the ratio between consumption by the top and bottom ten percentiles of the population generally, as well as between regions, linguistic and ethnic groups, rural and urban populations.

3. Employment pattern, with special attention to unemployment and underemployment.
4. Environmental considerations, measured by such factors as absolute pollution, increase in pollution, laws governing pollution and their enforcement, investments made to control pollution, etc.
5. Dependency patterns, or the degree to which development is enhancing or hindering self-reliance, within as well as between nations (noting that not all interdependence is bad).
6. Participation pattern, pertaining to the degree to which the people share in production and distribution decisions.
7. Quality of motivation, or the degree to which selfishness, greed, acquisitiveness, domination, exploitation are widespread, rather than love, service-mindedness, etc. Justice and sustainability imply concern for future generations as well as for the integrity of non-human nature along with human nature.
8. Human rights and freedoms, recognizing that in different cultures the emphases in human rights and freedoms may differ (right to free speech and free press, right to work, right to full health care, right to free education, right to travel at will, etc.)
9. Cultural freedom and creativity, perhaps including scientific and technological inventiveness.
10. Some negative parameters: prevalence of contagious diseases, accident rates, crimes, suicides, alcoholism, drug addiction, prisoners, bribery, corruption, etc.[12]

Why "justice", "participation", and "sustainability"? Have these grown directly and clearly out of the tradition and ethos of the Christian community, and pre-eminently from the Bible? With the exception of justice, it is not easy to find clear links in the historic teaching of the Christian community with the participation and sustainability themes, though such links are now being uncovered and traced. Have the concepts of participation and sustainability grown out of other cultural environments, and then biblical and theological justification been sought for them? Is some new ideology creeping into Christian theology, masked behind these terms? Such concerns are natural and important, if the integrity, power, and meaning of the gospel is taken seriously.

Yet the gospel, in all times, is rooted in the experience of the community of the faithful, and is affected by concrete historical events. The Bible is less a cosmology than a history of God's relationships with covenant people and with all creation. All theology is rooted in a sense of God's power and presence, not only through the historic community of faith known through tradition, but through the Spirit at work in the continuing fashioning of creation. Today an over-riding experience of the covenant community, particularly those on the "underside" of history, is that society, at national and international levels, is scandalously unjust. People ask what God's relationship is to this reality, and they conclude that God is on the side of those struggling for justice, wholeness and dignity; against those who stifle, cramp and oppress.

Thus the JPSS debate is firmly grounded in people's experiences of the struggle for justice and faithfulness, and new theological emphases are springing from the soil of real contemporary experience. An integral aspect of that theological reshaping is a deepening appreciation for the role of the poor in the theological task. Theological and biblical struggle is a manifestation of solidarity with the poor, not in the sense of providing a new top-down worldview to assist or strengthen the masses to better understand (and accept?) their predicament. Rather, it is an effort to shape theological discussion in response to the real hurts, pains and aspirations of the people.

That is why, for example, the emphasis on "stories of the people" (given so much prominence in recent Asian theology) is so vital for the JPSS effort. While such stories are not a substitute for an integrated, coherent theological worldview, they help the theological enterprise to take seriously the experiences of the people captured in fables, myths, and stories. We are reminded that the Bible itself is in a basic sense "stories of the people" more than cosmology or systematic theology.

Srisang warns that it is important not to minimize or misinterpret the significance of stories. He contends that stories of the people are not simply grist for the theologians' mill, something out of which theology can be manufactured; story-telling is at once theological and ethical. This view of the significance of stories appeared in the 1981 Cyprus meeting: "Story-telling by people is an integral part of political ethics and not merely a prolegomena to the analysis of situations and the articulation of ethical norms."[13] If treated as prolegomena to "real" theology, and not constantly related to living movements for social justice, there is danger that "in the passage from story-telling to analysis everything can be lost; people's struggle can be coopted once more".[14]

> The important point here is the need to underline that theology is called to overcome its isolation, not only from political and social sciences, but also from people's life and the way that people understand it. The method which we suggest is a combination of context, life, people's stories, social analysis and affirmation of basic values and non-negotiable assumptions.[15]

Some of the most stimulating contemporary biblical exegesis stems from small, lower economic class ecclesial communities, such as Cardenal reports in his *Solentiname*.[16] That is why the JPSS process has focused not only on global relationships, but has tried to regionalize and nationalize the discussions of development in order to take seriously particular cultural settings, and especially the experiences of the poor and oppressed.[17]

On the basis of these reflections, several important lessons have been confirmed. One is a deeper verification that, while they are still incomplete and not fully defined, justice, participation and sustainability are three litmus tests of an ethically adequate society. A second lesson is that there can be no facile resolution of these three objectives. The three concepts have to be integrally linked, though at the present time not all the links are clear. What is clear at present, however, is that while there appears to be more positive congruity among the three ideas than incompatibility, some of these linkages may be negative as well as positive. It is evident also that the three should not be separated, as is sometimes done – justice for the third world, participation for the second, and sustainability for the first. At one stage in the evolution of the JPSS concept there was a danger that the discussion might break up into such distinctions, but the Kingston Central Committee rightly insisted that the three concepts must be affirmed as dialectically relevant to all societies.

Thirdly, it is increasingly evident that, while the three concepts belong together, there is a certain priority for justice. "Justice has become the acid test of all engagement in society and the criterion of all possible programmes and strategies for society. Justice, in the perspective of the Kingdom of God, is not a principle, an ideal value which will never be realized in social life. Rather, as the historical embodiment of love, it indicates a quality of relationships in community, and a criterion for evaluating and changing social structures."[18] Justice itself demands participation as a constitutive element. Participation, therefore, is not simply a strategic consideration; it is a *desideratum* of justice. One cannot speak of having "given their due" to persons or communities (the classical understanding of justice, under attack today by those who want to avoid legalistic definitions of "due") unless they have been enabled to participate in the shaping of policy, especially those policies which most directly and deeply affect their own lives.

Similarly, sustainability is linked to justice, for justice vis-à-vis the entire creation, and the entire human community as part of creation, must take into account the legitimate and often unprotected claims of future generations upon the resources of the earth. Further, sustainability refers not only to physical sustainability, but to social sustainability as well, and a society characterized by injustice is socially unsustainable in the long run.[19] Thus issues of justice permeate the discussion at every level.

A fourth lesson emanating from the JPSS discussion is a deeper appreciation for the relationship between the global situation and a local setting. This has been most vivid in reflections on sustainability, including issues of "growth" or "no-growth", as were dramatically posed at the MIT conference in discussions between Daly and Kurien. But on a broader level, too, JPSS has been a reminder of the importance of maintaining a distinct but vital interplay, between the global and the more local perspectives. The JPSS clearly needs both the concreteness of local experience and the analytical perspectives emerging from more global descriptions and analyses. Without such reciprocal enrichment, the JPSS discussion would lose its vitality, credibility, and efficacy.

A fifth lesson is a new appreciation of the crucial question of power. Analyses of the development-liberation process have forced the ecumenical perspectives of development away from a "stages of growth" perception of poverty. Oppression and liberation have become key analytical concepts, grounded biblically in the exodus and in the continuing covenantal relationship which is central to the biblical testimony. This biblical perspective is substantiated historically and sociologically by an analysis of the way power affects individuals and communities. Of course, theological perspectives on power have been a significant part of the ecumenical debate for decades, but there is today a deeper sense of the central importance of a theological understanding of power for an adequate view of development-liberation issues.

> In biblical perspective power is both demonic, perverting human relationships, and liberating for the preservation of human life. This has led some to regard power as neutral, as functional, placing the emphasis on its good or bad use, while others have established a radical metaphysical distinction between sinful, selfish power and the good power of God. The essential objective in the struggle should therefore be to render all exercise of power accountable to God and accountable to the people who are subject to it [a concept stemming directly from the concept of the responsible society].[20]

Increasingly a Christian view of the positive and negative aspects of power (is power ever neutral when it is in the hands of people?) is perceived to be a central issue of the continuing JPSS debate, requiring far more systematic and sustained attention than it has received to date. Just how important and difficult that discussion of power is was evident in the Cyprus consultation. It was reiterated there that a central theological issue is power, and that Christians perceive power in significantly different ways (the report spoke of two views of power, while the typology would need to be more precisely elaborated). One quotation from that report, however, illustrates the theological and ethical ambiguity of power, and the difficulty of clear understandings of power. "For Christians, the messianic politics of Jesus is our paradigm. Jesus not only did not use power as we know it, but he could not use power, since he himself was the embodiment and reality of the Messianic Kingdom which is the powerless status of Jesus the Messiah and the people."[21] This statement indicates how much work needs to be done in the clarification of Christian views of power!

Finally, the JPSS discussions with their emphases on participation and local experience (parallel to a commitment to a global vision of society) have highlighted the importance of perspectives of people of other faiths and ideologies. Beyond the fresh and challenging insights generated by third world Christians, one of the most stimulating aspects of ecumenical life in the past decade has been a creative encounter with people of other worldviews and commitments. That interaction continues to raise not only profound ecclesiological and missiological questions, but also questions about the attributes of a just and ethical society. As the report to the Kingston Central Committee acknowledges: "Christians and churches have to ask themselves self-critically whether they have not taken for granted too easily that there is a universal validity in all cultures of the model of a 'secular' state and society, and even encouraged an apparent identification of Christian values with a secularized, pluralistic type of society."[22] In some societies the vision of the good society does not include the principles of pluralism and participation; in some societies the idea of justice is far more static than active; in some societies the emphases on change and creativity are not evident; in some societies there is great attention to sustainability as a part of living with all creation.

It is becoming more and more apparent that Christians, already a minority of the world's population, will have to face theologically, biblically and ethically (as well as practically) the question of the relationship of religious institutions and ideologies to political institutions and policies. "Religion-state" (not just "church-state" relationships) have become central issues in many nations, and in situations where culture and religion are closely intertwined the questions become even more acute and complex. In the decades ahead these inter-religious and inter-cultural issues will become

more significant items on the "development" agenda than they have
been in the past.

Out of this rich JPSS discussion several persistent key theological
questions require attention. Some important examples might be
cited.

1. What are authentic biblical meanings of justice, and to what
extent are they congruent with doctrines of justice characteristic of
contemporary society? For example, some contend that Western
notions of justice, stemming from classical Greece, are different
from the biblical notions. It is argued that they put far too much
stress on distributional justice, perceive justice in too atomistic and
non-communitarian terms, have a too juridical rather than covenantal view of justice, assume that justice is largely static, and not
under the constant pressure of love. Among Christians, too, there
are varying understandings of justice, and the primacy justice should
have in relation to other social objectives. For example, Brunner
contended that "order" has a higher chronological priority than
justice, but this is not self-evident to some current liberation theologians.[23] The JPSS debate has highlighted the importance of these
differences, and provided a framework for creative interaction about
them.

2. What is humanity's proper relationship with non-human nature – to dominate, to cultivate, to be a partner, or something else?
What is the proper balance between changing and cultivating non-
human nature, on the one hand, and sustaining nature as it is, on
the other? In this connection, are there appropriate limits to long-
term (e.g. genetic) changes in the interest of "improving" the germ
line genes?[24] What is the significance of the "participatory" emphasis
in relation to these decisions? Church and Society's explorations,
especially in the MIT context on "Faith, Science and the Future",
open a Pandora's box of thorny theological and ethical issues pertaining to non-human nature, among other matters, forcing a reconsideration of the relationship between stability and change, and
the appropriate rate and direction of change. Has current theology
become so futurist and change-oriented (so concerned with *becoming*), that it is losing a sense that God "saw creation, and that it
was good" (*being*)?

3. What are the biblical and theological roots for the notion of
participation? How does the Bible understand participation, or does
it even address the question in a direct way? Does the Western
tradition of basic human rights of the individual convey an atomistic
view of society unfamiliar to and inappropriate in a biblical context?
Is the concept of participation too broad to be applicable? The

Kingston JPSS document supplied its own notion of participation: "Participation means that each one takes initiative in formulating or changing policies and becoming involved in directing their implementation. This participation must embrace every sphere of life: political – in being allowed to exercise full political rights – economic, social, cultural."[25] Is the idea of participation intimately linked with biblical notions of community and *koinonia*? Is it sound exegesis to base this notion of participation on the image of the many parts of one body, as in 1 Corinthians 12? Is the organic vision of society implied in the body imagery consistent with, and possible within, the mass and urbanized society which characterizes our time? Clearly the JPSS discussion has established "participation" as a central feature of the good society, but the perceptions of how this is grounded theologically and biblically, and how it is to be practically realized, are still very hazy and obscure.

4. The JPSS discussion raises the perennial issue of the relation between the Kingdom of God and the kingdoms of this world. Some are disturbed by what appears to them a naive romanticism about human achievements and prospects, unwarranted utopianism about the prospects for social regeneration or transformation. Notwithstanding disclaimers to the contrary, is there a danger that JPSS will be confused with the Kingdom? Does JPSS take eschatological questions seriously? One participant at Cyprus noted that "we live on Saturday, between the Friday of the crucifixion and the Sunday of the resurrection".[26] Perhaps this uneasiness more than any other issue arose in the Central Committee's review of the JPSS report at Kingston. The report had stated:

> The biblical witness refers to this final aim as the Kingdom of God which embraces the two dimensions of redemption of the whole of creation and personal fulfilment for each human being. We call this Kingdom "messianic" because we believe that Jesus, as the Messiah, has brought, lived out and inaugurated the Kingdom on earth, in space and time. It is already at work, therefore not a futuristic or spiritual escape, but it is not yet fulfilled, indeed beyond historical achievement. The messianic Kingdom, while having entered history, transcends it; it is present for the eyes of faith, and yet it remains the object of hope. [We] derive inner power and strength from this active and waiting presence between the two comings, one historical, the other eschatological.[27]

Despite the balancing statement, it was felt by some that the relationship between the historical kingdoms (and visions of kingdom) and the eschatological Kingdom was not adequately defined (could it ever be?). Failure to make a clearer distinction, even a difference, led some to believe the document was too blind to personal and corporate sin. Indeed, is not the notion of the Kingdom implied in the document too institutionally and politically conceived, without sufficient openness to the transcendent power and relationship necessary for wholeness and redemption, either of individuals or of communities?

These are but a few of the theological and ethical probings emanating from the JPSS discussion. Through them the churches can be in solidarity with the poor at a very significant level. Through these questions, generated in part by taking seriously the situation of the poor and oppressed, the church itself is being renewed. But we reiterate that these theological and biblical reflections cannot be done adequately in abstract ways; they have to be learned and thought about in the context of the struggle for justice. That leads to the second programme area of the Council which illustrates the mode of solidarity through theological, biblical and ecclesiological reflection, rooted in the tempest of struggles for justice.

Ecclesiological reflection through base ecclesial communities

Similarly, the Melbourne conference of the Commission on World Mission and Evangelism, in 1980, was witness to solidarity with the poor through the process of theological and ethical reflection, especially but not exclusively on ecclesiological questions. It centred attention on another liberationist theme, the role of basic ecclesial communities in the renewal of the churches and society. Thus the effort to be in "solidarity" challenges ecclesiological understandings in fundamental ways.

One of the most noteworthy developments in the post-Nairobi period has been a resurgent vitality of local Christian communities, from the celebrated *communidades de base* in parts of Latin America, to communities of the poor struggling for justice and faithfulness in, for example, Korea, Indonesia, the Philippines, the USA, Zimbabwe, and Tanzania.[28] Often these communities have little direct relationship with, and seldom any dependence on, existing traditional churches or denominations.

> In 1968 base-level ecclesial communities were just coming into being. Over the past ten years they have multiplied and matured, particularly in some countries, so that now they are one of the causes for joy and hope in the church. They have become centres of evangelization and moving forces for liberation and development. They have been one of the sources for the increase in lay ministers, who are now acting as leaders and organizers of their communities, as catechist, and as missionaries.[29]

Speaking of liberation movements in Latin America in particular, where base ecclesial communities are perhaps most prominent and vigorous, participants in the International Ecumenical Congress on Theology (1980), noted that "a popular, ecclesial stream is emerging that expresses itself in various forms of Christian life and community. This movement takes shape in different types of basic ecclesial communities, where people find a space for resistance, struggle and hope in the face of domination. There the poor celebrate their faith in the liberating Christ and discover the political dimensions of love."[30]

Thus communities of the poor, while not always begun as political movements, do "exercise among the poor a liberating ministry (through consciousness-raising, popular education, the development of ethical and cultural values)".[31] The Congress spoke not only of the transformative power of such ecclesial communities in society at large, but also in the structures of the churches. The blossoming of basic ecclesial communities today illustrates that long-studied pattern of the contribution of the poor to the regeneration and reform of the church, so cogently described decades ago by Troeltsch and H. Richard Niebuhr.[32]

Not confined to third world contexts, the vitality of basic ecclesial communities is manifest in some local congregations in more materially affluent countries – congregations struggling to discover non-consumerist corporate and personal life-styles, congregations witnessing against nuclear energy, communities protesting against escalating militarism, racism, world hunger, transnational corporations. Surveying the church landscape one observes not only hopeless "institutionalitis" and obtuseness, but sprouting signs of hope, commitment and faith. Often these nascent groups take their power and direction from a commitment to justice, a conviction that the gospel presses Christians into the struggle. While that struggle is often frustrating, it is actually a source of renewed strength and commitment. Life, seemingly lost in the struggle, is discovered just there.

This implies that being in solidarity is not a process through which the powerful share their faith and their theology with the poor (though that is not completely absent), but pre-eminently a process through which the poor are able to share their gifts (openness, feeling the powerful presence of the Spirit, unsophisticated theology, social solidarity, ethical commitment) with the materially rich. It is like the black pastor in America who claimed that when he preached in a big integrated congregation he felt drained and tired, but when he preached to his own local congregation in Georgia he may have started tired, but ended exhilarated and refreshed.

Today's emphasis on a church in solidarity with the poor stems not only from *biblical* studies purporting to show that the Old and New Testament were rooted in communities of the oppressed, rather than communities of the *status quo* (Beato, Brueggeman, Gottwald) or *sociological* studies (Troeltsch, H. R. Niebuhr), or *political* studies, which stress a class analysis, and insist on the creative role of the underclass in history. The emphasis on the central re-creative role of the poor is not only a *conceptual* argument, but one sustained and confirmed by recent experience of many different Christian communities, several of whom are actively involved in the ecumenical family.

This learning from communities of the faithful poor could be discovered in the work of several WCC departments and commissions, but the recent CWME conference in Melbourne serves as a striking example of how perceptions of church and mission have been influenced by new experience and new reflection. Matthey, conference secretary, observes that "Melbourne was an ecclesiological conference, recognizing the impossibility of limiting God's reigning activity to the churches' boundaries, [yet affirming] that one must not separate God's Kingdom from the central and specific role and being of the church".[33] Melbourne built upon the Bangkok (1973) assembly, as Potter reminded the group in its opening sessions: "We understand salvation as newness of life – the unfolding of true humanity in the fullness of God. It is salvation of soul and body, of the individual and society, mankind and the groaning creation. Therefore we see the struggles for economic justice, political freedom and cultural renewal as elements in the total liberation of the world through the mission of God."[34]

How was the Melbourne understanding of the church and mission influenced by the experience of churches seeking to be in solidarity with the poor? Six main conclusions emerge. While not totally new, they do appear with new power and importance. The first is a deeper and chastened sense of the churches' own complicity with structures of domination, both in their own lives (such as the oppression of women within the churches, or the churches' class or ethnic biases), and in active or tacit support of oppressive institutions and value systems in society at large. Across the world most churches are perceived, at least by the poor, as part of the establishment, undergirding the *status quo* rather than promoting justice and newness. Churches themselves need to be evangelized.

Though Christians are called to participate actively as responsible citizens in all societies, they should be conscious of "the eschatological dimension of the Kingdom and should reject the temptation to develop an uncritical relationship to the governments of their countries. A church which becomes part of the establishment in a settled society is an anomaly."[35] Throughout the Melbourne section reports there is a clear call to the churches to repent of their past and continuing uncritical collusion with any socio-political system, a persistent warning against uncritical conformity to any society. "If a church or members of a church should choose to use Marxist or any other ideological instruments to analyze the social, economic and political situation in which they find themselves, it will be necessary for them to guard against the risk of being subtly instrumentalized by such ideologies so as not to fall into the same trap as many churches have done in relation to the ideology implied by capitalism."[36] The primary option is for the poor and the oppressed, and not for an ideological position or a political party.

A second emphasis growing out of Melbourne reflections, "solidarity with the poor", as manifest in basic ecclesial communities, is a deepened and sharpened conviction that knowing God is not exclusively, perhaps not primarily, an intellectual or philosophical enterprise. People learn about the nature of the gospel, know God, not theoretically, but by being engaged in what God is doing in the world. This means that the churches can discover what it means to be faithful, and to be the church, only in their own struggles for justice and wholeness. Knowledge and commitment are not abstract; they are discovered in the context of struggle.

Reflecting on the symbolism of the fact that Jesus was crucified "outside of the gates", the conference stressed that his life was a constant movement from the centre to the periphery, from the centres of power towards those on the margins of society. While it is dangerous to read too much into symbols (after all, *all* persons were crucified outside of the walls), Section IV saw "special significance in the role of the poor, the powerless and the oppressed. Might it be they who have the clearest vision, the closest fellowship with the crucified Christ who suffers in them and with them? Might it not be that the poor and powerless have the most significant word for the rich and powerful: that Jesus must be sought on the periphery, and followed outside the city? We see the poor churches of the world as bearers of mission: world mission and evangelism may now be primarily in their hands."[37] The poor already are in mission in trying to change their own situation, the conference argued. While eschewing a traditional charitable and condescending attitude, it is the role of the churches and mission bodies to support what these poor churches and communities have begun already.[38]

A third implication of solidarity is that the central focus which should shape the character and mission of the church is a zealous commitment to the Kingdom. Of course the Kingdom is eschatological, never totally realizable in human history or through human endeavour, but the Kingdom ("that promised new heaven and new earth in which justice abides") is already present as inspiration and challenge.[39] "The church of Jesus Christ is commissioned to disciple the nations, so that others may know that the Kingdom of God has already drawn near and that its signs and first fruits can be seen in the world around them as well as in their own life."[40] No matter how "the poor" may be defined, "this mission is for them". The poor, however defined, are blessed (not a state of being, but a quality of relationship initiated by God) "because of their longing for justice and their hope for liberation. They accept the promise that God has come to their rescue, and so discover in his promise their hopes for liberation and a life of human dignity."[41]

The essential trait of the church was seen, not in its liturgical or credal terms, but in its openness and commitment to the coming Kingdom of God. Consequently the churches' relationship with people of other faiths and ideologies is defined in a more fluid and positive manner than in many traditional discussions. Recognizing the danger of syncretism (a danger which must be risked, it is argued), and recognizing the sometimes ambiguous relationship with other religious communities, the conference found that often people espousing other religious allegiances have perspectives on the struggle for justice, dignity and human rights from which Christians should learn. "Wherever a religion or its revival enhances human dignity, human rights and social justice for all people, and brings liberation and peace for everybody, there God may be seen to be at work."[42] The Kingdom is wider than the church; perhaps God has fresh visions for us through other religions.[43] "His instruments often include the courageous witness of those who do not name his name."[44] But the acid test for all, whether Christians or peoples of other faiths and ideologies, is their commitment to justice, their struggle for human dignity.

Finally, the Melbourne conference pleaded for a fresh and serious ecumenical study of non-violence and power.[45] What is the power relationship of self-emptying in Christ (*kenosis*) and struggles for liberation?

> Jesus Christ rejected coercive power as a way of changing the world. The eye of faith discerns in the cross the embodiment of a God who out-suffers, out-loves and out-lives the worst the powers can do. An altogether new quality of power appeared to be let loose among humankind. The inexorable bondage of cause and effect appeared to be broken. The

principle of self-sacrificing love is thus enthroned at the centre of the reality of the universe.[46]

What does this imply for churches? Should they divest themselves of power, such as the billions of dollars they hold in corporations, financial institutions and property? What might this kenotic theme mean for the hegemony of Western theology, or the theology of the "winners" in history? The section posed these questions and gave its own answer. While recognizing the desperate situation of many oppressed peoples; recognizing that often what is perceived as violence is only counter-violence and self-defence; recognizing that many Christians are pushed to such extremes that they take up violence against oppression; recognizing, finally, the pervasive and escalating nature of violence, the group nevertheless argued that violence is "fact and not fate", and that "the practice of non-violence [is] an inalienable part of Christian obedience".[47] In spite of its own stand, the group recognized that the ecumenical debate on the legitimacy of violence is an unresolved debate.

Thus it will be evident from these two examples, the discussions surrounding the "Just, Participatory and Sustainable Society", and the Melbourne conference "Your Kingdom Come", that the issue of what it means to be in solidarity with the poor has stimulated profound biblical, theological and ecclesiological questions, sometimes reviving old issues in new and fresh ways, sometimes suggesting new aspects of theological reflection. It is not an abstract debate, carried on only in the minds of theologians and ethicists. Rather, it is nurtured in the experiences of individuals and communities of Christians struggling for local and global justice and liberation. That intensified theoretical discussion can catalyze a revitalization of Christian faith, and of Christian community. At the same time it may help to shape, direct and energize struggles for justice at both the local and global levels.

NOTES

1. Arce, *op. cit.*, p. 275.
2. The notions of "justice", "sustainability", and "participation", along with "self-reliance" have had a formative influence on the development thinking of other church groups, such as Church World Service, or the National Council of the Churches of Christ, USA, in its documents "The Nature of Church World Service" (pp. 4–5), and "Areas of Consideration" (pp. 3–5). Differing church groups develop their own content for each of these notions.
3. Central Committee of the World Council of Churches, *Minutes of the Thirty-First Meeting*, Kingston, Jamaica; Geneva, WCC, 1976, pp. 16ff.

4. Konrad Raiser, "Towards a Just, Participatory and Sustainable Society", speech given in Oslo, Norway, October 1980, p. 10.

5. *Ibid.*, p. 10. Not everyone is content to revive the notion of "middle axioms", however. Srisang reported that at the 1981 consultation middle axioms were "buried". Indeed, the consultation report stated that "rather than developing a blueprint for an ideal political order or defining middle axioms for an ecumenical political ethic, the consultation considered witness and solidarity as the areas needing priority attention in the further process". "Report of the WCC Consultation on Ecumenical Political Ethics", Cyprus, 18–25 October 1981, Geneva, WCC, p. 20. To this writer the report seems to set up a dangerous and unnecessary separation between engagement and the formulation of tentative or proximate social goals expressed in middle axioms. While agreeing that much more engagement should receive priority attention at the current juncture, it is also significant to note that action groups, as discussed in chapter 8, are constantly pushed towards formulations of an "ideological" position. Middle axioms, in the writer's view, are still valid, when they are responsive to new and diverse situations and not held dogmatically.

6. *Ibid.*, pp. 18–19.

7. Bucharest Conference, 1974, as quoted in Abrecht (ed.), *Faith, Science, op. cit.*

8. CCPD Final Report, "The Churches and People's Participation", consultation in Geneva, 18–23 January 1982, pp. 1–2.

9. Paton, *op. cit.*, p. 125.

10. Abrecht (ed.), *Faith, Science, op. cit.*, p. 5.

11. John Sewell (ed.), *The United States and World Development: 1977*, New York, Praeger Publishers, 1977, pp. 147ff. (for PQLI discussion). James Grant, *Disparity Reduction Rates in Social Indicators*, Washington, DC, Overseas Development Council, 1978 (for DRR longitudinal change discussion).

12. Abrecht (ed.), *Faith, Science, op. cit.*, pp. 47–49.

13. Cyprus, *op. cit.*, p. 24.

14. *Ibid.*, p. 24.

15. *Ibid.*, p. 28.

16. Reference 15, Chapter 5.

17. For example, in studies of transnational corporations major attention has been paid to the experiences of the poor vis-à-vis TNCs, and their perspectives on what TNCs do to their own lives. See chapter 6, note 31.

18. Report of the first meeting of the JPSS Advisory Committee, meeting in Geneva, 4–14 December 1977, p. 4.

19. Refer to the provocative book by Fred Hirsch, *Social Limits to Growth*, Cambridge, Massachusetts, Harvard University Press, 1976.

20. Report of the JPSS Advisory Committee to the Kingston meeting of the Central Committee, 1979, p. 10.

21. Cyprus, *op. cit.*, p. 9.

22. *Ibid.*, p. 9.

23. Emil Brunner, *Justice and the Social Order*, New York, Harper & Bros, 1945, especially chapter 20.

24. See chapter 1, note 23.

25. Report of the JPSS Advisory Committee to Kingston, p. 7.

26 Cyprus, *op. cit.*, p. 15.

27. *Ibid.*, p. 21.

28 Torres and Eagleson, *op. cit.* (see chapter 1, note 28).

29. Quoted from the Puebla (1978) bishops' message, in Torres and Eagleson, *op. cit.*, p. 7.

30. "Final Document, International Ecumenical Congress of Theology" (20 February to 2 March 1980), in Sao Paulo, Brazil, quoted in Torres and Eagleson, *op. cit.*, p. 234.
31. *Ibid.*, p. 235.
32. Ernst Troeltsch, *The Social Teachings of the Christian Churches*, New York, The Macmillan Company, 1931 (Volumes I and II); H. Richard Niebuhr, *Social Sources of Denominationalism*, New York, H. Holt & Co., 1929.
33. World Council of Churches, World Conference on Mission and Evangelism, Melbourne, 12–25 May 1980, *Your Kingdom Come: Mission Perspectives*, Geneva, WCC, 1980, p. xii.
34. *Ibid.* (as quoted on p. 17, referring to Bangkok Assembly Report), pp. 88–89.
35. *Ibid.*, p. 182.
36. *Ibid.*, p. 183.
37. *Ibid.*, p. 219.
38. *Ibid.*, p. 177.
39. *Ibid.*, p. 172.
40. *Ibid.*, p. 176.
41. *Ibid.*, p. 172.
42. *Ibid.*, p. 187.
43. *Ibid.*, p. 201.
44. *Ibid.*, p. 212.
45. *Ibid.*, p. 213.
46. *Ibid.*, pp. 209–210.
47. *Ibid.*, p. 213.

8: Working alongside the poor

Three illustrations

BUILD: ORGANIZING SLUM-DWELLERS (INDIA)[1]

I belong to a small action group, called Bombay Urban Industrial League for Development (BUILD) and we work among slum-dwellers in the city of Bombay.

The struggles of the three million slum-dwellers, who constitute almost 40 per cent of the population in this city, are related to food, clothing and shelter. In Bombay, particularly, they have to struggle to defend and protect their shacks from the bulldozers and police forces, for from time to time there are attempts to evict them from their place of residence, in the name of city improvement.

The city, which is kept going by the labour of its poorer sections – sweepers, casual and manual labourers, construction workers, etc. – is strangely insensitive to their basic rights. The so-called development efforts have not benefited them, and democracy and political participation are for them empty words. In addition to the obvious economic oppression, they are victims as well of cultural bondage, regional bias and caste prejudices. Thus they are not only unfree; they are also disunited.

Their problem cannot be solved through foreign aid or more economic development projects. Only an ongoing process of education, and organizing them to confront the immediate structures of oppression, thus starting a movement for the creative participation of all in the life and affairs of the country, can help them come into their own.

The method of operation is always dependent on the goals. We started working in the slums of Bombay, through efforts aimed at creating awareness and empowering the unorganized and powerless. We did not see our task as one of propagating any particular ideology. It was only to help people gain confidence, understanding and power to decide for themselves the kind of society they wanted to have.

With this in view, we concentrated on organizing people around immediate and conscious needs. Most of the slums in this city are devoid of the basic amenities of life: water, electricity, sewage, etc. Slums are seen as a nuisance and people living there are treated as second class citizens. The land where slums are situated is owned either by the government or by private individuals. People live under constant threat of eviction sanctioned by law, and with a sense of perpetual insecurity.

We organize people to take direct action against the authorities in order to press their demands. This takes the form of deputations, demonstrations, and similar confrontations with the power structures. The preparation for these consists in study classes, discussion groups, public meetings, audiovisual programmes, and publications. This process of confrontation, we believe, is an integral part of humanization. When for centuries people are made to believe that they are inferior or sub-human, without rights or privileges, they tend to conform to the understanding people have of them. But when they rise up and demand their rights in solidarity, then they enter a process of liberation, and they begin to feel free and human.

In a big city like Bombay, our efforts are rather small and insignificant. But we have begun to see that uprisings need to be multiplied at local levels before one can seriously talk about a national movement for liberation.

NORTH COAST PROJECT (COLOMBIA)[2]

Migration from rural areas to the cities is a phenomenon which exists throughout Latin America, but in the northern region of Colombia it has reached alarming proportions and the slum population is increasing all the time. These are the sectors which suffer the greatest deficit of education, because not even the state schools are within their reach, one of the reasons why they are becoming increasingly impoverished. In addition, the overcrowded conditions of life in the slums, the lack of the most elementary services such as light and water, plus unemployment, have led to a very high mortality rate, especially among children. We need only say that one of the highest infant mortality rates in Latin America, and some of the highest levels of malnutrition, illiteracy, and unemployment are registered in our country. Finally, a view of the Christian faith which is presented through the traditional churches has discouraged many people from working for social change, while alienating others from the church.

A project run by the Colombia North Coast Group aims to begin changing this situation. The project is run collectively, in order to make all decisions democratic and to maintain the ecumenical, political, and social principles which have inspired it. The programme of work has been divided into two parts. The first involves work with the people of the shanty towns, including the opening of a primary school for 180 pupils, a secondary school for 150 pupils, and a medical clinic. The second involves work in the labour sector, primarily organizing an association of the unemployed, the provision of legal and social advisory services, and the establishment of a production cooperative.

The North Coast Project works towards the political and theological enabling of workers and peasants, conscientizing them about their own interests, and contributing to the process of liberation which is neither conceived nor received as a gift, but is the outcome of a struggle with the exploited against the exploiters, by people following the example of Jesus Christ himself. The Project also aims to integrate its group into the basic communities through common action. This will enable them to identify those who might be given political leadership training through the Project's schools, clinics, cooperatives, workshops, and religious congregations. The ultimate goal is to move society in the direction in which we might perceive the breaking in of the kingdom of God.

TEMA INDUSTRIAL MISSION (GHANA)[3]

Soon after Ghana became independent, a new seaport was built fifteen miles east of Accra, the national capital; it was officially opened in 1962. The next task was to create a township to serve the harbour and the industries that would spring up around the port; thus Tema was born. Tema has grown very rapidly, combining port activities with an industrial and commercial network; the population is now well over half a million.

As a new town, Tema had no "citizens". No one regarded Tema as home. It was a place to work for a living, but workers *belonged* to the village; they went there on week-ends. Tema was built by the Tema Development Corporation (TDC) which leased houses to the people as the sole landlord. If rent fell into arrears and the defaulting tenant was evicted, the Corporation would demand the outstanding rent from the new tenant before he could move in. Or, if a tenant defaulted in his rent payment, he might move his family into a single room and then sublet the two remaining rooms to another family in order to pay his rent. To enhance living conditions, so that the people would feel part of Tema, they and the Urban-Industrial missioner formed an umbrella association called Tema Welfare Association (TWA) of twenty-three other organizations, the labour unions and the Tema Council of Churches. TWA identified several areas of concern: high market prices caused by a long series of middlemen; high rents and inflated costs for purchasing a home, and the cost of water. It saw itself as a corporate group for action in situations where services or policies were inequitable to the people of Tema, it also wanted to initiate self-help programmes whenever possible. In all confrontations, dialogue with the authorities would be the first step, but if this failed TWA would employ protest marches and other peaceful demonstrations to arouse public concern.

One issue which the TWA tackled was the water rate. Since 1963, tenants had been paying c1.00 for their water as a part of their rent. In July 1970, however, a Water and Sewerage Corporation took over rate collection directly and increased the rate to c3.00 without notifying the public until February 1971. At that point, the accrued bills were thrust upon the unsuspecting people for payment. The Tema Council of Labour appealed for a return to the c1.00 rate, but the request was ignored. TWA took up the issue and requested a rate reduction, but this also bore no results. Finally, a petition was forwarded to the Corporation's Ministry through Tema's member of parliament.

The people in Tema, mostly factory workers, dockers, and self-employed individuals, have an average income below c40.00 a month. With the high cost of rent and electricity, the increased water rate was more than they could afford. Delinquent water bills piled up in the Corporation's office, and authorities announced a mass disconnection of water lines to the houses where the bills were unpaid. Immediately, plans were made for a protest march to the Water and Sewerage Corporation offices on the day of disconnection.

Circulars and handbills inviting the people to the demonstration were distributed to every inhabitant of Tema. Arrangements were made for television coverage, and TWA members made placards protesting: "Treat Citizens as Humans", "Disconnection Means More Cholera", "Water for Man, Not Man for Water!"

Three days before the disconnection deadline, the national cabinet in Accra voted to reduce the water rate to c1.00 a month. The Water Office was notified and the disconnection was cancelled. The people of Tema gathered for the demonstration and were greeted with the good news of the reduction in the water rate. The people had won a small part of the struggle to make Tema their city.

These three examples illustrate a fifth mode of "being in solidarity with the poor". Perhaps it is the most complex and difficult of all the styles mentioned because it requires a level of engagement, sacrifice, and yielding of leadership to others which does not often characterize the previous four modes of churches' solidarity. George Todd, director of the Urban-Rural Mission Programme of the World Council, insists that real solidarity with the poor requires that churches actively engage in the struggles of the poor at a local level, that authentic solidarity must have a "cruciform" shape – a significant element of self-giving and suffering.

Features of this mode of solidarity

What are the main features of this kind of solidarity? One is an emphasis upon the leadership of the poor themselves. Those who wish to show solidarity must take their cues from that leadership. Leadership cannot be imported. Indeed, it may be more appropriate to talk about "organizers" rather than "leaders", for the main function of leadership in this model of solidarity is to help people express and manifest their own values, commitments and priorities. The function of an organizer is not to import an ideology, a strategy, or even a tactic; an organizer is not a mobilizer of persons to an already predetermined pattern of thinking or acting. An organizer's primary responsibility is to help people articulate and clarify their own thinking and help give coherence to their actions – to help people to sense and express their own power and capacities. Outsiders, such as overseas churches, can express solidarity only to the extent that they are willing to become partners on terms defined by the local community of the poor.

A second feature of this model is that the key issue is what happens to people in the process. External objectives may be achieved (e.g. shorter work days, adequate drinking water, protection of a community from so-called urban renewal). While these objectives are useful in their own right, their chief importance is that they provide a context for a community to gain a greater sense of its identity, its possibilities and its power. Achievement of specific proximate objectives only opens up new issues, and introduces new possibilities. The primary objective is achieved only when formerly powerless people, characterized by a sense of hopelessness and impotence, gain a new sense of their dignity and power, not only as individuals, but as communities. At the same time the attainment of certain measurable achievements for a better life should not be minimized, for often through concerted corporate action to remedy explicit evils, a new sense of personhood and community emerges.

Another feature of this style of solidarity is that it focuses on action groups. Action and engagement are essential to learning identity and community power. The normal way of imagining how social change occurs is reversed. Rather than assuming that changing people's minds and values will lead to changed actions, it is argued that the most significant way to change people's consciousness (their self-perceptions, their goals and values) is through their engagement in social movements to attain specific objectives. Conscientization comes through the struggle for, and exercise of, power; it is a by-product of the struggle. Saul Alinsky argues that often the poor and powerless seem not to have an idea of what they want. This "seeming not to have an idea" grows in part because

> if people feel that they don't have the power to change a bad situation, then they do not think about it. Why start figuring out how you are going to spend a million dollars if you do not have a million dollars? Once people are organized so that they have power to make changes, then, confronted with questions of change, they begin to think and ask questions about how to make the changes.[4]

The first requirement for communication and education is for people to have a reason for knowing. It is the creation of the instrument for the circumstances of power that provides the reason and makes knowledge essential.[5]

Efforts to change things create a new sense of power, a new capacity to take responsibility for shaping society, a new awareness of the relativity and vulnerability of the *status quo* which had seemed immutable, and a keener interest in thinking about what kind of society is desirable and possible. Action to eliminate specific problems emancipates participants to a new self-understanding, and awakens an active hope for a more just and desirable society. Moreover, participation in local political struggle also influences the way people think on a national and international level, too. Action contributes significantly, therefore, to the formation of both new consciousness and new visions of reality; it also generates greater commitment to making that vision a reality.

A fourth ingredient in this model of solidarity is that people's movements are usually tactically oriented, often towards a confrontation with the existing system. This model assumes that society is conflictual, that society is a melange of conflicting power interests (like a swirling field of energy composed of electronic impulses which obtain their energy and vitality from their interaction and conflict). Society is not a "structure of orders", but a " 'sea of influences' or a 'conflict of vitalities' ".[6] Society's task is to keep these vitalities in tolerable limits for cooperation, while not stifling their freedom. If society is a contest for power, with the "haves" tenaciously clinging to their power, the alternatives open to the "have-nots" are either to succumb to the power of the "haves" in docile or sullen fashion or to create their own power base to oppose the "haves". In this struggle the middle class, threatened by the possibility of becoming "have-nots", but also harbouring the hope of joining the "haves", play an ambiguous and usually conservative role. But because the "haves" are unlikely to relinquish their power voluntarily (which often they have rationalized and legitimized with religious arguments), and because the "have-nots" discover their identity and power in the midst of confrontation and struggle, this model generally is conflictual and confrontational – the poor challenging the system.

Naturally it is this confrontational character which makes this model of social change so controversial for those who have come to accept as normal or normative a harmonious and reconciling vision of society, for liberal reformists. It is threatening to those "haves" who want to maintain or expand their privileged position, or who think their power is a right based on hard work, superior intelligence and/or morality, or on superior economic and political systems. Also the conflictual approach is often unpopular even among the poor, since they find it difficult to break their age-old patterns (social, intellectual and psychological) of dependency and apathy.

> The first step in community organization is community disorganization. The disruption of the present organization is the first step toward community organization. Present arrangements must be disorganized if they are to be displaced by new patterns that provide the opportunities and means for citizen participation. All change means disorganization of the old and organization of the new. That is why the organizer is immediately confronted with conflict. The organizer dedicated to changing the life of a particular community must first rub raw the resentments of the people of the community; fan the latent hostilities of many of the people to the point of overt expression. He must search out controversy and issues. An organizer must stir up dissatisfaction and discontent. When those prominent in the *status quo* turn and label you an "agitator" they are completely correct, for that is, in one word, your function – to agitate to the point of conflict.[7]

We do not want to give the impression of undue reliance on Alinsky, since many groups, especially in Asia, have pushed their own thinking beyond his. Not all people's movements supported by the World Council of Churches (Urban Rural Mission alone relates to a network of over 500) would endorse an explicit and provocative view of the necessity for conflict. Many, however, are strongly convinced that power is the name of the game. Many believe that countervailing power exercised by the poor against the powerful is the only way to raise people to new consciousness, and the only tactic likely to change the existing order. For many Christians working within the context of the Council, this is a legitimate and compelling way to view social realities. For many, joining poor people in their struggle for countervailing power appears to be the only convincing and effective way for churches to exercise solidarity with the poor.

Another aspect of this model of solidarity is that such groups of the poor usually focus on issues in the local community. Believing that consciousness-raising has to be done through tangible actions, their emphasis is on micro- rather than macro-level changes. Why? Because local level issues capture people's attention, and that's where people are willing to adopt a cause. Clearly, there is risk that preoccupation with local issues will heighten a sense of frustration and alienation, when it is discovered that the solution of one issue always opens up new problems and expands one's expectations. There is also a danger that focusing on local issues will obscure the interconnectedness of issues. Piecemeal reforms often are made without significantly altering the basic pattern of unjust and oppressive relationships. But the greater danger is that the poor, convinced of their own impotence and of the invulnerability of the existing system, will think it useless to try to change anything, or will rely on an ideological elite for their ideas.

Ideology and organization form

Indeed, a crucial question being explored among many local people's movements today is whether they should encourage specific ideological analyses. There is a certain uneasiness, among some people like Todd, that people's movements will become dominated by externally defined ideological perspectives, and ultimately victimized by them; that the voice of the people, rooted in their own concrete experience, will be drowned out by ideologues who import an analysis into a local situation that does not do justice to that particular environment, or grow in the soil of the people's experiences. While uneasy about what he perceives as danger that people's movements will be coopted by externally formulated ideologies, Todd is so wholeheartedly committed to listening to the experience of the people that he accepts as natural, perhaps inevitable, that people's movements need a clearer ideological analysis and stance.[8]

Notwithstanding the dangers of an imposed or pre-packaged ideological stance, it is evident that ideologies are operative, even dominant, in all societies. If ideology is as a way of perceiving reality in a holistic way, of believing that certain factors are key to the way a particular society operates, of affirming certain goals or visions, then all coherent societies have an ideological base. In common parlance those positions with which we agree are not ideologies, but a worldview; while those positions we find unacceptable are labelled ideologies. Ideologies help to shape, and are shaped by, every society. Normally the ideologies of the ruling class are so assiduously cultivated and so tacitly accepted that they require little interpretation or reinforcement. On the other hand, ideologies of the have-nots have to fight for recognition.

A recent discussion under the auspices of the Christian Conference of Asia clearly raises some of these points. The discussion endorsed a truly prophetic vision of society, and explicitly rejected "a course of seeming to provide mere palliatives and social tranquillizers to ease the burdens of the masses and thereby to prop up a diseased social order weighing upon the people".[9] Referring to the danger of "patchwork solutions" (as might be implied in fragmented attacks upon specific social ills, without an overall strategic direction, a rudder), they opined that such piecemeal efforts might "distort or delay the genuine struggle of the people for their own emancipation".[10]

In a society divided into haves and have-nots, it is inevitable that the thinking of the people should be broadly influenced or coloured by ideologies which reflect such [class] interests. The dominant ideology would then be that of the haves, which would reflect the value of the existing social and economic structures and generally be the instrument of the ruling political establishment. A counter to this prevailing ideology would be an ideology reflecting the aspirations of the have-nots. But ideology need not be openly expressed or professed by any group in society. It could be implicit in their very existence. In such a situation, URM groups must learn to rigorously evaluate their own ideological positions as well as to test the ideological position of other groups engaged in social work so as to be able to recognize their allies more easily. In this situation, a critique of the dominant ideology becomes useful. For URM groups have a positive role to play in the cultural and religious spheres too as catalysts vis-à-vis the dominant myths and values of society. A structural analysis of society and an understanding of social classes and the role they play will be of vital importance in our strategy.[11]

The same group argued that URM does not act out of a given theology or ideology, but out of a "commitment to working with the poor and being involved in their struggles".[12] They concluded that, given the pressures against the people and people's movements, "a lot more ideology is required, not only to encourage, [but] also to discipline. Not only to defend rights, [but] also to make new ones. Not only to put together protest movements, [but] also to help build powerful people's institutions. URM has no choice but to seek to build more comprehensive systems of theological and ideological understanding."[13] A predominant concern is that these comprehensive systems should be built from the experiences of the poor rather than reflect the preconceived notions of the "organizers" and the churches attempting to be in solidarity.

Thus, the question of how fully people's movements should be informed by an ideology, and what that ideology should entail, becomes increasingly important. It is clear, however, that any discussion of the role of ideology in social movements and social change needs to take into account the differing understandings, conscious and implicit, of what ideology means. Aside from the importance of such ideological formulations for people's movements themselves, a whole range of questions pertain to what it means for partners who wish to be in solidarity. For example, to what extent

are partners obliged to accept and endorse the ideological interpretations of reality of a people's movement as a precondition for partnership? To what extent are experiences of people's movements in
one environment instructive for similar movements in another? Is
a homogeneous ideological stance a desirable goal?

Related to the question of ideology is the issue of organizational
form for people's movements. What will hold the people together
in the face of continuing hardship, partial success, or outright confrontation by the dominant society? If the horizon is ever-receding
and new challenges to justice are encountered and perceived, what
will sustain a common effort? What is the difference between a
church movement and a political movement, an ecclesial community
and a people's movement rooted in social issues or a political orientation? Some organization is required. But which? Can it be predominantly horizontally organized? Will it be based on an
ideological stance? On a prolonged series of encounters with the
system at hurting points? On leadership which itself tends to become
power-hungry? Will it be centred in a political organization or a
party? These are particularly vexing problems for people's movements predicated on constant openness to pressures from "below".

One of the greatest difficulties for a people's movement is to
maintain a sense of cohesion and direction in the midst of a plurality
of perspectives and goals among the people themselves. It is dangerous to assume a homogeneous entity called "the people" or "the
poor".[14] This danger is compounded by a commitment to keeping
the movement a genuine expression of the perspectives, priorities
and commitments of the people, rather than of a leadership which
is tempted to speak for the people. For constant tension exists
between leadership "from above" and impulses and directions "from
among the people". That is why the distinction between "leader"
and "organizer", referred to above, though seemingly trivial at first,
is nevertheless meaningful.

There is also a constant tension between a commitment to working to overcome particular "problems" which a pluralistic community identifies and agrees should be overcome, and the larger
systemic questions of which these "problems" are merely symptoms. There is a built-in tension between the piecemeal and more
comprehensive approaches, and between the short-term and longer
term approaches. Important as it is, for tactical reasons, to focus on
tangible problem solving, it is crucial to assure that attacks on
"problems" be treated as a first stage towards addressing the most
systemic aspects of economic and political injustice.

What kind of an organization can resist atrophy, or fragmentation, or sustain a diverse group of people in a common venture which invites hostility and suffering? Many people's movements can be mobilized for a specific cause, but then disappear; people's groups often proliferate but endure only briefly; they tend to become an extension of the personality of their organizer or leader; they constantly struggle with the question of a cohering "ideology" or stance; often they are bedevilled with questions of organizational style and frequently reach out for coalitions with similar groups. Why? Probably because they temporarily paper over inherent tensions which cannot be resolved, and perhaps should not be.[15]

These perhaps irreconcilable tensions are a significant, though not exclusive, reason for recent emphasis on the need to build networks of people's groups. These networks are increasingly prominent in the work of the entire Council, though they have been significant aspects of CCPD, URM, and PCR for some time. Such networks of kindred groups (e.g. groups working on transnational corporation issues, questions of the control of communications by a few centres of power, issues of nuclear energy development, development education questions – to cite examples more prominent in the "first world") spring up to provide mutual reinforcement, sharing of experiences, testing of ideas. For example, in India M. J. Joseph has been supported by the Commission on the Churches' Participation in Development to act as liaison among approximately 75 existing people's efforts towards social justice. He does not create such movements or groups; they have come into existence spontaneously. His task is to strengthen their witness by recognizing common bonds and mutual commitments.

This "network approach" has become a major feature of World Council of Churches efforts at solidarity for justice.[16] Struggling people's groups need the support and stimulation of similar communities in other environments. They also need one another for moral and spiritual energy. Strategically speaking, the proliferation of small-scale people's groups and movements, which sense their connectedness and enhanced power through association with one another, significantly broadens the base and potential impact of such groups, and defuses the widespread argument that local groups, stressing only the solving of local problems, are merely palliative. Major attention is now being given to ways in which the network approach can be developed on national, regional and perhaps global bases, although it seems prudent at the present juncture to emphasize national and regional groupings only.

One of the most interesting discussions about networks pertains to whether the current project system can be focused more on regional discussion and decision-making, making greater use of people's movements and groups in the decision-making and in operational phases of the project system. At present it is impossible to know how far this network approach can and should proceed, but the poignant words of a successful and committed community organizer from Bombay highlights the importance of such networks.

> All of us believe that unless we are able to contribute towards the emergence of a national movement of the oppressed, our efforts on the local scene will not mean much. We cannot hope to build a beautiful island in Bombay when the rest of society is submerged under a system of exploitation and oppression. The eighteen months of the Emergency Rule brought about a new desire among the action groups to come together and express their solidarity with one another. I had to travel more within India, and occasionally outside, in the interest of national and international solidarity.[17]

Tasks of the churches in this mode

What, then, is the role of churches in solidarity with people's movements? What are the limits of solidarity? What are the hindrances? These thorny issues need much more serious attention, to avoid romanticism. Of the many things which might be said, three are of greatest importance. The first is that the churches should perceive their task as generating power, but not their own power or status. Their task is to foster the power of the people, to strengthen the people's capacity for creating their own future, to take their directions from the way the people are struggling to overcome injustices and oppression. The churches are not to build up power vis-à-vis other social groups, in order to contend, even in the name of justice, against the principalities and powers. The churches are not to be leaders of mass movements, but a leaven in the lump, catalysts for helping the inherent strength of the people to become conscious and manifest. As Fr Edicio de la Torre said after his release from a Philippine prison: "When I say that Christians will always be a minority, I mean that, regardless of numbers, our position is not based on power, but on truth."[18] "One could say, 'the power of truth as expressed in the people's struggle'. In prison I often thought what would I shout if I were going to be shot. Long live the people? The movement? Church? Christ? I thought and thought, and decided it would be 'long live the struggle' for that includes everything."[19] From this view of social change, the people's struggle is the source of power and change, and the churches' task is to join that struggle rather than try to direct it along predetermined paths.

The second task of the churches is to incarnate in their own life their theological affirmation of the central role of the poor in history – God's special "option for the poor", as the Medellin conference of 1968 so eloquently claimed. "The strength of the people themselves is transformed as that struggle [the victory of the justice of God over evil in history] is revealed to be the dynamic of the messianic Kingdom. People discover themselves as the subject of the Kingdom, moving through their actions towards justice, *koinonia* and *shalom* for all humanity."[20]

To relate to people's movements, churches themselves need not only self-criticism, but also conversion. "We should understand the need to evangelize the churches. The church calls on others to repent, but the church itself needs to see the error of its ways and to repent, to be liberated from the shackles of the past."[21] That repentance can come only through incarnational involvement in the life of the people, by being in solidarity with their struggles for justice. "The expression that the gospel seeks is an 'incarnation' – a self-emptying act, an abdication of an exalted status and awesome might to assume the lot of the most forsaken condition of mankind."[22] "As Christ's body was broken on the cross for mankind, so our bodies must be broken and our lives shared in the common struggle for liberation against the demonic forces of the old order."[23] Or again: "The church's very reason for being – indeed the very nature of the church – demands a flesh and blood involvement in the struggle of the oppressed, the wretched of the earth."[24] Thus "we plead with the church to give in to the promptings of her heart, and not allow herself to be inhibited by concerns of security, safety and mere maintenance of church structures, or be compromised, intimidated or subtly pressured by big business. *Be the church!*"[25]

A third task of the churches deriving from this model of social transformation is that the normal way of looking at the churches' role vis-à-vis the poor should be reversed. The role of the churches is to interpret the "reality of the gospel through the experiences of the poor in their struggle for justice and wholeness, and to amplify those experiences so that others can hear". As Prof. Arce argues above, it is not the churches' task to initiate or direct the people's struggles, but to join them and interpret them to others. This is a far less pretentious task than the churches usually perceive for themselves. Most frequently the churches think of themselves as pioneers of justice, but those in many people's movements, on the periphery of society, have a different perception. They experience the churches as often on the side of the Establishment.

The churches are hardly the sole instruments of God's renewing and transforming power. There are many, especially among the poor, who also are agents even when they reject, or are indifferent to, the churches; even when they act for justice without explicit religious convictions.

The strengths of this mode of solidarity are self-evident: the psychological emancipation of communities of people; concentration on specific actions in explicit local environments; avoidance of abstract ideology; emphasis on actions instead of slogans and platforms; direct concern for the socially and economically marginated sectors of the population that are most victimized; dynamic and realistic views of social reality and the role of power in social change – an emphasis on the exercise of power which, ironically, may prevent the necessity for cataclysmic power and destruction at a later state.

What might be some major liabilities? One is the danger that emphasis on local actions might frustrate the possibility of widespread structural changes, i.e. small reforms rather than radical changes. In other words, will emphasis on achievable objectives become palliative? In stressing local issues or problems, will we lose a vision of the more global situation and its connectedness? Does a problem-solving approach undermine efforts to achieve more profound change? Will efforts for change be so unconnected that those holding power now will be able to retain it, and even increase their oppression, by manipulating people with small concessions (like small increases in workers' wages in transnational corporations)? Will those in power be able to "divide and conquer" when there is insufficient attention to macro-level issues, or will some people be "bought" by the system to curb dissent? Some advocates of macro-level solidarity feel these questions keenly, and are unwilling to invest their energies in micro-level problem-solving, even while recognizing that such micro-level efforts might be part of a larger and more comprehensive strategy for change.

Another question often raised is whether there is not a danger of romanticizing "the people", or assuming that the people are united in their commitment to justice, or believing that people's movements dedicated to confrontation can escape building their own, eventually oppressive, power base. Clearly far more attention needs to be paid to the meaning of "the people", and to the question of the role that people's movements are able to play in history. What has been their historic role, and that of leaders arising from the middle, sometimes upper, classes? Is there danger of being too romantic, or too naive, about the aspirations of "the people", and their ability to become long-term agents of social justice? In many

World Council documents there is healthy scepticism about making too many assumptions about the creative, catalytic role of "the people", but also enough uncritical remarks to make it important to keep the issue alive.

Another persistent question is whether what seems to amount to an exclusive emphasis on "the people" is consistent with the biblical narrative. Granted that the role of the poor is highlighted far more than much of historical theology and many biblical studies acknowledge, is the recent emphasis on the dominant role of the poor justified? Is the corrective an over-correction? Despite a rich recent literature demonstrating the central role of the poor in biblical testimonies, the haunting question remains whether, as with all newly recovered hermeneutical keys, the case is not made so vigorously that it distorts the gospel. I am aware of the danger of raising this even as a question, in view of the churches' long tradition and practice which have obscured the role of the poor, but the question must be kept before us in order to avoid a new truncated gospel, as seen through the lens of class or provincial cultural perspectives.

Finally, questions are raised about the strategy of confrontation which are central to the philosophy of many people's movements. Is a confrontational style consistent with the gospel, even when it is recognized that confrontation often results from the struggle for justice? Is there not a difference between aiming at confrontation, seeking it, encouraging it, and accepting confrontation as a normal by-product or consequence of struggling for justice?

But the question arises not only in the abstract. At the tactical level, too, the question is whether confrontation is preferable to less overtly conflictual efforts. Does a confrontational or conflictual style simply reinforce the powers maintaining the *status quo*, giving them an excuse to escalate violence? Who will be most adversely affected when violence erupts? Will it not be the poor and most vulnerable? Will the identity of a community built upon power, the capacity to command a response, to intimidate, be a sustainable and cohering community? Or will not the character of power and confrontation be constantly injected into that group, threatening to fracture and disintegrate it? Can a community based upon self-interest be transmuted into a longer-term community committed to the "common weal", even if that common weal entails relinquishment of some self-interest? Would a confrontational approach lead to a realistic view of a political order based on institutions and law as well as protest against them; to just structures instead of anarchy?

These are some of the basic questions being asked of a model of social change predicated on people's movements using confrontation and challenge as their basic strategy. Those who would be in solidarity with the poor through such people's movements continue to struggle with the implications of such questions for the way churches and Christians should express their solidarity for justice.

NOTES

1. George Ninan, "Organizing Slum-Dwellers", in D. Preman Niles and T. K. Thomas (eds), *Witnessing to the Kingdom*, Singapore, Christian Conference of Asia, 1979, pp. 58–9.
2. *Urban Rural Mission Askings List 1981*, Geneva, CWME/WCC, 1981, p. 85.
3. Joe Bannerman, "The Struggle for Justice in Tema, Ghana", in *Mission and Justice*, Geneva, CWME/UIM/WCC, 1977, pp. 38–41; and Bobbi W. Hargleroad (ed.), *Struggle to be Human: Stories of Urban-Industrial Mission*, Geneva, WCC, 1977, pp. 12–16.
4. *Rules for Radicals*, New York, Vintage Books, 1971, p. 105.
5. *Ibid.*, p. 106.
6. Edward Long, *A Survey of Christian Ethics*, New York, Oxford University Press, 1967, p. 216.
7. Alinsky, *op. cit.*, pp. 115–117.
8. In personal conversation with Todd, summer 1981.
9. Christian Conference of Asia, *Theology and Ideology* (a URM discussion), New Delhi, Kalpana Printing House, 1980, p. 29.
10. *Ibid.*, p. 29.
11. *Ibid.*, p. 31.
12. *Ibid.*, p. 2.
13. *Ibid.*, p. 3.
14. The Cyprus, 1981, consultation on political ethics recognized two meanings of the term "the people". One was geographically defined and the other defined by their marginated status in society; the consultation chose to focus its discussion on the latter. Here we refer to tensions not between these two understandings of "the people", but between different groups of "the people" within the latter definition. "Report of the WCC Consultation on Ecumenical Political Ethics", *op. cit.*, p. 8.
15. Acknowledging its indebtedness in Alinsky, the UIRM in Asia contends that power expressed through an organization formed initially on self-interest is the only reliable way to achieve social transformation. It must be expected that people, originally acting almost exclusively out of self-interest, "will grow towards a greater consciousness and responsibility towards the needs of the total community". They endorse the view that leadership in the organization is safer, more responsive, if it originates from among the masses rather than from the middle class. *Theology and Ideology*, *op. cit.*, p. 63.
16. "We have come to the conviction that local action groups at the grassroots level are the primary place of our work. But in order to counter the forces of inhumanity and injustice, our efforts go into establishing networks not only at local levels, but also at national and international levels." Christian Conference of Asia, *Struggling with People is Living in Christ*, New Delhi, Kalpana Printing House, 1981, pp. 121–122.
17. Leon Howell, *People are the Subject*, Geneva, WCC, 1980, p. 12.
18. Christian Conference of Asia, *Theology and Ideology*, *op. cit.*, p. 65.

19. *Ibid.*, p. 66.
20. Howell, *op. cit.*, p. vii.
21. *Ibid.*, p. 78.
22. Christian Conference of Asia, *Theology and Ideology*, *op. cit.*, p. 18.
23. *Ibid.*, p. 25.
24. Christian Conference of Asia, *Struggling with People*, *op. cit.*, p. 115.
25. *Ibid.*, p. 118.

Part Three:
Some personal reflections
on past experience
and future prospects

9: Some personal reflections

This brief reflective survey suggests the rich and varied efforts of churches working, through the ecumenical nexus, to express their commitment to act in solidarity with the poor and to promote global justice. What strikes this writer is the energy of the effort, together with the flashes of insight and the struggling creativity. It is also striking, but not surprising, that, owing to the exploratory and experimental nature of the struggle, there is a visible and sometimes debilitating diffusion of effort, and also an apparent duplication, if not contradiction, in it. A clear focus, both conceptually and institutionally, has not yet emerged. Indeed, one senses that to insist upon too much convergence and consensus would forfeit, at this stage, important insights and experimentation. A parallel concern which has evolved as we have studied the material is a great danger of abstract sloganeering, without sufficient attention to the content of certain key concepts. Some degree of abstraction and obtuseness is essential to keep open the search for new paradigms, but there is also a danger that vague and poorly defined terms will stifle rather than enrich the conversations, and lead to vapid ideologizing rather than intellectual and spiritual wrestling.

We would like to lift up six areas which seem to be particularly important for the Council's ongoing work in liberation-development, and global justice and human wholeness. These seem especially important in the life of the Council in view of the work of the past several years reviewed in this study.

More conceptual clarity

Thus we contend that one main task ahead is for the total ecumenical family to insist on more precision and clarity in key concepts. One such concept is "solidarity" itself. Because it has different connotations in the Anglo-Saxon and Continental worlds, and probably in the third world too, it is a particularly volatile word. Is anyone who cares vaguely about the poor really in solidarity with

them? Is a theology professor writing about biblical notions of
poverty really in solidarity with the poor? Is a church bureaucrat or
church pastor, by virtue of a general commitment to justice and
wholeness, on the side of the poor? Is a person who makes conscious
life-style changes in order to take less toll on the environment in
solidarity with the poor? Must a person live in a *favela*, or work
alongside the poor as a landless labourer or dump-picker, or take
up the arms of revolutionary struggle, to be in authentic solidarity
with the poor?

There is a double-edged danger that the notion of "solidarity"
will be coopted and cheapened by those who, in order to justify
their own action or inaction, use it to cover any and every kind of
action which vaguely "assists" the poor – comparable to the erosion
of the notion of "development" by all who argued that, after all,
they had been promoting development all along, and thus persisted
in practices which prevented genuine development from happening.
The opposite danger, equally fateful, is that solidarity with the poor
will be defined so narrowly that it excludes many from identifying
with or participating in the struggle for justice if they cannot become
involved in the precise manner advocated. At the least, the notion
of solidarity must include a genuine and "sacrificial" commitment
to justice; a practical and living contact with poor and oppressed
groups at some local level; a commitment to letting the voices and
experiences of the poor become a judgment on, and enrichment of,
one's own understanding of reality, and of the gospel; and a personal
and communal life-style consciously impacted by a commitment to
global justice.

To us, these are a few of the core notions of the meaning of being
in solidarity with the poor. However, much more definitive, corporate work needs to be done in the context of the WCC experience,
with care to avoid a premature narrowing of the concept, or a
careless expansion of it to include all things to all people. On the
practical and institutional levels the WCC needs to explore, in the
years just ahead, not only what it means more precisely to be in
solidarity with the poor, but also which tactics of solidarity are most
genuine, most effective, and most congruent with the gospel, and
with the churches' potentialities. This study has argued that there
are many ways of being in solidarity, at least as presently understood. But the churches need to assess which efforts are most urgent,
most useful and most congruent with the nature of the church and
the character of the gospel. Such an assessment may lead to a more
concerted, more focused expenditure of limited resources and energies. That, in itself, might constitute a significant contribution not

only to the struggle of the poor, but to the vitality of the WCC and of member churches.

Another term needing amplification and clarification is "participation", a concept clearly endorsed at the Nairobi Assembly, central to a full understanding of justice, and fraught with explosive implications for every existing political system.[1] A recent UNRISD publication indicates the same definitional problem in UN circles on the idea of "participation".

> "Popular participation" has for a long time been, and still is, one of the favourite catch words of the UN, as well as in national governments and in technical cooperative agencies. While we were astonished by the number of programmes and activities labelled under this title, we searched in vain for a clear definition of the concept and its implications. Where it had been spelled out more precisely it had been easily and eagerly coopted. There appeared to be a basic inability or unwillingness to discuss participation in decision-making processes, to discuss it in terms of the sharing of control by different social group.[2]

Indeed, it is increasingly apparent that every existing development paradigm has fallen short on this norm.

Participation implies that everyone will share more or less equally in the goods produced by society; that all persons will have their basic needs met; that persons as individuals and as communities (including religious communities) have a right to gather in associations not strictly controlled by the state; that persons have a right to the kind and level of information which will enable them to make informed and responsible decisions about their personal and corporate lives; that persons have a right to determine their own political leadership both in its overall shape and its particular political actors; that persons have a right to criticize or call political, economic and social structures into account. If the notion of participation means at least these, or comparable, conditions, then a participatory society is hard to find anywhere – and almost as difficult to envisage, if one takes seriously the potentially disruptive, contradictory and paralyzing possibilities of deep-penetrating participation.

Yet the larger, more complex, technologized and centralized societies become, the more urgent becomes the need for practical articulation and realization of the concept of participation. The more there is temptation to "escape from freedom", the more urgent is the need to restore or give birth to the conviction that significant levels of participation are both essential and possible, congruent with and mandated in a Christian view of reality. Insistence on self-reliant development, horizontal interdependencies, and appropriate technology are tentative beginnings for putting flesh on the notion of participation. Reflection on the non-participatory nature of the traditional churches (limiting the role of women, youth, lay persons, labourers and lower class persons) will continue to be one essential ingredient in that reflection and experimentation, as will a parallel reflection and experimentation within church agencies like the World Council of Churches. Such efforts at internal reform are essential not only for the credibility of the churches when they espouse participation, but also to provide a laboratory in which the actual meaning and limitations of the concept can become clearer.

It is very important that ecumenical discussions move as concretely as possible beyond the diffuse, though important, assertions that "people must be treated as subjects of history rather than as objects of other people's history", or that "people have a right to participate in all those decisions which shape their own future". Should all people be involved in all decisions? In everything that shapes their future? Should all share and shape at an equal level? In general policy matters, or also at specific implementation levels? Who will resolve inevitable conflicts? For "the people" is not a homogeneous group with the same commitments, the same convictions, the same "wisdom", the same aspirations. Ecumenical discussion, based upon experiences and perspectives shaped in a wide variety of cultural environments could pioneer a way through the brambles by forging a common understanding of the essential elements in "participation". This is not an appeal for an abstract theoretical definition, but for one shaped in dialectical relationship to living experience.

The participation theme, though prominent among the churches at least since the Nairobi Assembly, grows out of an experience of estrangement and powerlessness. It is keenly felt in both highly industrialized countries and in less materially developed nations. It is manifest in many ways: anti-nuclear energy demonstrations; major shifts towards political decentralization as shown by recent public policy in France, and by state's rights and local right's pressures in the USA; assertions of regional distinctiveness and independence in pluralistic third world countries; emphasis on the local church and local ecumenism within the churches. Thus, as the Council and member churches pursue further clarification of the idea of participation, their concepts will be sharpened by reality, and by the growing experience and concerns of theoreticians and practitioners from outside the churches as well as from within.

There are other concepts needing clarification as well. We too often speak as if "the people", or "the poor", or "the oppressed" were self-evident categories; obviously they are not. Without enumerating a long list of such ambiguous terms, suffice it to say that within the movement we are all prone to use concepts too vaguely, this writer among those too easily carried away!

Furthering the JPSS vision

A second theme on the WCC agenda which seems of crucial importance (in addition to clarification of key concepts like solidarity and participation) is to pursue the JPSS discussion in four major areas. Preston argues that "justice" includes "participation", so that it is necessary to refer only to justice and sustainability.[3] Yet we argue that since "justice" in the popular mind is primarily distributive, rather than distributive and participatory, it is important to highlight the importance of the principle of participation. One task is to explore more deeply the relationship between these three elements of the current JPSS formulation. It has been too simplistically assumed that there is harmony between these objectives, yet that complementarity and harmony are not always visible upon closer inspection. For example, participation and sustainability may be incompatible when people decide that in their own interests they will ignore ecological limits and the consequences of their own consumption for future generations. Or the demands for justice (full employment) within one nation may militate against sustainability or participation in another. Or the demand for justice at the distributional level may militate against the demand for justice at the participatory level within the same society (as when it is necessary to centralize decision-making for efficiency in production).

Related to this question of whether justice, participation and sustainability are harmoniously related is the issue of the overall adequacy of the JPSS concept. Should it be enlarged to include additional components? Four possible shortcomings of the current JPSS discussion may be suggested as examples. Is the notion too "horizontal", without sufficient attention to the relationship of human society to divine power and presence, to divine initiative, to accountability to God, to the integral but ambiguous relationship of the JPSS to the always-present but never fulfilled Kingdom? Does the JPSS stress contract more than covenant, law more than gospel, "Gesellschaft" more than "Gemeinschaft" – and is the dynamic relationship between love and justice sufficiently addressed and reflected? Is there sufficient attention to human wholeness, and its relationship to justice? Finally, does the JPSS give sufficient attention to "responsibility" and cost, or is there so much emphasis on freedom and participation that the element of responsibility is underplayed? Connected with this question is the possibility that the JPSS

discussion has not adequately reflected on the significance of redemptive and vicarious suffering as a distinctively Christian element
in a vision of the society to which Christians should aspire.

A third area of questions in the JPSS discussion pertains to political
ethics, including the need for a revival, in today's new context, of
the long-standing Oxford conference debate on the nature and functions of the state. Some exploratory initiatives have been taken, yet
the discussion is still at its beginning stages.[4] Major developments
have intensified the need for renewed political-ethical reflection: e.g.
growing power of the centre and increased dependency of periphery
nations on the centre (a paradox of heightened nationalism just when
nation states are becoming less sovereign in fact); internal frictions
and fissures; concentration of power through informational and
economic factors on the international scene which abridge the freedoms of *all* nations; the emergence of the "national security state";
erosion of the cultural assumptions which undergirded the evolution
of the modern nation-state; institutional forces which seem to operate by a faceless, nameless inner logic and are not manageable even
by those persons usually considered to be powerful decision-makers.

These are but some examples of major new world realities which
make the question of political ethics, along with the recent concentration on economic ethics, especially significant today. Not least
important in the discussion of political ethics are perceptions of
church-state relationships. Many new facets of that relationship require reflection, going beyond the juridical and formalistic discussions of church-state relationships of the past (important as these
were and are). Some of these are the following:

1. There is a greater awareness of the need to contextualize the
relationship: e.g. where the church and Christian community is a
small or even tiny minority (Thailand); where official government
ideology and policy are critical of the institutional church, yet pursue
aspects of justice congruent with the churches' mission (Cuba);
where the government officially endorses and actually pursues an
aggressive non-Christian (even anti-Christian) religious perspective
(some Islamic states); where the churches have become so aligned
politically and/or culturally with existing government that they exert little prophetic witness.

2. There is also a greater understanding of the overt and subtle
ways in which, historically and currently, government and church
often reinforce each other, thus repressing movements for change
and transformation. This mutual support is not only, or even primarily, at the institutional level, but also at the level of general
cultural assumptions and values.

3. There is deepening appreciation of the links between religious freedom and broader human rights, between freedom for Christians and for persons of every religious persuasion, and between rights of religious bodies or institutions and those of individuals.

4. There is increasing pressure to discover and spell out in clearer fashion the relation between the right to meet for narrowly defined liturgical and spiritual expressions, and the right (less frequently acknowledged) for Christians and churches to engage in broader aspects of their corporate religiosity, as, for example, in suggesting the public policy implications of faith, and in lobbying for specific political policies. Although there has been a rich and continuous reflection on church-state relationships during the whole history of the modern ecumenical movement, today's convergence of several pressure points makes deeper exploration, in the context of political ethics, a necessity.

A fourth aspect of the JPSS discussion, and one which warrants highlighting as a separate enterprise, is a new critical socio-ethical-theological reflection on a Christian understanding of power. The 1979 Central Committee called for such a debate, and its importance is affirmed constantly in documents emanating from different Council programmes and departments over the past several years. Despite the enormously rich and diverse discussion of power through recent decades, the *scale* of power in modern society has become so massive, so encompassing and pervasive, so subtle and yet overt, so fraught with positive possibilities and dire dangers, that a new reflection by the churches, based upon experiences in various cultural settings, is essential. This urgency is intensified by the widespread confusion that exists among Christians on the nature of power, and the ways in which Christians may use power for the transformation of society.

What are the different kinds of power? Do we need a new and more adequate phenomenology of power? Are Christians and churches called to be powerless? Does church power differ from the kind of power emanating from the state? Can power be neutral, and should it be? What is the relation between positive power required for social cohesion, and for life itself, and demonic power, which destroys vision and even life itself? Are these simply two different quantitative levels or ranges of power, or are they ambivalently present in every human relationship? What is the significance of the power of the Holy Spirit in the "divinization" of continuing creation? Are there unresolvable paradoxes in power, whereby competitive power bearing good for one group of people may, perhaps as a by-product, bring evil to another? Is competitive power, as well as cooperative power, advantageous for society as a whole? What is the relationship between suffering servant power – the power of the cross – and overt physical, or intellectual, or moral power to overcome, if not to convert? What is the legitimacy and efficacy of non-violent and of violent power? What is the proper relationship between the power of moral suasion and the power of confrontation? What is the relationship between the exercise of power (*taking* freedom), and the discovery or forging of one's identity, in a psychological sense, for an individual or for a community?

There are not simply theological and ethical conundrums, despite their pestering presence with the churches for centuries. They are made acute again and in a special way today, as they were in the midst of worldwide depression and Nazi Socialism in the 1930s. Pressures today are manifest on an ever larger and more threatening scale. Today these pressures exist in a context of a diverse and pluralistic cultural consciousness where the value assumptions of the West are being challenged by other cultures and are no longer even as acceptable in the West itself. Today the churches themselves assume a much greater moral and theological responsibility for social transformation. At the same time, both church and society have tended towards an ambivalent view of power – sometimes romantic about it, at other times able to see only its demonic aspects. There is too little sense of power's inherently ambiguous character, as it is always by human beings who have specific values, motivations and knowledge.

Programmatic consequences will result from this reflection on the nature of power. How should churches organize themselves and their work? How should ecumenical councils function? How should strategies of solidarity (confrontation, moral suasion, reformism, capillary change from below, networks of people's movements, etc.) be informed by the understanding of the nature, limitations and value of power in achieving global justice? In the entire reflective process, however, the concrete historical experience of people struggling for justice in the midst of power, especially those struggling in the context of Christian commitment, must play a decisive role.

New initiatives on militarism and peace

It has been difficult for us to avoid the conclusion that, perhaps more urgent than any other issue for the churches in their struggle for global justice is their fight against militarism. Why? Several reasons compel us to this conclusion. The world seems to be plunging headlong towards imminent and universal disaster, with militarism as a psychological attitude, as a way of perceiving reality, and as a system of mutually reinforcing weapon developments and expenditures – as the spearhead of this suicide. Judging by recent public awareness and demonstrations, the general populace seems to know this better than their leaders. Furthermore, militarism is not only a question of survival, but is also closely linked to and aggravates issues of global justice, development and liberation. Militarism concentrates power and gives aid, comfort and encouragement to forces of oppression, deflects scientific energies and resource from productive uses, depletes crucial natural resources and contributes significantly to ecological burdens. Fifteen million workers, including 400,000 high-level scientists (at least a quarter of all such people in the world) are engaged in the arms industry and in military research, with 50 million in military activity (e.g. the armed forces) and arms production. Military expenditures exceed by 40% all expenditures on education, and are 250% of government expenditures for health. Between 5 and 10% of all raw materials consumed are eaten up by the military. Militarism kills people even without a shot being fired, and it destroys human values even without a bomb being dropped.

In addition, the question of the use of force and of militarism traditionally has been a central ethical question for Christians, and could coalesce and focus a now fragmented church debate on a wide variety of issues which seem to have no common link, and no direct historic place in the churches' socio-ethical legacy.

Therefore, to focus on militarism as a key issue might bring a number of churches more willingly and authentically (in view of their traditions) into various aspects not only of the militarism debate, but also into the development-liberation arena. To address the issue of militarism could help demystify major assumptions about dominant growth and other development myths of Western society. Without suggesting a wholesale rejection of that total ethos and myth structure, we must assert that the easy, uncritical, passive or active acceptance of that "ideology" is a major obstacle to global justice and the kind of society envisioned in the JPSS discussions. Because the militarism debate is integrally tied to the development-liberation debate, there is great danger in that these two debates will be de-linked, and be treated either competitively or from only one side or the other. The connections between militarism and "underdevelopment" and oppression are only too apparent. This is also a key reason for resisting the current tendency to become preoccupied again with "East-West" tensions to the exclusion of "North-South" issues. Churches must struggle to keep a lively sense of the need to keep militarism and development-liberation, and East-West, North-South, issues in a complex but holistic global vision.

Beyond these more strategic and tactical considerations, militarism in the catastrophic forms exhibited today represents rebellion, hopelessness and faithlessness, a broken covenant and a fractured *koinonia*. Sociological considerations aside, the churches cannot ignore militarism and still act faithfully. That fact is perhaps more urgently evident today than ever before.

The question is not so much *whether* concern over militarism ought to be a central feature of WCC and the churches' agenda in the 1980s, starting now, but rather *how* to bring that concern inescapably, forcefully, and creatively onto the agenda. In many circles talk about "militarism" has become bland and, therefore, unable to capture the serious attention of Christians who have "heard all that before". To couch the discussion in terms of violence and non-violence would likely lead to a similar reaction, perhaps a *déjà vu* yawn, as well as an unfortunate narrowing down of the issue of militarism in ways which do not do justice to its larger reality. We have wondered whether using "security" and the doctrine of the national security state to revive the militarism concern might have the advantage of novelty (for some), but fear that this also might be narrowed down either by identification with an untenable ideological position, or by limiting the concern to one aspect of the militarism issue.

In short, although we are convinced that militarism is an absolutely crucial issue for the churches to tackle together, oddly enough (because Christians ought not to need prodding) we have not been bright enough to discover an angle of vision that could force this issue upon our consciousness, and mobilize the energies of all the churches. The task is so obvious and so urgent that, perhaps prompted by the wider society, the churches and the World Council will move in this direction. If existential fear is a greater power for change than reason, hope or vision, at least for the majority of us, there may be a kind of bizarre hope left.

Learning from and amplifying voices of the poor

Another major development-liberation concern for the Council should be to reflect on and experiment with more effective means to hear and amplify the perspectives of the poor and socially marginated. As the Council has stressed, solidarity is not primarily doing something for or to the poor, but with the poor. That requires taking seriously the unique contributions of the marginated in the partnership. Further experiments and reflections along such lines promise to be very enriching for more faithful perceptions of society, of the church, of the nature and demands of the gospel. Already attempts to understand the Bible from the "underside of history", to experience social oppression and prospects for liberation from the point of view of the oppressed, to take our directions from the lead given by marginated peoples at the front-lines of the struggle for justice, to discover new styles of partnership and decision-making in church circles which empower and strengthen rather than demean and create dependency – all these efforts have been extremely rewarding for the whole church. We believe, however, that churches and the ecumenical movement are still very much at the early experimental stages in this process.

Complementary to this conviction, however, is another concern, almost as profound, that in the years ahead the World Council not relinquish its promising work with morally concerned scientific, technical and professional leadership. This has been evident in such programmes as those on faith, science and the future, on dialogue with people of living faiths and ideologies. We recognize that such "status" groups already enjoy significant alternative channels of communication and public attention; society already is inclined to listen to them, owing to their presumed expertise and because they do not threaten the establishment in such direct ways. On the other hand, the poor have relatively few channels of social persuasion or for affecting social policy. Hence they are more often obliged to take a confrontational approach because society is not generally disposed to listen and respond to them on the basis of rational or moral argument, but primarily when it feels threatened.

Realistically speaking, the decision-making power of the world lies for the most part in the hands and hearts of this high level of expertise and leadership. That has to be considered seriously, lest we become hopelessly utopian. But the question for us as churches and Christians lies at a deeper level. We are concerned that the World Council should continue to exhibit in its own life and style of work attentiveness to the specific gifts, commitments and skills of all people – whether they are part of the status quo, or of the oppressed (a simplistic classist distinction which makes this writer restive, and one which he senses has become a too dominant, though helpful, tool of social analysis within the WCC). Human community is too rich in its diversity, too beset by ethical and cultural issues requiring the concerted efforts of all, to alienate in principle *any* class or group from the process.

In particular, we believe that a concerted emphasis on the insights and experiences of the oppressed peoples is warranted in the years just ahead, but not to the exclusion of sustained work with sophisticated, highly competent and committed leaders in science, government, business, medicine, social science, cultural and religious affairs. One would have to say that over the years reliance primarily on leadership of this kind has helped the churches and the ecumenical movement to reap a rich harvest of mutual growth in faith, in understanding, and not least, in ethical and moral sensitivity. It is on the basis of these learned sensitivities that we now are conscious of how far short we have fallen, and yet that we must not be paralyzed by that fact.

New cultural consciousness

If the 1950s and early 60s were years when the world became aware of political emancipation issues, and the 1960s and 70s a period when economic neo-colonialism became more evident, the 1980s and 90s promise to be a time when cultural penetration and domination will become more visible. This emerging consciousness of cultural invasions, coupled with a renaissance of more traditional cultures and a growing disillusionment of cultural values in more materially affluent countries, increasingly challenges dominant understandings of the nature of the churches' message for and in the world.

Three implications of this fact should be highlighted in the ongoing work of the Council. One is that, perhaps in contrast to the recent past, the function of the World Council is to be more a broker of ideas, initiatives and experiments, than a pioneer of new visions for the churches. That latter task has been an important role for the Council, and remains one function. But in many ways member churches, and specific groups within those churches, are ahead of the Council in their vision and practice of the gospel. Today the primary task is not to stimulate the ecumenical vision, not to raise issues of the nature of the church and its relationship to society. That vision is being animated and incarnated in literally thousands of places, and those issues are being dynamically explored by Christians in their own particular settings across the world. One thinks immediately of peace groups in the Dutch churches, Korean Christians struggling for human rights, South African Christians witnessing against apartheid, Indian Christians working side by side with Bombay slum-dwellers, etc.

In the face of this enormous dynamism within the churches, what is the task of the Council? Is it not, in part, to facilitate the interaction of these expressions of dynamic faith and hope, to enhance the sense of connectedness in the context of a common vision, a common struggle and a common Lord? Is it not to help people, especially in the churches, to sense their connectedness with each other, and to feel the vibrant variety and richness of responses of faith? Is it not to let "unity" become visible and manifest through the evidences people give of the hope that is in them? Can the Council become less a movement from the centre to the periphery, and more a movement from the periphery to other periphery, because of their sense of connectedness with the centre? Can the Council become less a movement animated from Geneva, and more a movement animated in Calcutta, the villages of Indonesia, the ecclesial communities of Hondoras, Nicaragua, Brazil and Scotland?

In this spirit the development of a "network" emphasis and style of operation is increasingly important in the life of the Council. Functional and regional networks of persons, committed to common objectives but working in very specific contexts, are a way of taking seriously the collegiality of the churches, of recognizing the particularities of each local circumstance, of enhancing self-reliance, of helping to maintain a rootedness of the church in the life of the people, of injecting into the life-blood of the churches people who are not only bureaucrats but activists. While there are many questions which should be raised about a network approach to the work of the Council, it is a promising concept which needs to be experimented with more fully throughout the range of the Council's work. CCPD, URM, PCR, and more recently the Project System, have been influenced by this style of operation.

A second implication of the "cultural consciousness" of the 1980s and 90s is a growing imperative for addressing some of the foundational assumptions which have been so formative in the past 150–200 years, especially in the West, but radiating from the West into other cultures. Many traditional assumptions and values are called into question not only because they are at odds with traditional values of other cultures, but because emerging conditions – such as new medical technology to postpone death, or to engineer new genetic materials – force new religious, ethical and moral questions upon us. What is our responsibility to non-human nature, especially where the "claims" of non-human nature are perceived as being in competition with human needs and desires? What are the physical and social limits to growth, and on what ethical bases are those limits defined? What responsibilities do present generations have towards future generations in a world which is depleting natural resources and compromising the carrying capacity of the earth? What limitations should there be in the invasion of space and other planets? What is the relationship between gainful employment and human identity? What are the proper limits to the centralization of economic, political, ideological and military political power, at a time when technology greatly enhances the capacity of a minority to control the masses of the people?

Driven by such issues which have basic moral, ethical and theological significance, it seems to us that a crucial role for the churches, probably acting more ecumenically than in the past, is to bring to bear their best resources for critical reflection on the profound value assumptions and convictions in the context of which more adequate (and faithful) perspectives can be articulated. The struggle towards a "Just, Participatory and Sustainable Society" is a significant part of that discussion, but it seems to this writer that more care needs to be taken to relate this JPSS debate to the kinds of theological, ethical and ecclesiological questions posed in the Faith and Order, and Church and Society, frameworks. Also it is clear that such reflection needs to be done in an intercultural context which brings the enormous riches of differing cultural environments into the discussion – demythologizing dominant assumptions, and contributing new visions of the real and the good. The Council has a major responsibility in the years just ahead for animating, nurturing and helping to integrate more foundational theological discussions.

This leads to a third implication of the cultural challenges before us. Needless to say, one of the assets of the Christian community is that it has grown in the soils of very different cultures. Thus there is a pluralism of perspectives even where Christians from different parts of the globe, and differing socio-economic situations, discuss foundational issues. But is that enough for the future? In a world where Christians are a minority, where God is cosmic Lord, and where the Spirit is working in all places for the "divinization" of the world, discussion about our common destiny and common aspirations must be (not only strategically "must be", but religiously "must be") both intercultural and inter-religious. As the Chiangmai consultation (1977) stated: "We are conscious of the formative influence of religions and ideologies which may be closely inter-related; but we recognize that these have themselves been shaped by other elements of the culture of which they are a part – language, ethnic loyalty, social strata, caste."[5]

The work of the Council's programme on "Dialogue with People of Living Faiths and Ideologies" is a critically important venture of the ecumenical movement and, building upon the solid pioneering work of the last ten years so evident in the Chiangmai consultation document, needs to be a major aspect of the Council's work of the next decade. As has been stressed so frequently in that programme, emphasis is not on abstract theological systems, but upon how communities of faith are responding to the critical human issues confronting us all. "We came to see how easy it is to discuss religions and even ideologies as though they existed in some realm of calm quite separate from the sharp conflicts and sufferings of humankind."[6]

In short, the issues of development–liberation, and of human wholeness and faithfulness, are increasingly perceived as requiring a reconsideration of basic value assumptions and orientations. That reconsideration, we are convinced, must be engaged in an intercultural and inter-religious framework, not only because it will fail if it represents the cultural hegemony of one part of the human family over others, but more basically because our vision of reality and of the future needs to be enriched by these diverse perspectives.

> We see dialogue, therefore, as a fundamental part of our Christian service within community. In dialogue we actively respond to the command "to love God and your neighbour as yourself". As an expression of our love our engagement in dialogue testifies to the love we have experienced in Christ. It is our joyful affirmation of life against chaos, and our participation with all who are allies of life in seeking the provisional goals of a better human community. Thus we soundly reject any idea of "dialogue in community" as a secret weapon in the armoury of an aggressive Christian military. We adopt it rather as a means of living out our faith in Christ in service of community with our neighbours.[7]

The continuing search for unity

Central to the life and purpose of the ecumenical movement has been the call to visible unity (not necessarily institutional oneness). The years just ahead will challenge us to pursue this question more vigorously for several reasons, in addition to the more traditional and still legitimate biblical, theological and historical preoccupations. Several main reasons come to mind: (1) The current mood in the churches seems to emphasize local manifestations of Christian community and to minimize the importance of big organizations and institutions; the ecumenical movement itself is under attack, as are large church bodies of all types. This is true of secular as well as religious organizations, especially where decisions made by the big organizations are controversial, remote, and not locally influenced. (2) The current involvement of the churches in controversial social transformation raises more visibly and critically questions concerning the *esse* of the church. Is the *esse* of the church defined more by traditional "marks", or by its commitment to being in solidarity with the poor? This issue became acute in Section II at

Nairobi.[8] It is raised in assertions such as that the rejection of apartheid has a *status confessionis* for Christians. (3) An almost phenomenal growth in "base ecclesial-communities", often appearing among the poor or marginated communities, often having only tenuous connections with established churches, clearly raises the issue of what constitutes the whole and true church. To this could be added the rise of Pentecostal and charismatic communities, challenging the claims of the established or existing churches. (4) The question of women's roles in the churches presents a strong ecclesiological challenge, especially for some church bodies, and certainly for the World Council. (5) Finally, legitimate pressures for the contextualization of the churches, and the gospel message (especially in what were formerly known as "mission fields"), brings a diversity of perspectives on the nature of the church, the demands of the gospel, and the nature of unity which are not yet reconciled with each other.

Within the ecumenical movement these ecclesiological questions are not abstractions; they have direct bearing upon the structure of relationships and work. Who speaks for the church?[9] Who represents the church in an area where there is scarcely concealed animosity between existing churches and their ecumenical agencies on the one hand, and groups struggling for justice and calling themselves Christian on the other? Who is the church when a group struggles for liberation, but has nothing formally to do with existing churches or base ecclesial groups? What is the meaning of the unity of the church in decision-making about service and development projects? Is the traditional distinction that the ecumenical movement "speaks *to* the churches" and not *for* the churches a tenable distinction in fact as well as in theory, given the prominence of ecumenical movement statements and the general confusion about their nature? Who selects delegates for consultations and who shapes the agenda, and what is the implication of such decisions for our understanding of unity? These questions represent both theoretical and practical dimensions of the discussion of the imperative for, and nature of, Christian unity. It is most urgent and also opportune that in the years ahead the issue of unity should be connected integrally with questions of justice, wholeness, solidarity and participation.

In connection with a deepening and more contextual discussion of Christian unity, it also seems important for the Council to take a lead in helping to achieve a more realistic view of what the church is. How shall we come to a modest and accurate view of the churches – neither too grandiose, powerful, and prophetic, as if the churches were always on the side of the righteous and always struggling for justice, nor abject, viewing the churches as unfaithful, always in collusion with the status quo, always spiritualizing and other-worldly, always triumphalistic? We seem unable to escape a "children of light" and "children of darkness" mentality. We fall into the trap of self-righteousness from either side, and we tend to simplify and exaggerate. This is also a temptation for churches and for the ecumenical movement. There *is* a tendency to inflate one's own righteousness if not one's own knowledge. There is a tendency to confuse one's limited analysis with a total perspective; to believe that one's own programme or way of doing things is somehow, if not normative, at least better. There is a creeping competitiveness, usually wrapped in the pretty paper of altruistic motives, but largely defined by personal ambitions or animosities. There is a disturbing escalation of the institutional rhetoric of self-righteousness which can only appear to the outsider as hypocrisy (possibly ineptness) when measured against performance. In short, the more visible and escalated the claims, even prophetic claims, the more searing the judgment.

This writer is struck with the immense energy, moral commitment, ability and faith, represented in the ecumenical family. It is also striking to note the many subtle, and sometimes not so subtle, ways in which – for reasons of impossible schedules, of limited resources, of partial visions, or even occasionally territorial imperative – some great promises become compromised or fractured. The ecumenical community, like the churches themselves, is called to be a sign community, living together liturgically, covenantally, diaconally. In many respects it now does, as anyone who has worked in its midst can joyfully attest. Yet the years just ahead, because of the pressures and opportunities alluded to above, present the movement with the challenge and possibility of greater visibility as a sign community, showing forth the proleptic unity of the church and of humankind, a sign of the kingdom.

NOTES

1. Cyprus consultation (1981), *op. cit.* The recent consultation on "ecumenical political ethics," held in Cyprus, and the consultation on people's participation, held in Geneva (winter, 1982), tackled the definitional problem (see Chapters 7 and 8 above), but there remain a number of conceptual and application problems related to "participation."

2. Matthias Stiefel and Andrew Pearse, "Inquiry into Participation," *Participation: Occasional Paper*, UNRISD/79/C/14, Geneva, May, 1979, p. 2.

3. Ronald Preston, *Religion and the Persistence of Capitalism*, London, Billings and Sons Limited, 1979, p. 44.

4. The October 1981 Cyprus consultation in the framework of the JPSS centred

on issues of political ethics and power and reiterated the need for far more serious and disciplined reflection on Christian perspectives on the political process, and on the relation between churches and states. However, "profound differences of perspective, approaches and contexts" were constantly experienced in the discussions, p. 22. As noted above, two major views were in tension: one group emphasized the need for the "powerless" to confront the systems of domination, alienation and oppression; the other stressed that churches with access to centres of power should use their power for justice, as salt of the earth, or as light of the world, p. 3.

5. Stanley Samartha (ed), *Dialogue in Community*, Chiangmai, Thailand, consultation (auspices of "Dialogue with People of Living Faiths and Ideologies,") 18–27 April 1977, Geneva, WCC, 1977, p. 11.

6. *Ibid.*, p. 9.

7. *Ibid.*, p. 17.

8. Paton, *op. cit.*

9. Paul Ramsey, *Who Speaks for the Church?*, Nashville, Tennessee, Abingdon Press, 1967.

Bibliography

Abrecht, Paul (ed.), *Faith, Science and the Future*, Philadelphia, Fortress Press, 1978.

Abrecht, Paul (ed.), *Faith and Science in an Unjust World* (Volume 2), Geneva, World Council of Churches, 1980.

Adams, Ruth and Cullen, Susan (eds.), *The Final Epidemic: Physicians and Scientists on Nuclear War*, Chicago, Educational Foundation for Nuclear Science, 1981.

Ahooja-Patel, Krishna, "Another Development for Women", in Marc Nerfin (ed.), *Another Development: Approaches and Strategies*, Uppsala, Dag Hammarsjkold Foundation, 1977.

Alinsky, Saul, *Rules for Radicals*, New York, Vantage Press, 1971.

Arce-Martinez, Sergio, "Development of People's Participation and Theology", *The Ecumenical Review*, Vol. 30, No. 3, July 1978, pp. 266–277.

Arruda, Marcos (ed.), *Ecumenism and a New World Order*, Geneva, World Council of Churches, 1980.

Arruda, Marcos (ed.), *Transnational Corporations, Technology and Human Development*, Geneva, World Council of Churches, 1981.

Arruda, Marcos, "The WCC Programme on TNCs: Some Lessons and Challenges", Geneva, World Council of Churches, 1982 (occasional paper).

Assman, Hugo, *et al.* (eds), *Dominación y Dependencia*, Buenos Aires, Tierra Nueva SRL, 1975.

Barney, Gerald (ed.), *The Global 2000 Report to the President*, Washington, US Government Printing Office, 1980.

Barnet, Richard, *The Lean Years: Politics in an Age of Scarcity*, New York, Simon & Schuster, 1980.

Bennis, Warren, Kenneth Benne and Robert Chin (eds.), *The Planning of Change*, London, Holt, Rinehart & Winston, 1970.

van der Bent, Ans J. (ed.), *Major Studies and Themes of the Ecumenical Movement*, Geneva, World Council of Churches, 1981.

Berry, Wendell, *The Unsettling of America*, New York, Avon Publishers, 1978.

Birch, Charles and John Cobb, *Liberation of Life*, Cambridge, England, Cambridge University Press, 1981.

(Brandt Commission: Independent Commission for International Development Issues), *North-South: a Program for Survival*, Cambridge, Massachusetts, MIT Press, 1980.

Cardenal, Ernesto, *The Gospel in Solentiname*, New York, Maryknoll, 1979.

Chin, Robert and Kenneth Benne, "General Strategies for Effecting Change in Human Systems," in Bennis, *et al.* (eds.), *The Planning of Change* (third edition), New York, Holt, Rinehart & Winston, 1976.

Christian Conference of Asia, *Theology and Ideology*, New Delhi, Kalpana Printing House, 1980.

Christian Conference of Asia, *People Against Domination* (report of a consultation, Kuala Lumpur, 24–28 February 1981), Tokyo, Christian Conference of Asia, 1981.

Christian Conference of Asia, *Struggling With People is Living in Christ*, New Delhi, Kalpana Printing House, 1981.

Christian Conference of Asia, *Struggling to Survive: Women Workers in Asia*, Hong Kong, Christian Conference of Asia, 1981.

Christian Conference of Asia, *Minangkabau: Stories of the People vs. TNCs in Asia*, Hong Kong, 1981.

Cline, William (ed.), *Policy Alternatives for a New International Economic Order*, New York, Praeger Publishers, 1979.

Dumas, Andre, "A Society Which Creates Justice", *The Ecumenical Review*, Vol. 30, No. 2, July 1978, pp. 211–219.

Fey, Harold, "Some Notes on the Global Zoo: Entering the 21st Century", *The Christian Century*, 1–8 July 1981, pp. 698–701.

Fraser, Ian, *Re-inventing Theology (As the People's Work)*, London, United Society for the Propagation of the Gospel, 1981.

Galtung, John, Peter O'Brien and Roy Preiswerk (eds.), *Self-Reliance: a Strategy for Development*, Geneva, Institute for Development Studies, 1980.

Garcia-Bouze, Jorge, *A Basic Needs Analytical Bibliography*, Paris, OECD, 1980.

"Global Brain Trade," *Asiaweek*, 3 July 1981, pp. 32–33.

Grant, James, *Disparity Reduction Rates in Social Indicators*, Washington, Overseas Development Council, 1978.

Hamelink, Cees, *The Corporate Village (Role of TNCs in International Communication)*, Rome, IDOC, 1977.

Hamelink, Cees, *Communication in the Eighties: a Reader on the Mac-Bride Report*, Rome, IDOC, 1980.

Hamilton, Roberta, *The Liberation of Women: a Study of Patriarchy and Capitalism*, London, George Allen & Unwin, 1978.

Hargleroad, Bobbi Wells, *Struggle To Be Human*, Geneva, World Council of Churches, 1977 (second printing).

Harrington, Michael, "Solving Poverty With Statistics", *Christianity and Crisis*, Vol. 1, No. 7, 27 April 1981, pp. 121–124.

Heilbroner, Robert, *An Enquiry into the Human Prospect*, New York, W. W. Norton & Company, 1974.

Hettne, Björn and Peter Wallensteen, *Emerging Trends in Development Theory*, SAREC (Report of the Wästerhaninge Workshop, August 1977).

Hettne, Björn, *Current Issues in Development Theory*, SAREC Report, No. 3, 1978.

Hines, Samuel, "Global Interdependence and the Process of Value Diffusion", in Sudesh Sharma (ed.), *Dynamics of Development*, Delhi, Concept Publishing Company, 1978, pp. 213–241.

Howell, Leon, *People Are the Subject: Studies in Rural Urban Mission*, Geneva, World Council of Churches, 1980.

International Labour Organization, *Employment, Growth and Basic Needs* (report of the 1976 ILO World Employment Conference), New York and London, Praeger Publishers, 1977.

Kim Yong Bock, *Minjung Theology: People as the Subjects of History*, Singapore, Christian Conference of Asia, 1981.

Kingma, Stuart, "Beyond Mere Survival to the Abundant Life", *Contact*, No. 62, June 1981, pp. 1–12.

Koshy, Ninan, "Introduction", in Viera-Gallo, *The Security Trap*, Rome, IDOC, 1979, pp. 5–10.

Kurien, C. T., *Poverty, Planning and Social Transformation*, Bombay, Allied Publishers Private Limited, 1978.

Liggett, Thomas, *Where Tomorrow Struggles To Be Born*, New York, Friendship Press, 1970.

Little, Charles, *Land and Food*, Washington DC, American Land Forum Report No. 1, 1979.

Lindberg, Carter, "Through a Glass Darkly", *The Ecumenical Review*, Vol. 33, No. 1, January 1981, pp. 37–52.

Lovins, Amory and Hunter Lovins, "The Surprises Are Coming", *Christianity and Crisis*, Vol. 41, No. 4, 16 March 1981, pp. 51ff.

Maglaya, Felipe, "Organizing People for Power", Tokyo, Asian Committee for People's Organization, 1978.

McGilvray, James, *The Quest for Health and Wholeness*, Tübingen, Institute for Medical Mission, 1981.

McNamara, Robert, World Bank Meeting in Nairobi, Kenya, 24 September 1973.

Meadows, Donella, *et al.*, *Limits to Growth*, New York, Universe Books, 1972.

Mesarovic, Mihajlo and Eduard Pestel, *Mankind at the Turning Point*, New York, New American Library, Inc., 1974.

Miguez-Bonino, José, "Christian Unity and Social Reconciliation" (brochure), Geneva, World Council of Churches, 1973.

Miguez-Bonino, José, *Room to Be People*, Philadelphia, Fortress Press, 1979.

Morris, David M., "Measuring the Condition of the World's Poor", New York, Pergamon Press, 1979.

Myrdal, Gunnar, *Challenge of World Poverty*, New York, Random House, 1970.

Nelson, Joan, *Access to Power: Politics and the Urban Poor in Developing Nations*, Princeton, New Jersey, Princeton University Press, 1979.

Nerfin, Marc (ed.), *Another Development: Approaches and Strategies*, Uppsala, Dag Hammarskjold Foundation, 1977.

Niebuhr, H. Richard, *Christ and Culture*, New York, Harper & Row, Publishers, 1951.

Niles, Preman and T. K. Thomas (eds.), *Witnessing to the Kingdom*, Singapore, Christian Conference of Asia, 1979.

Oldak, Pavel, "The Environment and Social Production: a Soviet View", in Paul Abrecht (ed.), *Faith, Science and the Future*, Geneva, World Council of Churches, 1978, pp. 215–225.

Pearson, Lester, *Partners in Development*, New York, Praeger Publishers, 1969.

Pierre, Andrew, *The Global Politics of Arms Sales*, Princeton, New Jersey, Princeton University Press, 1981.

Piven, Frances Fox and Richard Cloward, *Poor People's Movements: Why They Succeed, How They Fail*, New York, Vintage Books, 1977.

Presidential Commission on World Hunger, "Overcoming World Hunger: the Challenge Ahead", Washington DC, US Government Printing Office, June 1980.

Preston, Ronald, *Religion and the Persistence of Capitalism*, London, Billings & Sons, Ltd, 1979.

Puchala, Donald (ed.), *Issues Before the 35th General Assembly of the United Nations, 1980–81*, New York, United Nations Association of the USA, 1980.

Ramalho, Jether (ed.), *Signs of Hope and Justice*, Geneva, World Council of Churches, 1980.

Ramsey, Paul, *Who Speaks for the Church?*, Nashville, Tennessee, Abingdon Press, 1977.

Rawls, John, *A Theory of Justice*, Cambridge, Massachusetts, Harvard University Press, 1971.

Regehr, Ernie, *Militarism and the World Military Order*, Geneva, World Council of Churches, 1980.

Rogers, Barbara, *No Peace Without Justice*, Geneva, World Council of Churches, 1980.

Roxborough, Ian, *Theories of Underdevelopment*, London, Macmillan Press, 1979.

Samartha, Stanley (ed.), *Dialogue in Community* (consultation in Chiangmai, Thailand, 18–27 April 1977), Geneva, World Council of Churches, 1977.

Sampson, Anthony, *The Money Lenders*, New York, Viking Press, 1981.

de Santa Ana, Julio, *Good News to the Poor*, Geneva, World Council of Churches, 1977.

de Santa Ana, Julio (ed.) *Separation Without Hope*, Geneva, World Council of Churches, 1978.

de Santa Ana, Julio (ed.), *Towards a Church of the Poor*, Geneva, World Council of Churches, 1979.

Schot, Willem, "Do We Project Ourselves in Projects?", Geneva, World Council of Churches, 1977.

Sewell, John (ed.), *The US and World Development, 1980*, New York, Praeger Publishers, 1980.

Sharma, Sudesh (ed.), *Dynamics of Development: an International Perspective*, Delhi, Concept Publishing Company, 1978.

Shinn, Roger (ed.), *Faith and Science in an Unjust World (Volume 1)*, Geneva, World Council of Churches, 1980.

Shinn, Roger, "The End of a Liberal Dream", *Christianity and Crisis*, Vol. 41, No. 4, 16 March 1981, pp. 52–57.

Song, Choan-Seng, *Third Eye Theology*, Maryknoll, New York, Orbis Books, 1979.

Stavenhagen, Rudolpho, "Basic Needs, Peasants and the Strategy for Rural Development", in Nerfin (ed.), *Another Development: Approaches and Strategies*, Uppsala, Dag Hammarskjold Foundation, 1977, pp. 41–65.

Steinhart, Carol and John Steinhart, *The Fires of Culture*, North Scituate, Massachusetts, Duxbury Press, 1974.

Stiefel, Matthias and Andrew Pearse, "Inquiry into Participation: a Research Approach," *Participation: Occasional Paper*, UNRISD/79/C/14, Geneva, May 1979.

Talbot, Ross (ed.), *The World Food Problem and US Policies and Practices*, Ames, Iowa, Iowa State University Press, 1979.

Tinker, Irene and Michele Bo Bramsen (eds.), *Women and World Development*, Washington DC, Overseas Development Council, 1977.

Torres, Sergio and John Eagleson (eds.), *The Challenge of Basic Christian Communities*, Maryknoll, New York, Orbis Books, 1981.

Tinbergen, Jan (Coordinator), *Re-shaping the International Order*, New York, E. P. Dutton & Company, Inc., 1975.

Verma, S. P., "Systems Analysis," in Sharma (ed.), *Dynamics of Development*, Delhi, Concept Publishing Company, 1978, Vol. 1, pp. 243–256.

Verma, S. P., "Theories of Political Development", in Sharma (ed.), *Dynamics of Development*, Volume 1, Delhi, Concept Publishing Company, 1978.

Viera-Gallo, Jose-Antonio (ed.), *The Security Trap*, Rome, IDOC, 1979.

Weekes-Vagliani, Winifred, *Les Femmes dans le Développement*, Paris, OECD, 1980.

World Bank, *World Development Report, 1980*, London, Oxford University Press, 1980.

World Council of Churches, "Violence, Non-Violence and the Struggle for Social Justice", *The Ecumenical Review*, Vol. 25, No. 4, October 1973, pp. 3–19.

World Council of Churches (Urban Rural Mission), *Mission and Justice*, 1977.

World Council of Churches (General Secretariat), "Towards a Just, Participatory and Sustainable Society" (notes on presentation and discussion of the working group, mimeographed); meeting in Geneva, 11–14 December 1977.

World Council of Churches (CCPD), "Minutes of the First Exploratory Consultation of Transnational Corporations" (from the Cartigny consultation, 26–28 January 1977).

World Council of Churches (CMC), "Activities Report: January 1978 to June 1979", includes CMC Commission meeting in Bad Saarow, GDR, 1–8 April 1979.

World Council of Churches (CICARWS), "Project List Review", at the 1–3 November 1979 meeting in Cartigny.

World Council of Churches (ChSoc), "Energy For My Neighbour", *Anticipation*, No. 28, December 1980.

World Council of Churches (CICARWS), *Empty Hands: an Agenda For the Churches*, 1980.

World Council of Churches, "La transnacionalisación de America Latina y la misión de las Iglesias", consultation in Sao Paulo, Brazil, 1–5 October 1980.

World Council of Churches (PCR), "Churches Responding to Racism in the 80s", *PCR Information*, No. 12 (World Consultation on Racism, at Noordwijkerhout, The Netherlands, 16–21 June 1980).

World Council of Churches (CWME), *Your Kingdom Come* (report of the CWME world conference in Melbourne, Australia, 12–25 May 1980).

World Council of Churches (CCPD), "Towards a Church in Solidarity with the Poor", 1980 (pamphlet).

World Council of Churches (CCPD, CICARWS), "The Churches' Participation in Development Programmes and Projects in Latin America" (report of consultation at Itaici, Brazil, September 1980).

World Council of Churches (CICARWS), "Activities Report, 1980–81" (as presented at 8–13 June 1981 meeting of the Commission).

World Council of Churches (CCPD), "Report of the Second Indonesia Evaluation Team", June 1981 (mimeographed).

World Council of Churches (ChSoc), *Manipulating Life: Ethical Issues in Genetic Engineering* (report of a working group in Vogelenzang, The Netherlands, 15–19 June 1981), 1982.

World Council of Churches (ChSoc), "Faith, Science and the Future: the African Context" (report of a meeting in Jos, Nigeria, 20–27 June 1981).

World Council of Churches (CCIA), "Study Paper on Religious Liberty," *Background Information, 1980/4*, 1981.

World Council of Churches (CCPD), "The Way Ahead: Ten Years of Development Education: Summary and Conclusions" (report of the evaluation team, as reported to the meeting of the Commission at Salatiga, Indonesia, June 1981) mimeographed.

World Council of Churches (CCPD), "Report of the World Council of Churches Consultation on Political Ethics" (in Cyprus, 18–25 October 1981), draft 1, 13 January 1982.

World Council of Churches (CCPD), "The Churches and People's Participation" (report of a consultation in Geneva, 18–23 January 1982), mimeographed.

World Council of Churches (CICARWS, CCPD, CWME), "Consultation on a New Resource Sharing System" (report of a joint consultation held at Glion, Switzerland, 3–6 February 1982), mimeographed.

Appendices

1: A comment from Ghana

ANNIE JIAGGE

Reading through Dr Dickinson's comprehensive review of how the WCC's thinking on development, liberation and global justice issues has evolved since the Nairobi Assembly, one is greatly impressed by the tremendous efforts in studies, experimentations and concrete actions undertaken during the period.

However, the great efforts made by a number of churches to show solidarity with the poor and exert appropriate pressure to eradicate injustice in political, economic and social life during the period under review do not appear to have made any significant change in the conditions of life of the poor. Some churches as shareholders have demanded answers to pertinent questions that exposed injustice to workers in factories. A number of churches participated in the campaign against the sale of milk powder as substitute for mother's milk and exposed the dangers to which "bottle babies" are exposed in poor countries where sanitation and hygiene leave much to be desired. There have been pressure groups to stop banks from doing business with South Africa, and the WCC withdrew its investments from certain banks over the issue of apartheid. In spite of all these and more, the plight of the poor during the period under review has deteriorated. Namibia is still under apartheid domination, and South African police brutalities have taken a turn for the worse. But praise God, Zimbabwe is free and peace in that country is holding.

All this is not to suggest that the efforts made so far were not effective and so should be discontinued. Far from it. These efforts should be continued and strengthened in every way. However, it needs to be asked whether it is possible that efforts made so far lack the revolutionary impact that is necessary for solidarity with the poor to be meaningful. Further, are there urgent issues to which no great attention has been paid? As we go from Nairobi to Vancouver, are there new areas to which the churches' attention can be drawn in the struggle to do Christ's work on earth? I should think so, and let me think aloud on some of these issues.

In the 1960s international development aid was the talk of the developed world. The call from the United Nations' General Assembly for development aid to the poor countries was considered the key to alleviating suffering the third world. This hope was shared at Uppsala and the birth of the Programme to Combat Racism was one of the concrete steps taken in the struggle against oppression. PCR was endorsed at Nairobi and it proved so effective in providing access to information on the truth about the situation in Southern Africa that the South African government took steps and expended public funds to subvert the WCC's work on racism. The South African strategy achieved a measure of success in that church papers picked up South African propaganda and, without verifying the source of the information, published articles and items of news which created the impression of a house fighting against itself.

However the truth has a way of asserting itself and the state machinery behind the "Muldergate" scandal was exposed in due course. The South African propaganda against the work of the WCC on racism and the churches' reaction to it can be taken as one of the factors that prompted the decision in Jamaica to accept the proposal of the General Secretary that a process of consultation be set in motion as soon as possible "on how the churches may be involved in combating racism in the 1980s may be given priority".

These consultations have taken place and we know a lot more today about racism. In South Africa, human beings are made homeless everyday – human beings are being dumped so regularly on arid lands without water, without food, without shelter that this is no longer news.

Much good work has been done by the churches since Nairobi along the line of being in solidarity with the poor, but the suffering of the poor is greater now than ever before. The pertinent question is: are the churches' efforts directed to the sort of remedy which the situation demands? Has there been a proper diagnosis of the situation? What else is there to be done and why is it not being done?

In the 1960s, the United Nations General Assembly called on the rich nations to give one per cent of the Gross National Product in development aid in a bid to narrow the gap between the rich and the poor nations. It was considered that the situation in the world where one-third of the world's population appropriated for its own use two-thirds of the wealth of the world and left two-thirds of humanity to wallow in poverty and squalor should not be allowed to continue. The rich nations must give development aid to the poor nations and that, it was thought, would solve their problem. However today 78% of the world's population live in the developing world where the total expenditure on health is 6% of the world health expenditure, on education it is 11 per cent of the world education spending, 18% of the world export earnings, 8% of the world industry and 5% of world science and technology. The pay rise an American can expect in a year is greater than what an Indian can expect in a hundred years. The international aid did not work the miracle anticipated in the 1960s.

Right at that time third world voices came out to say: "Not charity but justice in trade and in compensation for the exploitation of natural resources." Of course the world mass media are controlled by the rich countries and so the views of the third world on the help to be given for their "benefit" were not heard or, if heard, not taken seriously.

There was in fact very little genuine aid and what little there was was often "tied aid". The process was a device where all the materials for any given project and the skills had to be purchased from the donor country and imported to the project area in the third world even though similar or even superior materials were available at cheaper prices on the world market. The freight and insurance were paid to companies of the donor countries, and the aid was in the form of loans with interest. The tied aid principle was carried out to ridiculous and quite obnoxious lengths. Take for instance the contract for the construction of workers flats in Tema (a new harbour town in Ghana) pre-financed by a TNC under tied aid. In this instance even the wood for the project was imported. But Ghana is the home of some of the world's must durable and beautiful timber and this was on the local market at much lower prices than the cost of the soft white wood imported for the project. The expensive but inferior wood could not stand the rigours of the Ghanaian climate or the ravages of white ants and termites. Naturally the cost of such projects was highly inflated and payment had to be made in hard-earned foreign exchange. (The magnificent technological contribution made by the Dutch to the textile industry in West Africa is one of the few exceptions).

Transnational capital moves only on the policy decisions taken in its home country on the basis of profitability. Transnational corporations are not primarily concerned with development issues in poor countries. If their activities bring development, well and good, but the target is the greatest profit investment. Letting loose transnational corporations on young independent nations in the name of development in the 1960s was disastrous to these nations which were vulnerable and inexperienced in such matters. The highly developed skill of high pressure salesmanship was new to them and they were taken in by the smooth persuasiveness of the agents of the TNCs. The result was that projects of little viability but of great profit potential for the TNCs were sold to the unsuspecting young nations in package deals, upsetting the national priorities.

Take the example of Ghana, once again. There was the need for a small dry dock to service fishing boats and a small merchant navy. The TNC interested in building the dry dock put forward a package deal consisting of a dry dock, a steel mill and a motorway. The local feasibility report indicated that there was not enough scrap in the country to justify the construction of Tema steel mill. However, a road connecting Accra and Tema was one of the country's priorities. The package deal was a "take-it-or-leave it" offer and Ghana accepted. Of the three projects only the motorway answered a real and immediate need. After a few years, the steel mill completely exhausted all the local scrap and Ghana now imports scrap with scarce foreign exchange. The dry dock constructed is so big that it can handle many of the world's biggest ocean liners. Twelve years after its completion the dry dock is still under-utilized. The country cannot afford even now to equip it fully. However, the repayment of the loans plus interest must be made to the TNC involved.

There are several similar white elephants in many developing countries which drain their poor resources. These were not national priorities but they answered the search for good investment by TNCs. It is not an area in which *caveat emptor* can apply. It is immoral to take advantage of inexperience to satisfy self-interest. When politicians began to learn from bitter experience, a new element was introduced, playing on human weakness – bribery and corruption of politicians and government officials to accept project proposals from TNCs.

The 1970s, after a decade of international aid, found the poor countries of the third world groaning under huge external debts; in some cases as much as 40% of all foreign exchange earnings is needed to pay such debts and the interest thereon. This does not however mean that the host countries derived no benefit whatever from the operations of TNCs. Apart from creating some job opportunities, some goals of national development were achieved. Ghana wanted to harness the waters of the Volta River to produce electricity for industrial development and domestic consumption and required vast sums of money for the purpose. International finance would take the risk of lending money to a poor country only when the repayability prospects are good. Kaiser Aluminium and Reynolds, by offering to purchase most of the electricity produced for an aluminium smelter to be constructed, provided the favourable conditions required for international capital to move. Kaiser and Reynolds considered the risk involved in investing in a young, developing, independent country and drove a hard bargain to safeguard the interest of Valco, the company set up for the project. The result was a contract with most favourable terms for Valco.

The risk paid off and Valco became one of the most profitable ventures of our age, but the company continues to pay very low prices for electricity and water. Power is being sold by Ghana to Togo and Benin at the rate of 2.5 US cents per unit, but Valco continues to pay 0.5 US cents a unit. Ghanaian industries pay ¢5.85 (or US $2.13) for 1000 gallons of water but Valco continues to pay 30 pesewas (US $0.11) in strict accordance with the original contract. Now Valco makes extremely generous finance provisions to a fund instituted for scholarships and other charitable purposes for the benefit of Ghanaians. Though this gesture is highly appreciated, it did not prevent the growth of bad feeling between Valco and young Ghanaians.

The realization that what is given in aid is only a tiny fraction of what is lost by the developing countries through injustice in trade, tariff barriers and other discriminatory practices is making the poor countries more and more impatient and restless. The numerous development theories have failed to produce the anticipated results; some have indeed proved to be a camouflage for self-interest on the part of the developed world. The trickle-down prosperity theory was a dismal failure – very little prosperity in fact ever trickled down to the poor, on the contrary they were made poorer.

Further, a new class of comfortable citizens was created in developing countries and this class operates outside the traditional norms and values. The conditions of life at the grassroots level deteriorate as the new alien structure introduces foreign practices into local society. And so the growing gap between the rich and the poor nations of the world is reproduced at the national level.

Meanwhile the cry of the poor countries continues to fall on deaf ears. The demand is for fundamental structural changes in world trade, the monetary system, free access to the markets of the developed world, equitable compensation for the minerals exploited in the third world and participation in decision-making on all the issues concerning the third world. These and similar remedies as incorporated in the UN New International Economic Order will provide at least some relief and lay a sound foundation for eradicating poverty and closing the gap between the rich and the poor nations.

Many leaders in the third world underestimated the strength of the external forces in the struggle for economic and cultural freedom after political independence. The enemy was indeed the same as in the struggle for political independence. Colonial self-interest after independence operated in the more subtle and smooth form of neo-colonialism. The struggle against the preservation of the *status quo* in economic and cultural domination has proved even more difficult to overcome than the battle for political freedom. In Ghana three civilian and one military governments have already fallen as victims in the struggle for economic and cultural freedom. The old tranquillizer of little changes here and there, little improvements here and there no longer seems to work. It is becoming clearer that the third world cannot be incorporated into the global economic system without first a radical change of that system itself. Piecemeal improvements to the present global structures do not seem to have any lasting effect.

In Ghana, changes after independence were merely cosmetic and of no lasting effect. The educational system remained essentially the same, producing clerks (as in the colonial days) for white collar jobs while the basic needs of the country are agricultural and technical. Agricultural production continued to be geared to the production of export crops to feed the factories of the old colonial powers at the expense of food crops, and a country like Ghana with vast acres of arable land and a good climate imports food to feed the nation with its hard-earned foreign exchange. On the other hand, however, the prices paid for the export crops such as cocoa and coffee and other primary commodities are determined by the purchasers of these products. They fix the price they wish to pay. The so-called free market is in fact carefully manipulated for the benefit of the purchaser of primary products in the developed countries. Prices have been depressed even for political reasons. Price fluctuations have a destabilizing effect on the economy of poor countries and were partly responsible for the overthrow of three governments by military coups d'etat in Ghana.

However the producers of the primary commodities are denied the privilege of the purchaser fixing the price when it comes to buying manufactured goods from those who purchase the primary products at their prices. The prices demanded by the manufacturers in the developed countries include such variants as cost of living, inflation and so on. But the same manufacturers were the ones who fixed the prices of primary commodities irrespective of the cost of production and with the hope of securing even bigger profits, on the basis of a "take-it-or-leave-it" policy. Lack of storage facilities and of the skill necessary to preserve perishable primary commodities means that such low prices have to be accepted. If prices of raw materials are indexed to the price of the manufactured goods the producer will receive equitable prices for his products. But this just proposal is vehemently opposed by the developed countries because it would mean lower profits on manufactured goods. And so the UN New International Economic Order remains substantially inoperative.

Local experience with TNCs has shown that comparatively very little foreign capital is brought into the host country; the bulk of the finance required for operations is borrowed from local banks. On the other hand, what the TNCs taken out of the country as profits is several times more than the capital invested. The remission of these profits becomes a drain on the scarce foreign exchange earnings of the host countries. Where the TNCs reinvest their profits in the host country, the indigenous entrepreneur is unable to compete on equal terms because of the superior advantages of the TNCs in research, development experience and the skills in advertising. The host country has to choose between two evils – the loss of foreign exchange through remission of profits and the killing of local initiative or entrepreneurship.

The inequities in the mining industries are even worse. The Ashanti Goldfields for example are reputed to be some of the richest gold mines in the world. They have been mined since the 1890s by fully owned foreign companies. During the colonial days, practically nothing was paid for the gold. It was mined and taken away in its raw state to be processed abroad. Some of the poorest people in Ghana live in the mining towns, their children suffer malnutrition and hardly any of the basic amenities are available to them. And yet the Ashanti Goldfields provided the exploiters with millions and millions of dollars over the years. The same story is true of diamonds, bauxite and mangenese.

It was only in 1975 after the Investment Policy Decree that the government of Ghana (this was after the introduction of the New International Economic Order at the UN) took over the majority shares in the mining companies. However, the day to day administration is still in the hands of the TNCs and Ghanaians have no effective control over production policy which is determined in the home country of the TNCs. The policies of the TNCs are not in consonance with African concepts of exploitation of natural resources. In Ghana, for instance, land and other natural resources

belong to this and future generations; the present generation holds
in trust for itself and future generations, and must apportion development and exploitation equitably between present needs and those
of future generations.

The minerals extracted continue to be washed and exported in the
raw state, just as was done during the colonial days, and they are
subjected to all the price fluctuations of raw materials. All the processing is done outside Ghana by either the subsidiaries of or companies in which the TNCs operating in Ghana hold several shares.
This country loses even the duty on the enhanced value of the
processed minerals. In view of the fact that these natural resources
are irreplaceable, their indiscriminate exploitation to maximize the
profits of foreign companies without payment of equitable compensation is a great injustice.

These are some of the injustices that create restlessness in poor
countries and some of the reasons why these countries continue to
be poor. People work hard on export crops but are not able to meet
their basic needs because of the inequitable prices paid for raw
materials. Their few manufactured or semi-manufactured goods are
not allowed free access to the markets of the developed countries.
They are met with protectionism tariff barriers and many other
discriminatory measures. On the other hand, the developing countries provide a good market for the goods from the developed
world. Mass-produced consumer durables compete with local production and traditional producers are pushed out of business. Indigenous local agents of the TNCs penetrate the ranks of national
decision-makers and ensure that the interests of the TNCs in production and distribution are safeguarded.

This is the area of economic suppression in which I think the
churches must concentrate action in the coming years. There is need
for awareness-building among shareholders of TNCs that the huge
profits they share in dividends are made possible because the producers of the raw materials are denied equitable prices for their
products and labour. The situation must induce in people the same
indignation they feel towards a big bully cruelly beating up a
defenceless child. The churches in the home countries of the TNCs
should endeavour to bring some sort of morality into their operations in the developing countries which have little or no bargaining
power. Research, development and managerial experience, plus accumulated capital, have together given the TNCs great power. This
power must be used for the benefit of mankind and not to enslave
people. In my part of the world we have the saying that the nations
of the world are like the fingers of the hand. They are not all equal.

There are long fingers and short ones but they all belong to the hand and the whole hand suffers pain when the smallest finger is hurt. In the same way injury to the poorest nation must be felt as injury to all humankind.

Lest I give the impression that all poor people do honest and hard work but are always at the mercy of exploiters, I hasten to state that the situation is not that simple. Among the African professionals and technocrats, there was a high standard of efficiency, dedication to work and managerial skill during the colonial days. But unskilled labour, especially in the public sector, put in minimum effort and expected maximum pay. Unlike professionals and other technocrats, they did not give themselves to their work which they considered just a means to earn a living in the service of a foreign government. Among the lower paid workers there was no sense of vocation and the majority of workers were in this group. This colonial mentality persisted after independence. Labourers on the state farms for instance, kept civil service hours, and animals requiring attention at night perished. Moreover, politicians anxious to gain popularity and win the next elections, interfered with management in the state enterprises and made staff discipline difficult. Management was frequently forced to employ people with no qualifications for the job. When this was resisted, the conscientious managers in the state enterprises were replaced with persons chosen by government ministers for political reasons. The result was, instead of making profit the state enterprises became a drain on the national economy.

There are however hopeful signs of changes in some of our countries. The realization that what needs doing to improve the conditions of life of the poor must be undertaken by the poor themselves has brought a new awakening, a new spirit of self-help in voluntary communal labour to meet some basic community needs. Self-reliance I think is an authentic response to the problems of development. Self-reliance has indeed a psychological and intellectual liberating effect on the "colonial mentality" – a plaque which has proved extremely difficult to eradicate.

The new awakening at the grassroots level today in Ghana must be nurtured to grow. The growing disenchantment with foreign culture and life-style and the desire to go back to cultural roots are healthy signs. The growing self-confidence of the poor must be maintained and nurtured. In this respect the formation in Ghana of People's Defence Committees to act as a catalyst, to expose corruption and ensure people's participation in decision-making is a positive step. There is need for education in the exercise of the new found power in the hands of the poor. The few PDCs that asked the management to retire, soon found that they could not operate without management. When people who had all their lives taken orders realize that they have the power to make decisions, abuse of that power in the initial stages cannot be ruled out, but it is a price worth paying for people's participation in decision-making.

Self-reliance releases creative energy and encourages initiative. It eliminates the urge to continue to imitate, and promotes efforts to innovate, minimizing dependence on foreign consumer durables. The struggle to rediscover their true identity, their cultural heritage, the African world view and way of life, all form part of an uplifting educational experience for people especially the grassroots level. The African way of life is one of caring. The individual belongs to the community and the community takes care of the individual. The rich have a duty to the poor in the same community. The African concept of life is holistic. They live their religion. To them the welfare of the spirt is inseparable from the welfare of the body which is healthy only when the spirit is at peace.

The poor in our societies are better acquainted with these and several other traditional and cultural values than the new class of comfortable citizens.

God in his great wisdom has revealed himself to humankind all over the world through the ages. Although human perception is imperfect, certain truths have registered in the encounter with God. These truths have formed the basis of traditional and cultural values. A return to these is a step in the right direction.

The demand today is for more and more research in these matters and the churches have been called upon to play a leading role. In the African tradition, there is a lot more to life than self-interest and the individual lives not only for oneself but for the community as well.

At a recent WCC/AACC consultation in Kitwe, Zambia, AACC was called "to commit itself to programmes of Africanization in consultation with those groups (such as the Catholic University in Kinshasa and the Association of African Theologians) who are already addressing their attention to this need. Such programmes ought to address themselves essentially to African values and life-style and not merely to the introduction of African songs and styles of worship. These programmes ought to be designed in such a way that they incorporate the research already being undertaken by in-dividuals in various parts of Africa. It is felt that such a study could go a long way towards the alleviation of fears concerning the conflict between capitalist and socialist ideologies in Africa". This is indeed a great challenge to the church in Africa.

On 31 December 1981 there was a revolt against corruption in Ghana led by Flt Lt J. J. Rawlings, the young man who in 1979 took over power from the military goverment for what he called "a house cleaning exercise". Corruption at that time seemed institutionalized and those in the business of buying and selling became rich overnight through corrupt practices. Flt Lt J. J. Rawlings led a revolt by the other ranks of the army against corrupt senior army officers and their civilian associates.

During the "house cleaning exercise" general elections were held and within three months, a new civilian government was installed. Rawlings took an undertaking from the new civilian government that the house cleaning exercise would continue until corruption was eradicated from society. However, the problems were more complex than the young rulers realized when they handed over to the civilian government. The new president, himself an honest man, could not control members of his political party who made their fortunes through corrupt practices and were still great advocates of such practices. Corruption became so rampant that even the TNCs in Ghana realized that the climate was bad for investment.

J. J. Rawlings and his "revolutionary boys" took over power a second time with the declared intent to put things right. Miraculously, the price of cocoa immediately shot up from around US ¢80 to ¢101.50 a pound on 5 January 1982. Then as it became clear that what the new rulers want to establish is people's participation in decision-making at all levels, the dangers to foreign investment in Ghana were obvious. TNC policy decisions are taken outside Ghana in the home country. Gradually the price of cocoa on the world market took a downward trend from 28 January at ¢97.64 to the low of ¢68.63 a pound on 14 June 1982.

The new goverment in Ghana needs the help of the churches and has said so. The aims of the revolution cannot be achieved without a firm moral basis, and the churches have a wonderful opportunity to participate in shaping the destiny of Ghana. Neither sitting on the fence nor throwing in the towel is meaningful in the present situation. Some church leaders have spoken strongly against the excesses in the conduct of affairs and the lack of discipline in the armed forces.

The government has clamped down heavily on the importation of all the goods that make life comfortable, and people are being urged to go back to the land and produce more food to feed the nation and for export. The distribution of the scarce essential commodities available is firmly controlled, and preference is being given to meeting the needs of the poor in the rural areas. Living in Ghana suddenly has become a problem but the young rulers keep promising a better future. Having a laudable aim is one thing, achieving that aim is another and the method of achieving makes all the difference. The process of social transformation initiated by the young rulers is one of people's participation in decision-making at all levels. With the enthusiasm to return to traditional and cultural values, the poor at the grass roots level have an important role to play as they are, at the moment, the custodians of such values. This is going to give them, I hope, the confidence to rise above the pressures of poverty in the struggle to be self-reliant. However, they are woefully ignorant of the complexities in development in modern life.

Development must be bottom-up and top-down simultaneously. The young rulers seem to distrust many of the intellectuals and technocrats, but it is obvious that the revolution cannot succeeed without the full utilization of knowledge and skills available in the country. Fortunately the Presbyterian Church of Ghana took the first step to bring together the intellectuals and the young rulers. A series of symposia has been planned for the purpose. On 22 June 1982 one member of government, himself an intellectual, and three other intellectuals presented papers on "Liberation Theology in Ghana". All the four members of the panel are ordained church leaders. They spoke on vital issues relating to the moral direction of the revolution and their convictions on the methods that must be adopted to achieve the desired goals. They were frankly critical of some government actions and the lack of discipline in the armed forces. It was a most uplifting experience and the audience fully participated in making contributions and asking questions.

This of course is a very small beginning but it is significant because it was on the initiative of Christians and took place in the church.

In the debate on violence, I would like to suggest, if I may, that we miss the point in our over-enthusiasm to condemn violence. Let me put it this way – one man in his desire to obtain a good view of his favourite football team at play climbs on to the head of another. From his vantage position he wants to maintain the *status quo* – the man carrying his weight must quietly endure: any action to overthrow him is violence and must be condemned. But to the man on whose head he stands, the *status quo* is violence and peace for him is the overthrow of the man on his head. Violence from the point of view of the oppressed is different from violence from the point of view of the oppressor. I do not think it is exactly Christian to condemn the overthrow of the man committing violence by standing on the head of the other when we cannot claim that we can by our efforts pursuade the oppressor to climb down. The man bearing the oppressor's weight is also a child of God.

To conclude my comments, I think the churches, with the grace of God, have made great strides since Nairobi in the area of justice for the poor and the oppressed. The fact that no dent has been made shows the magnitude of the problem and must inspire the resolve to strive even harder. We know a lot more today about the poor and the oppressed and their conditions of life than we did at the time of Nairobi. I think our next step should be to allow that knowledge to inspire appropriate action in our own countries, with our own people who, with the power of the ballot box, select decision-makers, and with our own governments. If shareholders in Lonhro for instance, will take the plane, after sharing dividends, to Ghana and travel on our bad roads to Tarkwa and Obuasi to see the devastation of good agricultural land by the mining operations, the poverty of the miners, the rampant occupational diseases, the malnutrition of the children, the inadequate housing and health facilities provided for the miners, their families and other inhabitants of these towns, they will see for themselves what those profits cost in terms of human suffering. The miners are the people who bring up the gold and make good dividends possible. Is it too much to ask for an equitable share of the profits for these poor people?

In South Africa, human degradation hits you in the face. After physical violence one can pick up the threads and start afresh, but institutional violence is the worst type of violence. In addition to physical injury, it suppresses the spirit of people to such a point that they are unable to cry Abba-Father. This is the violence in South Africa – the violence that dehumanizes and seeks to separate people from their Maker. This is the violence that South Africa's trading partners support for greater and greater profit. What does it profit one to gain the whole world and lose one's soul? Listen, please listen to the muted heartbreak of a mother carrying her dead daughter shot by the police in support of apartheid. Is the South African blood money worth it? Why continue to be unconcerned when our country's trade with South Africa makes apartheid viable? The theory that support for South Africa is necessary for national security is false – those who propound that theory know it is false. National security does not lie in nuclear weapons. It lies in the realization of the truth that like the fingers of the hand all humankind belong to the same Father who loves us all so well that he did not spare his only Son but gave him that whosoever believes in him should not perish but have everlasting life – the Jesus who described his mission in these words:

The spirit of the Lord is upon me because he has anointed me
He has sent me to announce good news to the poor
to proclaim release for prisoners and recovery of sight for the blind,
to let the broken victims go free,
to proclaim the year of the Lord's favour.

Dare we keep these broken victims in fetters?

2: A comment from Indonesia
T. B. SIMATUPANG

We are indeed very much indebted to Dr Richard Dickinson for his lucid review and analysis of the World Council of Churches' thinking and actions on development, liberation and global justice, to some extent going back to the beginning of the ecumenical movement but primarily focusing on the post-Nairobi period. His reflections on what has been done and his suggestions for the years ahead should be studied seriously as part of our preparations for the Vancouver Assembly.

With the aim to complement and, where needed, to challenge Dr Dickinson's views, which he himself considers as reflecting a predominantly first world perspective, two World Council presidents from the third world have been invited to make their comments.

I have always felt a great uneasiness with the terms first, second and third world. They may well reinforce prevailing concepts of a hierarchical order, in which the so-called first world is the centre of the universe while the second and the third worlds are respectively the inner and outer periphery. For want of better terms West, East and South will be used in this essay instead of those expressions though, rather confusingly, the East and the West together constitute the North.

Granted that Dr Dickinson's view reflects a Western perspective, inviting the World Council presidents from the South to contribute their reflections, while leaving out the president from the East, gives the impression that the search of humankind for development, liberation and global justice is only and exclusively a West-South affair without the involvement of the East. By implication this could strengthen the notion that the search for global peace is only and exclusively an East-West affair without the involvement of the South.

For the years ahead we must see the search for global justice and the search for global peace as two inter-related challenges, with the very survival of the whole of humankind at stake. In many respects, especially in terms of the stages in their modernization process, the West, the East and the South are living in different historical times. And yet they are contemporaries in our present world, which has become a global village. Living in different historical times, they share a common responsibility and a common destiny in the search for global justice and global peace.

The churches in the West, in the East and in the South are called together to discern how God's kingdom is present and active in our contemporary history, judging the world more radically, more critically and more realistically than the world is able to judge itself, but at the same time opening up a vision of hope which the world needs but cannot generate for itself. In responding to this common call the churches in the West, the East and the South see the world from different historical perspectives.

Churches always face the temptation to adapt themselves totally to the pattern of the world around them and to become captives of a specific historical perspective. In order to fulfill their common task to discern the will of God for our present world, the churches in the West, the East and the South need to be in continuous dialogue, thus challenging and enriching one another. One of the main functions of the World Council of Churches is to facilitate this continuous dialogue.

It is the burden of this essay to provide a contribution to that ongoing dialogue from an Asian perspective. Of course nobody can presume to provide "the Asian perspective". In fact the Asian perspective reflected in this essay will inevitably be coloured by the involvement of the author in the life of the nation and the life of the churches in one of the Asian countries, Indonesia.

In this perspective the emergence of the World Council of Churches in 1948 can be seen as a response of the churches to the historical situation of the post-World War II period. This response of the churches, though rooted in the history of the ecumenical movement, especially since the beginning of the twentieth century, and also rooted in the understanding of the church's very nature, was made possible because secular history had created the reality of a secular oikoumene manifested, among other things, in the formation of the United Nations. If we consider secular history and church history as two ways in which God is working in history, then we can say that church history was responding to secular history.

From its inception the World Council of Churches had to respond to the East-West ideological division, and to the emergence of the newly independent countries (now called the South), which directly or indirectly have been living under Western dominance for a few centuries. Most of the churches in those countries have been established during that period of history.

It is clear that the first assemblies of the World Council of Churches, while deeply influenced by the Cold War between the West and the East, did not pay adequate attention to the struggle for national independence in Asia and Africa. At the time of the Amsterdam Assembly (1948), the Indonesian struggle for national independence, in which the author was actively involved, was not yet resolved. And yet the Assembly, which was held in the capital city of the colonial power, was totally silent on this matter. Had we in Indonesia started our struggle for national independence about twenty years later, we could have applied for a grant from the World Council of Churches! Perhaps this can still be considered retroactively.

The emergence of the World Council of Churches coincided with a period of transition in the long march of humankind. During this period of transition humankind was struggling to grow beyond the structures and value systems which had been created during the three-to-four centuries of dominance and exploitation of the rest of the world by the modern West. Inspired by a vision of global peace and global justice humankind is at present struggling to build a better world, free from domination and exploitation of nation by nation, of race by race, of man and woman by man and woman – free also from an uninhibited and greedy exploitation of non-human nature.

A period of transition is always a period of crisis. Depending on the ability or otherwise of the people who are living in such a period to respond creatively to the challenge of the time, a period of transition can be followed either by a better future or by catastrophy. It is in such a dangerous period in the history of humankind that the World Council of Churches, together with the churches in the West, the East and the South, in witnessing to the kingdom, participate positively, creatively, critically and realistically in the search for global justice and global peace.

The modern West was able to dominate and exploit the rest of the world during three to four centuries, not because it had any inherent superiority, nor because it was inherently more greedy, nor because it was "Christian", but simply because it had a virtual monopoly of modernity in its scientific, technological, economic, political and military expressions.

Basically this absolute monopoly of modernity by the West has run its course. As a byproduct of its domination over and exploitation of the rest of the world, the modern West has united the world and has exported modernity throughout the globe.

Non-Western nations have acquired enough of modernity to stand up against the modern West. Colonial countries have regained their independence, developing nations are making efforts to overcome their underdevelopment and there are areas where non-Western nations have already surpassed the modern West in its own game.

It has been our experience in Indonesia that all our efforts to get rid of Dutch colonialism met with failure as long as we opposed the Dutch with pre-modern methods of struggle. We became successful in our efforts to bring an end to Dutch rule after we acquired enough of modernity to become a modern state, organizing an army and waging war and conducting diplomacy along modern lines. Modern Indonesian history is basically a record of the gradual acquisition, and later the gradual internalization, of the elements of modernity in all spheres of life, exposed to all the tensions involved in such a process of transformation. Christians in Indonesia constituting less than 10% of the population of which about 85% are Muslims, have tried to avoid both total conformity and total withdrawal, and to participate positively, creatively, critically and realistically in this historical process in the light of the gospel of the kingdom.

Some Asian countries, notably Indonesia and Vietnam, went through years of war and revolution in the struggle for national liberation. Others became independent through less turbulent methods of struggle. Some twenty to thirty years ago many people in Asia saw the future of the newly independent nations as a linear development, more or less along the same road which had been traversed by the European nations during the last three to four centuries. This view was expressed dramatically by Prof. Masao Takenaka from Japan, the first non-Western country which has become a fully modern nation, at the 1958 Inaugural Assembly of the East Asia Christian Conference (at present the Christian Conference of Asia) in Kuala Lumpur, when he spoke about telescoping within a few decades in the history of the Asian nations all the European revolutions since the renaissance, including the French Revolution, the Industrial Revolution, the American Revolution and even the proletarian revolution in Russia. At present we in Asia are no longer sure whether the telescoping of all the European revolutions will ever happen in the life of many Asian nations, and there is also a widespread feeling of doubt as to whether it would be a good thing if it does happen. Because in the meantime two things have become evident.

The first is that despite the attainment of independence by most of the countries in the South, the consolidated and institutionalized superiority of the modern West, based on its accumulated wealth, accumulated skills and accumulated achievements in science and technology, is still a fact of life. The second is that the very structures and value systems which have been created as a result of all the European revolutions and which partially have been exported throughout the world in more crude forms, constitute the source of the reality of domination, exploitation and ecological crisis, at the global, regional, national and local levels in our present world.

This situation confronts the developing countries with two problems, or rather two levels of the same problem, in their efforts to raise their capacity to master and generate modernity in its scientific, technological, economic, political and military expressions, and to achieve a fully competitive position in the world. The first is how to relate themselves to the West and also to the East, (which in many respects is in a position comparable to the West), so that they can benefit from the accumulated wealth, skills and achievements in science and technology of the West and of the East, without being subjected to the old relationship of dominance and exploitation. It was in this context that the word neo-colonialism was coined. The role of TNCs must also be seen in this light. The second is to develop alternative models for modern societies by gearing modernity to structures and value systems which are less subjected to domination and exploitation, including the exploitation of non-human nature.

We may now pass on to an assessment of Asian ecumenism. Compared to the other ecumenical regions – Africa, Europe, North America, South America, the Middle East, the Pacific and the Caribbean – geographically Asia is the most extensive and the most broken-up area. Speaking about Asia in ecumenical terms we have in mind the area situated within the triangle formed by Pakistan in the West, New Zealand in the South and Japan in the North, which is served by the Christian Conference of Asia. It is the most populous and the most pluralistic among the ecumenical regions. In view of the differences and even contrasts between and within the various countries in this area, the question can be raised whether anything sensible can be said about the area as a whole. M. M. Thomas, the former moderator of World Council of Churches Central Committee and one of the most penetrating Asian ecumenical thinkers, on one occasion made the remark: "In spite of its plurality of cultures, political ideologies and social structures, we can discern certain common features in what Asian peoples are revolting against and are struggling for."

A Philippine theologian, Dr Emerito P. Nacpil, mentions seven features which he considers to be characteristic of the region.

First, plurality and diversity in races, peoples, cultures, social institutions, religions, ideologies, etc.

Second, most of the countries in this region have had a colonial experience.

Third, most of the countries in this region are now going through the process of nation-building, development and modernization. They want to modernize through the use of science and technology. They want to develop and achieve economic growth, social justice and self-reliance.

Fourth, the peoples of this region want to achieve authentic self-identity and cultural integrity in the context of the modern world.

Fifth, Asia is the home of some of the world's living and renascent religions, and these religions have shaped both the culture and consciousness of the vast majority of Asians. They represent alternative ways of life and experiences of reality.

Sixth, Asian peoples are in search of a form of social order beyond the current alternatives. There is an apparent resort to authoritarian forms of government as an emergency measure. There are efforts to revise and reformulate alternative forms of socio-economic systems and adapt them to the Asian context. All this is an indication that the human issues in Asia today are of such a magnitude that none of the current ideological systems seem adequate for dealing with them. And so, like the rest of the peoples of the world, Asians are looking for a form of social order which would enable them and all humankind to live together in dignity in our world.

Seventh, and finally, the Christian community is a minority in the vast Asian complex!

Perhaps nowhere in the world is the religio-cultural substratum as strongly influential as in Asia, linked to problems of demography and poverty of a magnitude which seems to defy solution. In addition to the ancient Asian religions we have also Islam. Though Islam is a latecomer in Asia, most of the world's Muslim population live here, Indonesia being the country with the largest Muslim population in the world. In the vast area and among the tremendous population of Asia, less than 2% of the people are Christians. Asian ecumenism indeed bears a heavy responsibility for the wider ecumenism.

Except for Australia and New Zealand, which in ecumenical terms are part of the Asian region, in all the Asian countries the ancient religio-cultural-social forces have by no means been dislodged totally in the encounter with the modern worldview, which originated in the modern West. What is going on is a prolonged process of what M. M. Thomas referred to as the "transformation of all spheres of Asian life-forms, of state and politics, structures of economic and social living, cultural values and spirituality which form one inter-related bundle". It is in this sense that the word revolution is referred to in many Asian writings, though there have also been revolutions involving the widespread and prolonged use of violence in Indo-nesia, Vietnam and China.

The management of this total transformation, which constitutes a prolonged and painful crisis of order in which the old and the new forces and worldviews are competing for predominance, is a task of nearly superhuman dimensions.

The most successful in mastering this task up till now has been Japan; it managed the process of transformation becoming a modern industrial nation under a reformed imperial system. In the process, however, it became militaristic and totalitarian, and only after its total defeat in World War II had Japan the opportunity to reorganize its life along the pattern of the Western industrial democracies. It is at present for all practical purposes part of the modern West.

Of all the countries of Asia, China has been going through the longest period of revolution and in many respects it underwent the most violent crisis of order since the breakdown of the imperial system, both during the nationalist and the communist period of its modern history.

Most of the other countries in Asia entered the process of mod-ernization as national movements for independence, reacting to the colonial domination of modern Western powers (except in the case of Korea which was colonized by Japan). After the independence achieved through a war for national liberation or otherwise, in many countries the initial democratic political system based upon Western models collapsed for a variety of reasons. In Indonesia that system could not cope with a war for independence, armed separatist re-bellions, and threats both from the radical left and fanatical religious movements. An enlarged role for the bureaucracy, both military and civil, gave way to a kind of a modernizing bureaucratic state. Some of the states in Asia under the free market system at present have the fastest growing economies of the world. And yet there are many questions with regard to their future. Will they face a total failure like Iran under the Shah? Will they become militaristic and totalitarian modern industrial states like Japan before World War II? Will they go through a prolonged stagnant and unstable period, like many of the Latin American countries? Or will they succeed in gradually enlarging the areas of freedom, widening participation and bringing about more social justice, along with stability and economic growth? It is clear that what is going on in Asia can only be understood in a historical perspective, which transcends the continuously changing and fashionable modes of analysis, theologically and otherwise. No uniform theory of development is applicable to the variety of situations in the Asian countries. Nacpil noted that the human issues in Asia today are of such magnitude that none of the current ideological systems seem adequate for dealing with them. Class analysis alone seems to be unable to do justice to the historical, cultural, social and religious realities. Each country has to struggle to formulate the most adequate theory of development to undergird its efforts to manage the transformation of the country into a viable modern society – a society which while preserving its identity, at the same time institutionalizes in its life as much as possible the basic elements of the universal principles of humanity, justice, freedom and participation.

Can the churches which, except for the Philippines, Australia and New Zealand, constitute a numerical minority, have an impact on the direction and the nature of the process of total transformation of the Asian societies?

When representatives of the churches in Asia met in Prapat (Indonesia) in 1957, a year before the Inaugural Assembly of the East Asia Christian Conference, they formulated what through the years has functioned as a Magna Carta for the social responsibility of the churches in Asia. It reads as follows:

> The churches of East Asia are called to be witnesses together of the gospel of Jesus Christ. What is this gospel?
>
> Firstly it is a gospel of redemption of the whole human race and of the whole created world. By his death and resurrection Jesus Christ has reconciled "all things to himself". His purpose is not to withdraw individual spirits one by one from their involvement with material things and human communities, in order to set them in a "purely spiritual" relation to himself. Rather, his goal is "to unite all things in him". Therefore the church's witness to the redemption of Christ must inevitably include the message of the renewal of society.
>
> Secondly, it is a gospel of the kingship of Christ over the world. Therefore the meaning of world history, including that of modern Asian history, is to be discovered in that kingship, which today is hidden and will be revealed at the end of time. The church must endeavour to discern how Christ is at work in the revolution of contemporary Asia, releasing new creative forces, judging idolatry and false gods, leading peoples to a decision for or against him, and gathering to himself those who respond in faith to him, in order to send them back into the world to be witnesses

to his kingship. The church must not only discern Christ in the changing life but be there in it, responding to him and making his presence and lordship known.

It is this that is the substance of the church's witness amidst social change in Asia today. It is our common conviction that the church should be a full participant in the new life of Asia, if she is to be effective in witnessing to Jesus Christ as Lord and Saviour.

At a recent meeting held in Kuala Lumpur to commemorate the beginning of Asian ecumenism 25 years ago, M. M. Thomas gave a brilliant account of the creative role this Magna Carta has played during the past history. It is a measure of the changes which have taken place during the last 25 years that the discussion became much more difficult when the question was raised about the implementation of it in facing the very difficult and sometimes confusing situations in most of the Asian countries at present and probably also in the future.

We may now offer a few general comments on Dr Dickinson's overview and analysis of the past and his reflections and projections for the future, from an Asian perspective.

The first comment is a repetition of the argument already presented on the necessity to relate the search for global justice more intimately to the search for global peace, which calls for a continuous dialogue, continuous mutual challenging and continuous mutual enrichment between the churches in the West, in the East and in the South.

The second comment is related to a feeling of being on a "different wavelength", which the author sometimes has during ecumenical discussions on the social responsibility of the churches in our present world. To start with there is the impression that when we in many countries and in many churches in Asia were living in a revolutionary mood, the mainstream of ecumenical thought was primarily preoccupied with the post-World War II problems between East and West. By the time many in Asia were in a post-revolutionary mood, which does not necessarily mean being anti-revolutionary, many voices in ecumenical gatherings from the other parts of the world gave the impression of reflecting a pre-revolutionary mood, directly or indirectly inspired by a dogmatic class analysis, and not giving enough weight to the historical, cultural and religious dimensions, which are very strong elements of the Asian reality. In fact in many Asian countries Christian social ethics can only be developed in a dialogical relationship with the historical self-understanding of the nation and with the inner dynamics of the cultural and religious value-systems among the people, in order to enable Christians to participate positively, creatively, critically and realistically in the common task to overcome the tremendous challenge of poverty and population and to bring about the transformation of society. We must consider the possibility that at present we are at the beginning of a long historical process leading to the emergence of modern non-Western civilizations, each with its own strong and specific characteristics, alongside the present modern civilization which is basically Western in origin and in inspiration. The unity of the church, then, is to be understood as the unity of churches living in different historical, cultural and religious realities. While a common "centring focus" is needed, Christian ethics in our present world should not be a recipe for an universal standard menu like Kentucky chicken.

Then there is the problem with regard to the relationship between our thinking and action at the macro and the micro levels. Dr Dickinson refers to this problem when he speaks on the one hand about the "centring focus" and on the other hand about "partial visions". There is no need to see the macro and micro approach and also the "centring focus" and the "partial visions" as two contradictory methods. In fact when we are witnessing to the kingdom we must be concerned both with the macro and the micro as well as with the personal level. A strong critical stance *vis-a-vis* the "establishment" and the "status quo" and a sincere solidarity with the oppressed and the poor do not relieve us of the concern and responsibility for macro problems, where sometimes painful decisions have to be made in the use of power to bring about an acceptable balance between the static (order, stability, security), the dynamic (economic growth, structural changes) and the human (justice, freedom, participation). The concept of the "just participatory and sustainable society" can have a creative and critical significance in this respect, not as a neat, comprehensive and consistent system, but rather as broad pointers expressing a rejection of the present realities and a determination to work creatively for new structures and value systems which express more effectively the concern for justice, participation and sustainability in the different situations where the churches are living.

A commitment to eradicate absolute and dehumanizing poverty throughout the world and especially in the developing countries must certainly be the main preoccupation for Christian social responsibility in the years ahead. This implies on the one hand a concern and a responsibility with regard to comprehensive and long-term plans both at the international and the national level. In addition to this approach "from above" there must be also a concern and responsibility for participation or even struggle "from below" in solidarity with the poor and the oppressed, without falling into the pitfall of what M. M. Thomas at one occasion referred to as "idolatry of the people" and "identifying the people with the Messiah". The crucial element is to generate among the poor and the oppressed a new hope, a new confidence and an enhanced sense of their role and responsibility.

My last comment is on the church. Dr Dickinson's concluding note about the ecumenical movement as a sign community of proleptic unity of the church and of humankind, a sign of the kingdom, is very apt. It indicates what the ecumenical movement should be and should do during this dangerous period of transition. Dr Dickinson also refers to the necessity to relate the view of what the church should be and should do to a far more realistic, a more modest and a more accurate understanding of what the church is. We in the ecumenical movement cannot idealize or romanticize the future task of the church, while speaking cynically about the reality of the church. In many parts of Asia the church consists of small congregations, economically weak, socially and politically without much significance, theologically unsophisticated and physically scattered among huge masses of people of other faiths. Ecumenism in Asia and elsewhere does not only imply speaking, writing, thinking and working for global peace and global justice in solidarity with the poor and the oppressed. It also means praying and working for the renewal, the strengthening, the growth and the unity of the church in a joyful spirit, because we know that "to shame what is strong, God has chosen what the world counts weakness".